Ordinary Objects | Enduring Legacies

The Atlantic Beach Collection

Edited by

SUE TALANSKY

First published in the United States of America in 2021
by drew design & printing co., inc.
Charleston, South Carolina

ISBN 978-578-86442-6
Library of Congress Control Number: 2021912658

Editor: Sue Talansky
Art Director: Andy Allen
Dust Jacket, Design & Layout: Andy Allen, drew design
Cover Illustration: Collage of artifacts

First Edition, August 2021, Printed & bound in Québec, Canada

$60.00
ISBN 978-0-578-86442-6
56000>

9 780578 864426

Ordinary Objects | Enduring Legacies

The Atlantic Beach Collection

A Collection of Holocaust-Related Stories and Artifacts
Gathered from Members and Friends of
The Jewish Center of Atlantic Beach

Edited by

Sue Talansky

אחרי מותי ספדו ככה לי:
"היה איש— וראו: איננו עוד;
קדם זמנו מת האיש הזה,
ושירת חייו באמצע נפסקה;
וצר! עוד מזמור אחד היה לו —
והנה אבד המזמור לעד,
אבד לעד!

After my death say this when you mourn for me:
There was a man – and look, he is no more.
He died before his time.
The music of his life suddenly stopped.
A pity! There was another song in him.
Now it is lost
lost forever.

- *"After My Death" by Hayim Nahman Bialik*

Dedicated in loving memory to

Dr. Mark Ramer z"l

1947-2019

*whose visionary leadership, legendary generosity and infinite energy
proved how just one life can have a lasting impact on so many others.*

We still hear the music of his song ….

When the great Rabbi Israel Baal Shem-Tov
Saw misfortune threatening the Jews
It was his custom
To go into a certain part of the forest to meditate.
There he would light a fire,
Say a special prayer,
And the miracle would be accomplished
And the misfortune averted.
Later when his disciple,
The celebrated Magid of Mezritch,
Has occasion, for the same reason,
To intercede with heaven,
He would go to the same place in the forest
And say: "Master of the Universe, listen!
I do not know how to light the fire,
But I am still able to say the prayer."
And again the miracle would be accomplished.
Still later,
Rabbi Moshe-Leib of Sasov,
In order to save his people once more,
Would go into the forest and say:
"I do not know how to light the fire,
I do not know the prayer,
But I know the place
And this must be sufficient."
It was sufficient and the miracle was accomplished.
Then it fell to Rabbi Israel of Rizhyn
To overcome misfortune.
Sitting in his armchair, his head in his hands,
He spoke to God: "I am unable to light the fire
And I do not know the prayer;
I cannot even find the place in the forest.
All I can do is to tell the story,
And this must be sufficient."
And it was sufficient.
God made man because he loves stories.

From the preface to Elie Wiesel's ***The Gates of the Forest*** *(1964)*

INTRODUCTION

The idea for this collection was conceived at the Young Israel of Great Neck in 2011. The shul's Yom Hashoah program that year was a viewing of the film *Conspiracy of Silence*, depicting the heroic work of Chiune Sugihara, Japanese consul in Lithuania, whose visas to Japan saved the lives of thousands of Jews. A woman in the community approached me afterwards and showed me a paper she had clutched in her hand. It was her mother's stamped visa, signed by Sugihara himself. It suddenly occurred to me that buried somewhere right in our own homes were treasures of comparable significance. All we had to do was dig. And dig we did. An excavation crew of volunteer researchers was assembled and the result was an exhibit in 2012 displaying our incredible findings. The exhibit led to the publication in 2016 of the book *Ordinary Objects/Enduring Legacies: The Great Neck Collection* in which over one hundred synagogue members shared their stories and the photos, documents and other artifacts that they had stored for years in basements, attics, closets and drawers. In the summer of 2019, at a Friday night meal in Atlantic Beach, I observed that almost all around the table were, it turned out, children of survivors. It seemed to me then, that it was time to begin another excavation with a new set of subjects. And so, on the eve of Thanksgiving 2019, our Holocaust Remembrance project was launched, a questionnaire was sent out, and the digging began anew. As always, persistence and patience were the key. A lot of patience. The result, after nearly two years, is the volume you now hold in your hands, *Ordinary Objects/Enduring Legacies: The Atlantic Beach Collection*.

Over the past many, many months I have had the privilege of speaking to dozens of our synagogue members, sometimes even with their parents, children and siblings, and learning the details of their relative's wartime experiences. The work of transcribing, translating, deciphering and highlighting the extraordinary tales of courage, fortitude and resilience of the survivors proved to be once again an endeavor that seemed like a *mitzva*. Certainly, this collection is testimony to the fulfillment of what has been termed the 614th commandment of *zachor* – remember! And as the Rambam teaches us in *Sefer Hamitzvot* with relation to the Seder night, to tell the story is an act of holiness itself. Elie Wiesel illustrates this so beautifully in the Chasidic parable above. The Rabbi of Rizhyn simply retells the story of his masters and it is enough to merit a miracle.

After the texts were created, we combed through the precious documents, letters, postcards, and photos that were unearthed. The artifacts too, like the implements in the Temple, carry a holiness within them. A kiddush cup, a siddur, a luggage tag, a bus pass, a nurse's bag – all ordinary objects with enduring legacies. And the photos - what heart-wrenching loveliness in all those beautiful portraits of families assembled in their Shabbos finery, posing with no inkling of the tragedy about to engulf them. By printing these stories and reproducing images of these artifacts, we honor the kedoshim and create a time capsule for generations to come.

That one small congregation tucked away in a tiny beach community on Long Island should yield such a rich and varied array of material is remarkable. We present here survivors from great cities like Paris and Berlin, as well as from backwater shtetls and mountainous outposts. We have survivors hidden in monasteries, attics, basements, tunnels, cloisters and forests. We have saviors coming from the clergy, the farmlands, the diplomatic corps and the resistance. We have, again and again, survivor stories hinging on sheer mazel or pure miracle – a door not opened, a road not taken, a disguise not discovered. And, perhaps most poignant of all, we have countless stories of faith and trust, *emunah and bitachon*, in the face of unspeakable tragedy and horror.

One might legitimately ask, do we need yet another book about survivors? And my answer is a resounding yes! Each and every story in this volume is what my father would regard as *"a shtick golt,"* a piece of gold – the ultimate compliment in his lexicon. And when set together in this manner, our stories, our individual pieces of gold, achieve the status of a priceless jewel.

We are, after all, a people for whom history is ever present. I remember learning that when the farmer presents his *bikurim* or first fruits at the Holy Temple in Jerusalem his prayer does not begin with an expression of gratitude for his bounty but rather with the strange words, *"Arami oved avi,"* my father was an Aramean…. This phrase, uttered at this moment, puzzles the rabbinic commentators. Many conclude that *Arami oved avi* points to the fact that nothing is created in a vacuum; everything begins with a history. The grateful farmer is tasked with remembrance even before gratitude. As Jews we have an imperative to look back and to see from whence we came.

I wish, in turn, to express my own gratitude to all the people whom I harassed, cajoled and stalked in order to get this job done. I hope you will agree that the effort was worth it. In all cases, I have tried to respect the wishes of the contributors who each had the final sign-off on their pages. Some families escaped the Holocaust early enough with many of their keepsakes intact. Others possessed barely a scrap of anything at all. Some children of survivors were well versed in the minutiae of their parents' ordeals. Others had hardly a clue. The results you see presented here vary according to the particulars of each individual case.

A great debt of gratitude goes to Andy Allen of *drew design* whose vision and aesthetic are evidenced on each and every page of this book. His dedication to this undertaking was passionate and his respect for the subject matter was unparalleled.

Thank you also to Rabbi Elie Weinstock, Rabbi Simcha Willig, Jayne Luger, Lisa Bechhofer, Shira Golden and Shaul Rabinowitz who were so supportive of this project from its inception. And special thanks to my husband, Arthur Talansky, who, in this, as in all my endeavors, has been at my side throughout, encouraging me, cheering me on, and providing me with the expert computer and technical advice that an old *AOL*-user needs on a daily basis.

I am sure that some subjects and material were left out of this volume and I apologize in advance. It surely was not for lack of trying. But, as the poet Paul Valery once wrote, *"A work of art is never finished, only abandoned."* By the summer of 2021, abandonment was the only option.

Treasure these stories, these photos, and these artifacts as they represent our histories, individual and collective - our *"Arami oved avi"* incantation. Each page has inscribed upon it tragedy and triumph, miracle and resilience.

Sue Talansky
Summer, 2021
Atlantic Beach, New York

Sponsors

Bari and Dani Erber
Anne and Natalio Fridman
Nina and Andrew Gaspar
Laura and Jonathan Heller
Jean and Armand Lindenbaum
Smadar and Jonah Meer
Elisa and Alan Pines
Naomi Ramer
Sue and Arthur Talansky

Debbie and Tommy Furst
Elly and Steve Hammerman
Jerry Kestenbaum
Esther and Motti Kremer
Judith and Joe Packin
Blima Safrin
Barbara and Mendy Silber
Lili Stawski
Linda and Steve Weissman
Taisa and Alex Yusupov

Jennifer and Saul Burian
Rachel and Barry Cooper
Rita and Fred Distenfeld
Frances Gleitman and Barbara Gleitman Samuels
Sarah and Martin Goldman
Marisa and Ben Kest
Ruth Kestenbaum
Faye Klausner and Allen Rosenberg
Bea Peyser
Ruthie and David Schwartz
Rebecca and John Steindecker

Raphael Amoona
Bella Borg-Brenner and Stephen Brenner
Shirley Boyarsky
Aviva and Andrew Feinman
Sylvia and Bert Fisher
Fred Fox, Karen and Steven Fox, Helen and Jeff Kramer
Family of Fred Frenkel
Danielle and Jason Friedman
Sonia and Tommy Gelb
Dasha and Ben Gelbtuch
Marla and Jerry Goldberg
Debbie and Howard Goldschmidt
Georgie and Steven Gross
Estie and Barry Hollander
Charlene Khaghan
Helen and Arnold Klein
Rosalie and Harry Kleinhaus
Rena and Alan Kohn
Amy and Darren Landy
Jayne and Steven Luger
Linda and Albert Marshak
David Ohayon
Elizabeth and Michael Pinewski
Patricia and Shaul Rabinowitz
Judi and Marty Schaffer
Howard Schulder and Louise Weadock
Jane and Willy Senders
Devora and Morris Smith
Michelle and William Spielfogel
Pammy and Michael Talansky
Heidi and Jonathan Talansky
Miryam and Israel Wahrman
Naama and Rabbi Elie Weinstock
Geet and Hersh Wolf
Erica and TJ Zuckerman
Shellie and Steve Zuckerman

Gita and Jay Gruenfeld
Helene and Harvey Kaminski
Mlra and Herschel Sennett

"For the dead and the living, we must bear witness" -- Elie Wiesel, 1928-2016

"Some books are born in solitude, others among people."
*Yaffa Eliach, **Hasidic Tales of the Holocaust**, 1983*

The People

Inna Abramov
Sonya Begelman
Joyce Bendavid
Lea Bernstein
Michael Bernstein
Anouche Billet
David Billet
Richard Born
Jennifer Boyarsky
Jonathan Boyarsky
Shirley Boyarsky
Saul Burian
Leslie Capobianco
Suri Cohen
Rachel Cooper
Fred Distenfeld
Rita Distenfeld
Bari Erber
Aviva Feinman
Nicole Fisher
Steven Fox
Eda Frenkel
Fred Frenkel
George Frenkel
David Fridman
Danielle Friedman
Debbie Furst
Tommy Furst
Andrew Gaspar
Nina Gaspar
Ben Gelbtuch
Dasha Gelbtuch
Mendi Gertner
Frances Gleitman
Mark Gleitman
Jerry Goldberg
Miriam Goldberg
Shira Golden
Sarah Goldman
Howard Goldschmidt
Georgie Gross
Steven Gross

Jay Gruenfeld
Hilda Heller
Jonathan Heller
Dwight Hershman
Carrie Hirschfeld
Barry Hollander
Estie Hollander
Marcel Junger
Danna Kalter
Jessica Kaplan
Charlene Khaghan
Faye Klausner
Arnold Klein
Helen Klein
Harry Kleinhaus
Rosalie Kleinhaus
Rena Kohn
Ben Kest
Jerry Kestenbaum
Rina Kestenbaum
Ruthie Kestenbaum
Zachary Kestenbaum
Motti Kremer
Esther Kremer
Amy Landy
Armand Lindenbaum
Bennett David Lindenbaum
Linda Marshak
Jonah Meer
Joel Nessim
Sarah Cooper Oberman
David Ohayon
Daniel Ottensoser
Joseph Packin
Natan Packin
Ronit Packin-Ymar
Bea Peyser
Josh Peyser
Allen Pilevsky
Shoshana Pilevsky
Alan Pines
Elisa Pines

Tali Goldberg Pines
Elizabeth Pinewski
Michael Pinewski
Shaul Rabinowitz
Mark Ramer
Erynne Rennert
Allen Rosenberg
Gabriella Safdieh
Saul Safdieh
Blima Safrin
Barbara Gleitman Samuels
Marty Schaffer
Jesse Scherban
Ariel Lindenbaum Sebag
Willy Senders
Mira Sennett
Barbara Silber
Mendy Silber
Esther Kahan Smith
Michelle Spielfogel
John Steindecker
Abigail Masha Tambor
Arthur Talansky
Sue Talansky
Israel Wahrman
Rabbi Elie Weinstock
Avrum Weiss
Rosalie Weiss
Avi Wilensky
Jill Wilensky
Rabbi Simcha Willig
Eva Wolf
Geet Wolf
Hersh Wolf
Myron Wolf
Alex Yusopov
Julie Yusupov
Erica Zuckerman
TJ Zuckerman

SONYA BEGELMAN

Marsha Baranov, the mother of Sonya Begelman, was born in Vilna, Poland on June 27, 1919. She was one of seven children born to Sonya and David Baranov, who was a successful businessman. Marsha studied to become a nurse and midwife and functioned in that capacity in the Lodz ghetto. Just a few days before the liquidation of the ghetto, a Polish doctor, with whom she had previously worked, successfully petitioned the Germans to transfer her to a Polish hospital in Lodz. Marsha became the chief midwife at that hospital. Her skills saved her from deportation to Auschwitz, where, with the exception of one brother, the rest of her family perished. With most Polish doctors assigned to the front, Marsha's services as a midwife were much in demand in the local Polish hospitals in Lodz.

After the war, Marsha went to a DP camp in Munich, Germany, where, in 1946, she met and married Louis Schwindelman, another survivor, who had spent the war years fighting as a partisan. Louis was born in Russia on November 10, 1919 and worked as a Hebrew teacher before the war. The couple had twin daughters in the DP camp and finally immigrated to New York in 1951 and settled in the Bronx. Upon entering the United States, Schwindelman became Schin. Louis and his wife opened a jewelry store on 138th Street in the Bronx. Tragically, in 1968, they were both shot in a robbery. Only Marsha survived, although medical complications disabled her for more than a year.

A widow at forty-nine, with two children, Marsha once again demonstrated her courage and strength by eventually re-establishing her store on 47th street in New York City and continuing on.

Marsha Baranov, despite a life filled with difficulties, would never complain. "All that is important is your health. If you have your health you have everything."

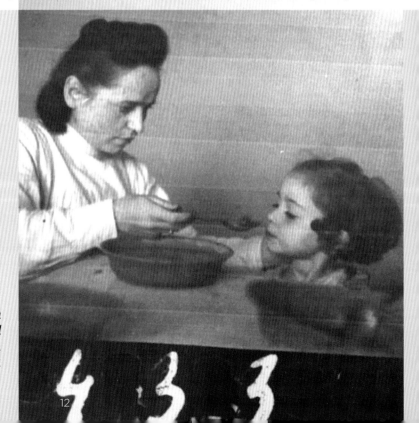

This photograph with the caption "Nurse feeding child in the Lodz ghetto" was found on Twitter by the Begelmans in March 2020. The unidentified nurse is Marsha Baranov.

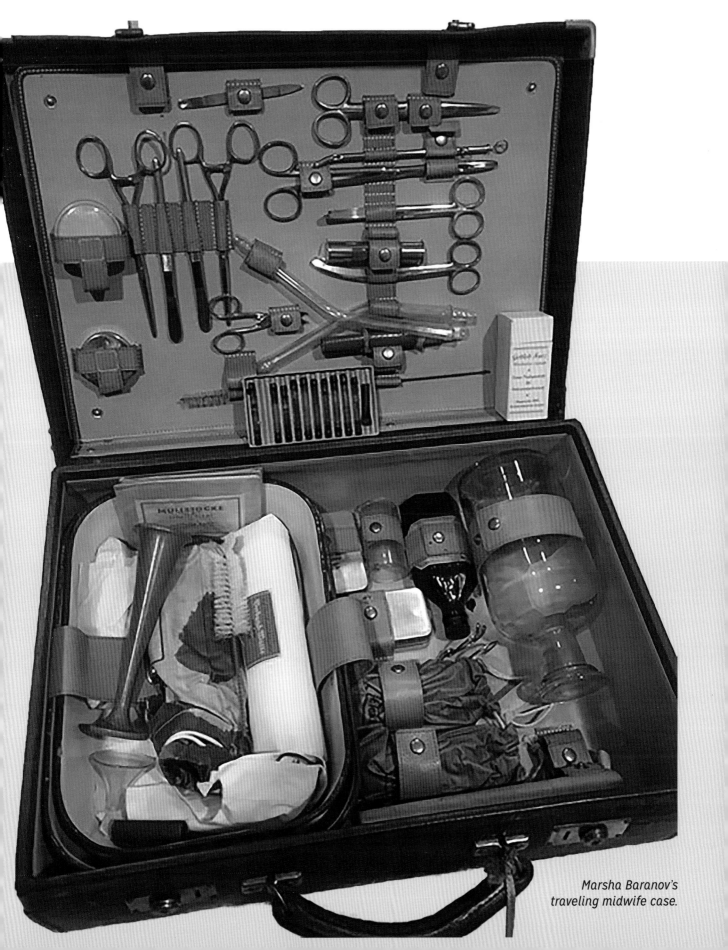

Marsha Baranov's traveling midwife case.

JOYCE BENDAVID

In 1911 Nussa Natan Rubinstein left his wife, Chana Chaya, and three small children in his hometown of Wohyn, Poland in order to try establishing a life in the United States. In her husband's absence, Chana Chaya supported this young family by working as a *sheitel macher* (wig fashioner) and managing a small grocery store. Ten years later the family was reunited in America and their fourth child, Moshe Mordechai, was born on October 19, 1921. Moshe attended Yeshiva Torah Vodaath but dropped out at age sixteen and worked in the ladies millinery business until he was drafted in 1942. He was stationed in Verdun, France where he worked in radio communications. After the war, he met Minnie Pion, whom he married in 1950. They raised their two daughters, Joyce Bendavid and her sister, Carol Goldberg, in Brighton Beach. Moshe worked in the frozen food business for the remainder of his life, working for an old army buddy, Sammy Baum.

After Moshe Rubinstein's death, his family discovered a photo album filled with postcard size photographs of Nazi atrocities, most of them depicting scenes from Dachau. During his lifetime, Moshe had never mentioned them nor had he spoken much about his wartime experience. Many of the images in this album originated in the Parisian photo agency Roger Viollet and were widely distributed in postwar Europe. According to archivist Bonnie Gurewitsch, American GI's purchased such souvenirs in the hopes that they would help convince those back home that the horrors of Hitler's Final Solution were real. Included here are the most benign images in Moshe's album.

> Amongst Moshe's papers were letters written to him by survivors thanking him for his kindness and generosity. One such letter dated October 1945 from Feldafing DP camp reads, "We shall never forget you! I wonder that you are still so yong [sic] and you had not suffered so much as we and you are able to understand our pain and you come to help us."

Moshe Rubinstein. Verdun, France, 1942-3.

Moshe Rubinstein. Verdun, France, 1942-3.

MORRIS RUBINSTEIN

To you who answered the call of your country and served in its Armed Forces to bring about the total defeat of the enemy, I extend the heartfelt thanks of a grateful Nation. As one of the Nation's finest, you undertook the most severe task one can be called upon to perform. Because you demonstrated the fortitude, resourcefulness and calm judgment necessary to carry out that task, we now look to you for leadership and example in further exalting our country in peace.

THE WHITE HOUSE

President Harry Truman's letter of thanks to Morris Rubinstein. 1945.

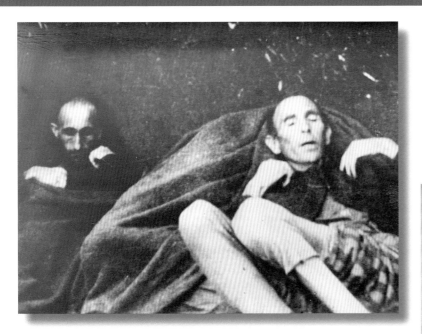

*In a letter from **General Dwight D. Eisenhower***
to Army Chief of Staff, General George C. Marshall,
written after visiting Buchenwald. April, 1945:

"The visual evidence and the verbal testimony of starvation,
cruelty and bestiality were so overpowering as to leave me a bit sick...
I made the visit deliberately, in order to be in a position to give first-hand evidence
of these things if ever, in the future, there develops a tendency
to charge these allegations to "propaganda."

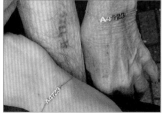

LEA BERNSTEIN
David Billet

Arthur (Aharon HaKohen) Katz, father of Lea Bernstein, was the second of five children of Irving Katz and Ruth Manischewitz. He was born in Williamsburg, Brooklyn on August 20, 1923. Arthur was called "Sonny" by his family and friends. He attended the Yeshiva Torah Vodaath through grade 8, Seward Park High School, and graduated from Brooklyn College with a degree in mathematics. His grandfather, David Meilech Katz, had emigrated from Galicia in 1905 and in 1906, established a furniture business called M. Katz and Sons on Essex Street on the Lower East Side. Sonny's father, Irving, worked in the business with two of his brothers. Sonny was drafted into the U.S. Army, and because of his excellence in mathematics, was sought by the Manhattan Project, but did not end up with that assignment. After basic training, he was shipped to the European front to fight the Germans. He sustained a shrapnel wound to his leg while crossing the River Our with C Company of the 319th Infantry Regiment. After receiving a Purple Heart and an honorable discharge, he joined the family business and worked there till the end of his life, seeing his own son take over. He married Phyllis Gross, whose outgoing, vibrant nature was a great match for his quiet, thoughtful personality.

Their wonderful romance produced four children: Rookie Billet, David Katz, Nissan Katz and Lea Bernstein.

When his children asked him, "Were you afraid when you went to war?," his reply was "All soldiers believe they will come home. If they didn't, there would be no armies."

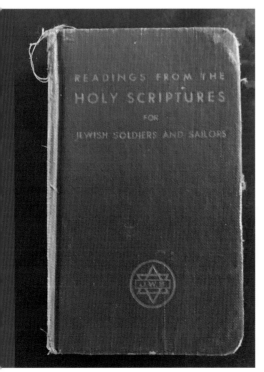
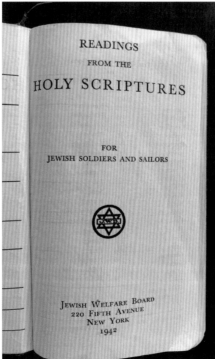
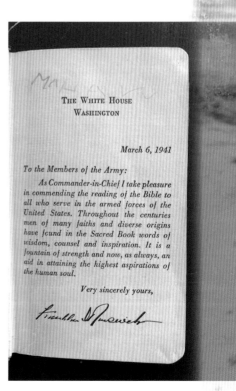

Arthur Katz's Bible, distributed to Jewish soldiers and sailors by the Jewish Welfare Board.

Purple heart and bronze medal awarded to Arthur Katz.

Arthur "Sonny" Katz at his military training camp.

Letter home to family in Brooklyn.
"I would appreciate if you would send me a salami, cookies or anything else you can get into a package, that would not perish on the way over."
Luxembourg, January 30, 1945.

MICHAEL BERNSTEIN

Michael Bernstein's father, Henry Weisblum Bernstein, was born in Wieliczka, Poland on December 12, 1912 to Naftali and Yehudis Bernstein. Henry was the youngest of their six children – David, Moshe, Yitzhak, Baruch, Lola and Henry. When the Germans entered Wieliczka, they marched most of its inhabitants outside the town and shot them. Among the dead were Henry's parents and, except for Lola, all of his siblings with their families. Henry himself was serving in the Polish army, and after an injury put him in an army hospital, he ran off, first to Hungary, and eventually to Italy. In Italy Henry was interned in the Italian concentration camp Ferramonti in Calabria. There Henry met another survivor, Lisl Schiff.

Lisl was born on March 24, 1924 in Vienna, Austria, to Lola and Binyamin Schiff, who was in the textile business. When Binyamin died in 1934, Lola was left to fend for herself with two daughters, Lisl and Annie. Lisl clearly remembers Kristallnacht and her mother's humiliation when she was forced to clean the streets on her knees with a toothbrush. It was then that Lola and her girls made the perilous trek on foot over the Alps, eventually ending up in Ferramonti, Italy.

Lisl and Henry were married in Ferramonti on December 28, 1943. The Bernsteins remained in Italy after the war, living in Rome, where Henry earned a living in the import export trade. A daughter, Ruth, was born there. In 1950 the Bernsteins immigrated to the United States, settling first in Washington Heights and later in Hillcrest, Queens. The family now included another daughter, Lola, who tragically succumbed to cancer in 1958. In 1962 twin sons, Michael and Mark, were born.

Henry established a successful business in packaging supplies which is today run by his sons.

Naftali Bernstein in Polish army uniform. He served during World War I. Binyamin Schiff served on the German side.

Lisl Schiff in Ferramonti, Italy. 1942.

Llsl and Henry. Ferramonti. 1943.

Bernstein family wedding. Naftali Bernstein, first row, right, with beard and glasses. Yehudis Bernstein, first row, fourth from the right. Lola Bernstein, standing between the bride and groom, her brother. Henry Bernstein, back row, center, between a taller man and a young boy. Of the over 30 people in this photograph, only two survived. Poland, pre-war.

ANOUCHE BILLET | MOTTI KREMER

Sofia Zisl Erdman, the maternal grandmother of Anouche Billet and Motti Kremer, was born in 1918 in Felsztyn, Poland, a town on the outskirts of Lvov. She was the youngest of six children born to Yehuda Arieh and Yocheved Erdman. Sofia lost her mother when she was young. At the onset of the war, she had the opportunity to join the Youth Aliyah group and move to Palestine, but she gave her spot to her oldest sister, Tonia. When Hitler invaded Poland in 1939, Sofia was twenty-one and she quickly realized what was unfolding. She colored her hair blond and with her advanced language skills she was able to pass as a gentile outside the ghetto. As the situation worsened, danger lurked around every corner. Once stopped at a checkpoint by German guards and their dogs, she ran in panic, jumped into a river and knocked out her front teeth. She then found a hiding spot with a Polish family and lived out the remainder of the war in a small hallway the size of a bathtub, subsisting on a diet of potatoes. Sofia and two sisters (who left Poland before the war) were the only survivors of her immediate family.

Like Sofia, Moshe Erdman came from Felsztyn where he was born around 1908, one of the eight children of Mordechai Aryeh Erdman and Miriam Erlich Erdman. Miriam supported the family through money lending while her husband sat and learned. Moshe was a kind son who, like his father, spent his early mornings learning in the *Beit Midrash* and worked as a merchant during the day to help support his mother and family. He married and had three children. When the war broke out, the family was forced to relocate into a ghetto/labor camp near Przemysl. One day in 1942, Moshe returned home from work, to realize that, while the men were away, his wife, his three young sons, and his brother's family had been deported to a death camp along with other Jewish women and children. In the years that followed, he managed to escape and survive by jumping off a transport truck and by going into hiding with two different gentile Polish families. He lost his parents, wife and children and all but one of his siblings in the Shoah.

In 1945, when the war ended, Moshe looked through Red Cross lists of surviving relatives, where he found Sofia Erdman, a distant second cousin. A few months later, they married in the presence of a rabbi and two witnesses. They settled in Berlin and later on in Antwerp, where they raised their two daughters, Miriam Yocheved (named after both grandmothers) and Ida.

For the rest of his life, Moshe Erdman was plagued by nightmares and declined to talk about the war, leaving his family with few details about his early life, before and during the war.

(l to r) Sofia Erdman, her brother's wife, their baby, and Sofia's father Yehuda Arieh Erdman. Felsztyn, Poland, 1939. Only Sofia survived.

DAVID BILLET

Leib Jakob (Yehuda Yaakov) Billet, or Jack Billet, was the paternal grandfather of David Billet. Jack was born in the Polish shtetl of Tulyiglow in 1910 to Gitel Tretany and Avraham Billet. One of five siblings and half siblings, he was raised for a period of time by an aunt and uncle, until in the 1920's he followed his parents to Cologne, Germany, where they had gone in pursuit of a better life. There he studied in the Carlebach School. In August 1930, Jack saw Hitler with his own eyes, speaking in front of a crowd of 20,000 in Cologne. One Friday night in the mid-1930s, Nazi Brownshirts cut Jack's father Avraham Billet's beard on his way home from shul. Jack and his parents emigrated in 1937 on the *Queen Mary* from Cherbourg to New York. Jack courageously smuggled out many anti-Semitic publications, including two copies of Julius Streicher's *Der Stürmer* tabloid, to show what was happening in Germany.

And so, for the third time in a third country and in a third language, Jack Billet set out to build a new life in America. He mastered English and cast off his foreign accent almost entirely. He married Pearl Turer, settled in Sheepshead Bay, Brooklyn and had one child, Rabbi Hershel Billet. Jack and Pearl lived a modest life and Jack made a living as an upholsterer for his half-brother's Imperial Leather Furniture Company. He was a lover of Zion and a man of faith. Having escaped from Europe with little but Nazi newspapers in his boots and a souvenir bar of soap from the *Queen Mary*, his most prized possessions were his grandchildren. Jack died in 1999 at the age of 88.

(Cartoon close-up) "A Jewish Ritual Murder"

*Front page of the **WestDeutscher Beobachter** (the West German Observer) Cologne, Germany, October 28, 1928, accusing Jews of the ritual murder of high school student Helmut Daube.*

WestDeutscher Beobachter Cologne, Germany, March 29, 1933. Headline calling for the general boycott of Jewish businesses ("Jewish filth") in Germany for Saturday, April 1, 1933.

Der Deutsche Berlin, June 3, 1934 headline regarding the efforts by the Jewish lawyer and activist Samuel Untermeyer to organize a boycott of German goods and services in the United States.

Front page of Julius Streicher's **Der Stürmer** with its recurring bottom banner "Die Jüden sind unser Unglück!" (The Jews are our Misfortune!) The phrase was coined by Heinrich von Treitschke in the 1880's. Nuremberg, October, 1934. The cartoon depicts the Jewish press as a "shameless whore" and the caption contends that ritual murder still persists.

Niniejszy rysopis osoby winien być potwierdzony przez policję ob... **3 Goldmark** a pobytu.

Diese Personalbeschreibung ist von der Polizeibehörde Ihres jetzige... **DREI GM**

ortes zu beglaubigen.

3 Goldmark

RYSOPIS OSOBY: / PERSONALBESCHREIBUNG:

Imię i nazwisko
Vor- u. Zuname — *Leib Jakob Billet*

Zawód
Beruf — *ohne*

Dzień, miesiąc i rok urodzenia
Geburtstag, Monat und Jahr — *20 November 1910*

Miejsce urodzenia
Geburtsort — *Tuligłow*   Gmina / Gemeinde *Tuligłow*   powiat / Bezirk *Jarosław*

Kraj
Staat — *Polen*

Miejsce przynależności wzgl. zapisania do ksiąg stałej ludności *(Pruchnik) Tubjecko*
Ort der Heimatszuständigkeit bezw. Eintragung in die Liste der ständigen Einwohner

Wieś / Dorf *Tuligłow*   Gmina / Gemeinde *Tuligłow*   Powiat / Bezirk *Jarosław*   Kraj Polska / Staat Polen

	ojca / des Vaters *Abraham Billet*	rok urodz / Geburtsjahr *14 Januar 1877*
Imię i nazwisko / Vor- und Zuname	matki / der Mutter *Gütel Billet*	rok urodz. i naz. rodowe *2.2.84* / Geburtsjahr u. Mädchenname *Trolteuer*

Imię męża / Vorname des Ehegatten	miejsce urodzenia / Geburtsort	data urodzenia / Geburtsdatum

wzrost / Statur — *klein*

twarz / Gesicht — *rund*

włosy / Haar — *schwarz*

oczy / Augen — *braun*

usta / Mund — *oval*

nos / Nase — *normal*

znaki szczególne / Bes. Kennzeichen — /

Photographie ist auf der Bildseite (Vorder-seite) von Passwerber eigenhändig zu unterschreiben.

Jacob Billet.

Die Identität der auf obiger Photographie abgebildeten Person mit dem Passwerber und die eigenhändige Namensunterschrift wird mit dem Bemerken bestätigt, daß der (die) Genannte seit dem *7.7.1920* ununterbrochen hierorts gemeldet ist; in Deutschland hält sich Passwerber ohne Unterbrechung seit dem auf.

Köln , den *11. 6.* 192 *4*

3 Goldmark a

DREI GM

oldmark

RICHARD BORN | RITA DISTENFELD
Michael Distenfeld

Esther Wittlin Born, mother of Richard Born and Rita Distenfeld, was born on July 15, 1933 in Zolkiew, Poland, a town not far from Lvov. Her parents were Klara Klein and Abraham Wittlin, who was a wheat broker. She and her brother Harry lived a peaceful existence until 1939 when the Germans invaded Poland. The entrance of the Red army gave the town's Jews a two-year reprieve until June of 1941, when the noose of restrictions, confiscations and deportations became tighter and tighter. As the ghetto became more dangerous and the Aktions more frequent, the Wittlins, in April 1943, escaped into the nearby woods where they remained for the remainder of the war, scrounging for food and narrowly escaping detection time and time again. Several Ukrainian and Polish farmers hid them periodically but only for short intervals, as they themselves feared detection. Miraculously, despite extremes of thirst and hunger, cold and heat, sickness and delirium, the four Wittlins survived and were transferred to a DP camp outside Munich and then to another in Austria. In 1949 they finally procured the papers allowing them to immigrate to the United States. Esther was only sixteen and entered Thomas Jefferson High School in Brooklyn.

Esther Wittlin, age 14, outside Munich.

Pages from Esther Wittlin's Diary and Autograph books.

Courtesy of USHMM United States Holocaust Memorial Museum archive.

Esther Wittlin's autograph book with entries from 1945–1947.
In Polish a friend writes "When you leave the Wegsheid barracks and go into the wide world, remember your happiness and remember your nice friend from an earlier time. Remember school in the 24th Barrack."

Another entry with the Hebrew "If I am not for myself, who is for me? And if I am only for myself, what am I? And if not now when?" is incorrectly attributed to Herzl rather than to Hillel in Ethics of the Fathers.

rodziłam się w roku 1933 w Żółkwi obok

...wowa. Mam rodziców i brata, życie upływa

...m bardzo dobrze. Mija szczęśliwie rok za

...iem i następuje rok 1939. Który przynosi

ze sobą dużo zgrozy. Wybucha wojna.

...o dziesięciu dniach Niemcy są u nas.

Znęcają się okropnie nad narodem żydowskim

Biją i katują żydów. Panika obejmuje całe

miasto. Na ulicę nikt nie wychodzi. Każdy się

Class picture. Esther Wittlin, top row left.
Wegscheid DP camp near Linz, Austria, 1947.

przygnębiony

...o trzech dn...

armia. Ży...

stanu. Ja...

Ten spokojny...

mija.

W roku 19...

nad miastem naszem niemieckie...

Którą przynoszą ze sobą jakąś skrytą tajemn...

...ikt z nas wyobrazi...

A page from Esther Wittlin's diary, 1942.

Robert Born, father of Richard Born and Rita Distenfeld, was born on November 20, 1926 in the Polish town of Wegrow, about 100km from Warsaw. He was the only son among the five children (Gitl, Regina, Fayga, Masha and Robert) born to Rachel Friedman and Abraham Borensztein who was a successful wine merchant. He grew up in a well-to-do family that gained some fame when they won $1000 in a national lottery. As a young teenager, Robert loved sports and current events and, in his own words, to simply "hang out" with his friends. By September 1939, when the Germans took over Warsaw, the Borenszteins were forced to move into smaller quarters and struggle for food. At fourteen, Robert was assigned a job in the Presidential Palace which gave him more opportunities to get food for the family. By the winter of 1940 the Warsaw ghetto streets were filled with the starving and the dead. Robert was transported to a series of concentration camps including Buchenwald and Majdanek. In a memoir written in 1992, he describes his work as prisoner number 14922. "The work in Majdanek was really not productive work. We loaded lorries with heavy rocks from one end of the camp to the other end. Most of us were teenagers. We were stripped of our clothing and also told to drop gold, money and jewels into big wooden containers. We were brought into shower rooms before barbers shaved our hair...." Robert and his sister Regina were the only survivors of the Borensztein family. Robert spent the post war years, first in a DP camp and then in Berlin with other young and ambitious survivors. In 1950 Robert Born had saved enough money to emigrate in style, arriving in the U.S. by plane and settling into the Paris Hotel on Manhattan's Upper West Side. He immediately set out to teach himself English and he purchased a multi-volume set of *The History of the United States*, which he committed to memory. He went into the real estate business and at a Purim ball in 1953 he met a beautiful nineteen-year-old survivor, Esther Wittlin, whom he married on March 14, 1954. The Borns raised their two children, Rita and Richard, in Forest Hills, Queens.

Robert Born, Berlin, post-war.

An excerpt from Robert Born's memoir, 1992.

JENNIFER BOYARSKY

Jennifer Boyarsky's paternal grandfather, Isidor Gelb, was born on December 12, 1913 in Cop, Czechoslovakia, one of six children of Chaya and Moshe Gelb, who was a *melamed* (teacher). The Gelbs had four sons, Martin, Ludwig, Eugene and Isidor, and two daughters, Rose and Bozenka. When Isidor was three, the entire family moved to Berehevo where Isador's father, Moshe Gelb, established a kosher wine business which prospered. In his twenties, Isidor left the family business and struck out on his own. He became a sheet metal worker, married his first wife and had a son. When the Hungarians seized power, he, along with most able-bodied men, was sent to do forced labor. The Gelbs were herded into a ghetto and soon transported to concentration camps. Isidor's parents, wife and child were killed. After the war ended, Isidor reunited with his surviving siblings and seeing no future in the Ukraine, they moved to Usti nad Labem, a larger town not far from Prague. Isidore resumed work as a sheet metal worker and welder and married another survivor, Rose Mermelstein, on June 6, 1946.

Rose Mermelstein was born on June 21, 1921 in Kivijazd, Czechoslovakia to Malka and Baruch Mermelstein, Polish Jews who had fled the pogroms and who became farmers in their new homeland. Rose was their only daughter and she had seven brothers, Martin, Wolf, Moshe, Leiser, Yitzhak, Isaac and Berl. When the Nazis took power, the family was forced into the Munkacz ghetto and then transported to concentration camps. Rose's parents and three brothers were murdered. After surviving not only the camp but also a torturous death march, she managed to reunite with her four surviving brothers in Kivijazd, a town that now held nothing for them save a buried pot containing Jewish artifacts and some jewelry. Rose then relocated to Usti nad Labem where she met Isidor.

The young couple remained in Czechoslovakia and had two sons, Michael in 1947 and Thomas in 1949, the latter named after Tomas Masaryk (1850-1937), the first president of Czechoslovakia, and a great friend of the Jews. With their two teenage boys, the Gelbs immigrated to the U.S. in June 1964 and settled in Boro Park. Isidor again earned his livelihood working with sheet metal and Rose worked as a seamstress.

Malka Mermelstein. Moshe Gelb.

(opposite page) The four Gelb brothers. Berehevo, Czechoslovakia. Winter, 1940. Top row, left to right, Martin and Ludwig. Bottom row, left to right, Isidor and Eugin.

*Rose Mermelstein, the little blonde girl on the left, with five of her seven brothers,
leaning against her mother, Malka Mermelstein. Her grandparents, Malka's parents, to her left.
Kivijazd, Czechoslovakia c. 1931.*

*Thomas Gelb's parents, Isador & Rose Gelb
Usti nad Labin. Czechoslavakia, June 6, 1946*

Spice boxes, ranging from the 17th century to present.
Collection of Thomas Gelb. Thomas's own design, **The Freedom Tower**, front, left.

Earrings dug up from a hiding place in the Mermelstein yard. Kivijazd, Czechoslovaki

The Freedom Tower spice box, created by Thomas Gelb.

Jennifer Boyarsky's maternal grandfather, Ilia Katz, was born on June 7, 1907 in Stuzice, Czechoslovakia to Malka and Moshe Katz, who was a landowner and farmer. He had one older brother, Joseph, and two older sisters who immigrated to the U.S. before the war. When the Hungarians took power, Ilia was put into a forced labor camp, where he toiled in underground mines under conditions so intolerable that he suffered from emphysema for the rest of his life. Later still he was transported to Auschwitz, where the rest of his family perished, save for his brother Joseph who settled in Israel. Ilia returned to Czechoslovakia after the war and settled in Decín where he married another survivor, Helen Braun.

Helen Braun was born in Cinidavo, Czechoslovakia on October 1, 1924 to Sara and Moishe Braun who was the owner of a small local mill. The Brauns had four children – Rose, Helen, Samuel and Otto. With the invasion by the Hungarians came forced labor, ghettoization and ultimately deportation to Majdanik and Auschwitz death camps. Sara and Moishe perished, but the four siblings survived. While Rose left for the States, Helen and Otto followed Samuel to Decín where she met Ilia Katz. Otto headed for Palestine, where he joined the Haganah.

Ilia and Helen raised their three children, Otto and twins, Sonia and Jack, in Decín, where Ilia became a foreman in a state-owned chocolate factory. By the time the children were teenagers, the couple began to fear for their future as Jews in Communist Czechoslovakia. They decided to immigrate to the U.S. in December 1966 and with help from HIAS they settled in Brooklyn and Ilia earned a living in a company that manufactured desk sets.

Helen & Ilia Katz with their children, Otto center and twins Sonia & Jack.

Helen Braun Katz wedding portrait. Her dress was hand-sewn by a friend from either American or German parachute material. Decin, Czechoslovakia. June, 1946.

SHIRLEY BOYARSKY
Jonathan Boyarsky | Nicole Fisher

Sam (Osias) Krakowski, father of Shirley Boyarsky, was born in Piotrikow, Poland in 1907, one of eight children of Menachem Mendel and Shprintze Krakowski. In 1928 he moved to Vienna where he met and married Sara Freida Krupnik and made a living as a furrier. Their daughter Esther (Ellie) was born in 1931.

Sara Freida Krupnik Krakowski, mother of Shirley Boyarsky, was born in 1908 in Vienna, one of five children born to Dvora Chaya and Yitzhak Krupnik who, with his brother Julius, owned and operated the prestigious Krupnik Department Store. In March 1938, months before Kristallnacht, the store was looted by Nazi storm troopers, the property plundered and Julius Krupnik was arrested. Shortly thereafter, Sam procured the necessary paperwork and he, Sara, her parents, and their young daughter left for Palestine. With their experience in retail, they opened a shop called Chatzi Bechinam on Dizengoff Street in Tel Aviv. By the end of the war, Sam had lost his parents and all but three siblings to Hitler's killing machines. In 1948, urged on by Ellie's desire to immigrate to the U.S., the Krakowskis moved once again. In New York, Sam set up a sweater business and another daughter was born, Shirley, whom they named Shprintze after Sam's late mother.

Sara with her parents, Yitzhak and Dvora Chaya Krupnik. Vienna, 1928

Sam and Sara Krakowski, wedding photo,
Vienna, 1929.

Shprintze Krakowski with three of her eight children
Manya, Bronia and Duvza. Piotrikow, Poland, 1917.

Krakowski family, Sam and Sara with
daughters Ellie and baby Shirley,
New York, 1948.

Sam Krakowski (seated far left, front row, in a hat) at the forest dedicated in memory of the fallen Jews of Poland. Israel, 1949.

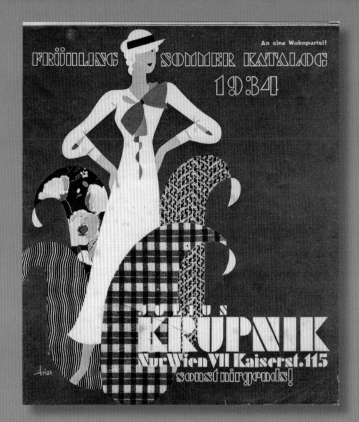

Above: Advertisements for the Krupnik Department Store. Vienna, 1930's. Courtesy, Claus Jahnke Collection

Below: Bus advertisement featuring Krupnik Department store. Courtesy, Austrian National Library | Austrian State Museum.

SAUL BURIAN

Andrew (Ondrej Mojzis) Brandstein was born on December 12, 1930 in the small town of Bustina (then Czechoslovakia, now Ukraine). His parents, Ernest and Matilda (née Bruckstein), and his older brother, Tibi, made up his nuclear family, but he was always surrounded by a large and loving extended family - the Brandsteins, who ran a profitable lumber business, and the Brucksteins, who owned a successful cane and herb establishment. Sheltered and loved, Andrew's childhood was nothing short of idyllic. A few months after his much-anticipated Bar Mitzvah, Andrew's world was shattered. His wartime odyssey began with deportation from his hometown to the deplorable conditions of the Mátészalka ghetto in Hungary. From there, boxed in cattle cars, Andrew and his family were later deported to Auschwitz-Birkenau where his mother, grandfather and great uncle were immediately murdered. Although Andrew was initially together with his father and brother, their paths soon separated and they were only reunited, miraculously, after the war.

In Auschwitz-Birkenau, with bravery and ingenuity, Andrew managed to survive countless selections and harrowing near-death experiences for more than seven months. In the freezing winter of 1945, by placing mind over matter and focusing on one goal at a time, Andrew survived the infamous death march from Auschwitz-Birkenau and then another horrific transport by cattle car to the Mauthausen concentration camp in Austria, where he witnessed unimaginable atrocities. Andrew was ultimately liberated from the Gunskirchen concentration camp by the U.S. Army, with African-American scouts leading the way. The surviving Brandsteins – father and two sons – decided for safety's sake to change their name to Burian, after the Czech actor Vlasta Burian. One week before the Communist regime took over Czechoslovakia, Andrew Burian began an arduous journey through Europe and, at the age of seventeen, aboard the SS *Washington*, he arrived in the U.S. and started life anew. He graduated with honors from Theodore Roosevelt High School and on November 23, 1960, he married an American girl, Ruth Yellin Allerhand, who was enchanted by this dashing European gentleman. Andrew and Ruth raised three children, Matilda, Saul and Lawrence, and were blessed with many grandchildren and great-grandchildren. In 2016, Andrew Burian's masterfully written and poignant memoir *A Boy from Bustina: A Son, A Survivor, A Witness* was published by Yad Vashem Press. Andrew Burian passed away in 2020.

In 1943, ruthless Hungarian gendarmes seized Andrew's most cherished Bar Mitzvah gift, a Tissot watch.
Seventy years later, on the occasion of his grandson Jonah's Bar Mitzvah and his own second Bar Mitzvah, they each received a new Tissot watch - a symbol of how far the family had come and how fortunate they were.

*Yisroel Natan and Rachel Bruckstein
(Andrew's maternal grandparents). Bustina, pre-war.*

*Eliezer and Amalia Brandstein
(Andrew's paternal grandparents). Bustina, pre-war.*

Bruckstein family reunion. Bustina, 1925.

The Brandstein home. Bustina.

Matilda Bruckstein (center, rear) with her sisters Gigi (left), Val
(right) and Fanny (center, front). Bustina, 1925.

Matilda Bruckstein and Ernest Brandstein, engagement photo. Bustina, 1926.
Matilda Bruckstein and Ernest Brandstein, wedding invitation. Bustina, January 4, 1927.
The Brandstein family (l to r) Tibor, Matilda, Ernest, Andrew. Bustina, 1935.

DIE TRAUUNG UNSERER KINDER

MATILDE und ERNST

WIRD AM 4. JÄNNER 1927. 4 UHR NACHMITTAGS IN SEVLJUS
STATTFINDEN, ZU DER WIR SIE SAMMT W. FAMILIE
HÖFL. EINLADEN.

BUŠTINA IM MON. JÄNNER 1927.

ISRAEL BRUCKSTEIN & FRAU.
LAZAR BRANDSTEIN & FRAU.

ABENDMAHL UM 6 UHR.

TELEGRAMMADRESSE: BRUCKSTEIN, HOTEL EUROPA SEVLJUS.

Andrew Burian, 1945

Children going to cheder with their rabbi. Tibor Brandstein in the rear. Bustina, c. 1935.

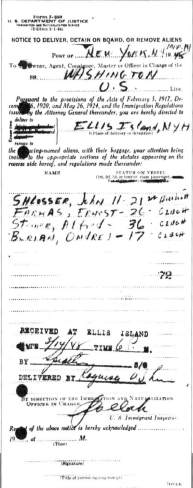

Andrew Brandstein's registration card for Mauthausen concentration camp.
January 30, 1945.

Andrew Burian's Ellis Island ticket. March 14, 1948

LESLIE SLOMOVITS CAPOBIANCO

Leslie Capobianco's father, Samuel Slomovits, was born to Yisroel Tzvi and Mindel Slomovits in Ruscova, Romania on December 20, 1910. He was one of eight children, two of whom, Benny and Pearl, had immigrated to the U.S. before the second World War. Samuel was working as an accountant, married and the father of a toddler son when Hitler invaded.

Rose Slomovits, Leslie's mother, was born on August 18, 1922 in Ruscova, Romania to Baruch and Leah Slomovits, one of their six children, Blanche, Yankel, Lazer, Pearl, Yitzhak and Rose. Baruch, Rose's father, was a grocer and cattle dealer and also the older brother of Samuel Slomovits. When her husband died in 1934, Leah was overwhelmed and her daughter Rose, only twelve at the time, trained to become a seamstress in order to support the family. Rose, her sister Blanche, and her mother were deported to Auschwitz where Leah perished and Rose was assigned work in an ammunition factory. Her sewing skills proved life-saving as she created wallets out of scraps of discarded leather and gave them to her German guards in exchange for extra rations which she shared with her relatives in the camp.

Samuel spent the war years in slave labor camps and after the war ended, he learned that he had lost his parents, four siblings, his wife and his child. After liberation, both Rose and Samuel found each other in a DP camp in Lampertheim, Germany. The couple, uncle and niece, married in Germany on May 1, 1946. Samuel immigrated to the U.S. in 1948; Rose followed in 1949. They settled in Brooklyn where they raised their two daughters, Leslie and Marlene. Samuel earned a living as a butcher and Rose continued to do seamstress work.

Rose Slomovits entered Auschwitz holding on to her mother on one side and her sister on the other. When asked to identify her companions she did so. "Meine mutter und meine schwester." Leah was then sent immediately to her death while Blanche remained with Rose. For years afterwards Rose regretted with sorrow and guilt not having answered that both women flanking her were her sisters, an identification which might have saved her mother's life.

Seated: Rose and Samuel Slomovits. Standing, left to right: Louis (Lazer) Slomovits (Rose's brother), and Freidel Slomovits (Samuel's niece). Lampertheim DP camp, Germany. 1947.

Rose holding Leslie. Williamsburg, Brooklyn. 1951.

Rose and Samuel wedding portrait. Lampertheim, Germany. May 1, 1946.

SURI COHEN

Goldie Berko, grandmother of Suri Cohen, was born on June 2, 1913 in Sasvar, Hungary. She lived with her parents, Moshe Yankel and Chana Berko, and her brother, Zalman, on a large family-owned farm. When she was nine, her mother died and when her father remarried, he had two more children, a daughter, Chana, and a son, Mendel, who died before the war. Moshe Yankel was a religious and spiritual man who worked hard on his farm. Goldie, too, was busy helping with the farm work and the household chores.

The Nazis came to that part of Hungary in March 1944, and within a month all the Jews who lived around Sasvar were captured and sent to Auschwitz and to almost certain death. Goldie was not well and was placed in the hospital for the medical experiments done by Dr. Josef Mengele. Every morning Mengele would come to the barracks and randomly select a certain number of people as experimental subjects. Most never returned. Goldie tried to encourage her younger sister to be brave, often pinching her cheeks to create a rosier, healthier appearance. She also witnessed the painful sight of her handsome, well-dressed brother, Zalman, a textile salesman, arriving on a transport, not long after her own arrival. Goldie Berko miraculously survived Auschwitz and returned to her home in Sasvar, hoping to find these beloved siblings. Neither returned. Goldie never learned exactly what happened to her sister, but she was later told by an eyewitness that her brother was shot dead on a death march from Auschwitz.

Soon after the war ended, Russia took over the land she lived on and it became a part of USSR, now Ukraine.

In 1945 Goldie married Yisroel Solomon, who was born in 1903 in Sirma, Hungary. He was a widower who had lost a wife and three children. The couple lived on a collective farm where Yisroel functioned as a watchman and also sold produce grown on the farm. Their first child, Jacob, was born in December 1946. A religious man, Yisroel cherished the quiet hours of guard duty when he could daven in private, undetected. A daughter, Henia, was born in 1948. In 1952 Yisroel was thrown in jail by Stalinist henchmen, but was released with the amnesty declared upon Stalin's death in 1953. Chana, another daughter, was born in 1954.

Despite the hardships imposed by the secular Soviet regime, Goldie and Yisroel raised their family in a kosher and observant home. In 1971 they sold their home in Sasvar and moved to the city of Vinogradowa. Jacob and Henia married, and Chana followed suit, marrying Gabriel Friedman in 1974. All anxiously awaited papers to emigrate. Tragically, Yisroel died in Moscow, just as he and Goldie were about to board a plane out of the USSR. Eventually the remainder of the family reached New York and settled in Brooklyn. Chana and Gabriel, with one-year-old Suri, arrived last, in 1976. Goldie lived with Henia and spent her later years caring for her many beloved grandchildren.

Goldie Berko Solomon's legacy is now honored by her seven grandchildren, thirty-three great- grandchildren (three of whom are named Goldie) and, so far, five great great-grandchildren.

The three children of Yisroel Solomon.
Sirma, Hungary, pre-war. All perished in the Shoah.

Right to left, Chana, Zalman's fiancée, Zalman, a friend, and Goldie.
Sasvar, Hungary, c.1937.

Goldie Berko.
Sasvar, Hungary. c. 1928.

Zalman Berko. Sasvar, Hungary, pre-war.

Chana Solomon Friedman
with Suri.
Vinogradowa, U.S.S.R., 1976.

Goldie Berko with Henia and Jacob. Sasvar, Ukraine, c. 1952.

RACHEL COOPER
Sarah Cooper Oberman

Rachel Cooper's father, Asher Anchel Ganz, was born in Vonihove, Austria-Hungary (now in the Ukraine) on January 18, 1901, the youngest of the nine children of Nissan and Rachel Ganz. According to family lore, he spoke seven languages and even had the opportunity to learn with the Satmar rebbe. He was married before the war to another native of Vonihove, Sarah Leah Ganz, born in June 1912, one of the seven children of Golda and Shmuel Ganz.

Asher and Sarah Leah had three children - Nissan, Shmuli and Sruli and lived in affluence as Asher's business as a bridge contractor grew. Their home was a stately structure with pillars and a wide front staircase. Details of their wartime experience are incomplete, but what is certain is that at some point all five were deported to Auschwitz, where the three little boys were murdered.

After liberation, Asher and Sarah Leah were reunited and they spent several years in a DP camp outside of Paris, where two daughters, Goldie and Rachel, were born. At this time Asher adopted the last name Berkovic, his mother's maiden name. In 1948 the family came to New York and settled on the Lower East Side where a brother Samuel was born. Tragically, Sarah Leah died in 1955, at the age of 43, leaving Asher to raise and support his young family alone.

Golda and Shmuel Ganz with their seven children. Sarah Leah is standing, center, rear. Vonihove, Austria-Hungary. c. 1927.

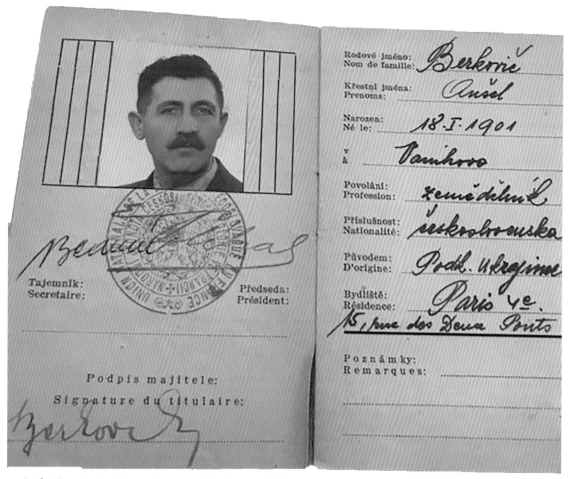

ID card of Asher Anchel Bercovic. Issued in France, 1946.

*Asher (standing, left) and Sarah Leah (Ganz) Berkovic (seated)
with baby Goldie and two other relatives. Paris, 1947.*

*Home of Asher and Sarah Leah Ganz.
Vonihove, Austria-Hungary, pre-war.*

FRED DISTENFELD
Michael Distenfeld

Joseph Distenfeld, father of Fred Distenfeld, was born in Lvov (Lemberg), Poland on March 17, 1912. He and his three siblings, Rivka, Yechiel and Chana, grew up in the comfortable home of their mother, Rivka, and father, Isaac, who ran a general store. Joseph was educated in a cheder and graduated from gymnasium and then became a furrier. During the period of Russian occupation, on March 17, 1941, Joseph married Matilda (Lucia) Goldwurm, the orphaned child of Ephraim and Pepi Landau Goldwurm, who also hailed from Lvov.

The young couple's joy was short lived since the German occupation, which began that June, transformed their lives forever. Ousted from their Lemberg apartment by German officers, they returned briefly to the village of Joseph's parents, Potok Zloty and along with the other Jews of Potok, they were soon thereafter transferred to the ghetto of Buczacz. By the end of 1943 Matilda's sister, and Joseph's parents and siblings had all been murdered. The young pair survived for ten months hidden beneath a barn in a space only four feet high. In March 1944 when the Russian army liberated Galicia Joseph and Matilda spent a year and a half wandering through Europe hoping to find a place where they could begin a new life. In December 1945 they reached Milan, Italy where at last they settled. Their seven year sojourn in Milan were years of tranquility and happiness, much of it due to the arrival of their only child, Fred, born on April 21, 1950. Their deep commitment to Yiddishkeit and their desire to provide their son with a proper Jewish education were essential factors in their decision to leave Milan and move to the U.S. They arrived in New York City in March 1952 and settled in Queens where Joseph began a successful career in business.

Isaac and Rivka Distenfeld

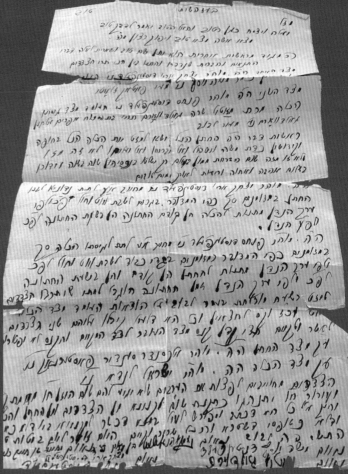

T'naim, or engagement contract between Joseph Distenfeld and Matilda Goldwurm.
Lvov, July 22, 1940 - 16 Tamuz, 5700.

Joseph and Matilda Distenfeld
with their son Fred. Milan, 1950.

Joseph Distenfeld Identity Card issued by the city of Milan, Italy , January 11, 1951.

Matilda Distenfeld Identity card for alien refugees issued by the International Refugee Organization, Italian Mission. Milan, Italy, January 17, 1951.

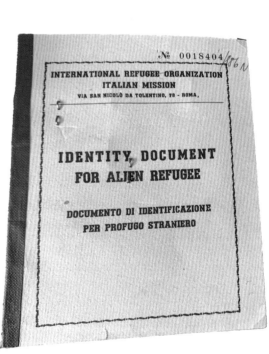

Joseph Distenfeld's registration certificate permitting both industrial and commercial business, issued by the city of Milan, August 10, 1946.

Receipt for a contribution to the new State of Israel. March 15, 1949 by "Gino" Distenfeld.

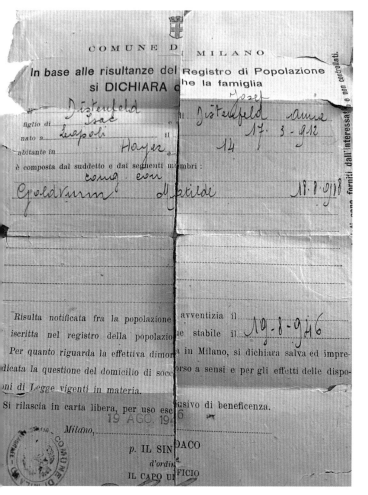

Registration of residence in Milan, issued to Joseph Distenfeld residing at 14 Hayer, August 19, 1946.

AVIVA FEINMAN

Aviva Feinman's father, Harry Levinson, was born on November 14, 1935 in Warsaw, Poland, the only child of Freeda and Joseph Pinchas Levinson. Freeda was the family's breadwinner while her husband, a Torah scholar and rabbi, sat and learned. The family traveled from Warsaw to Vilna in 1939 and was fortunate enough to procure the last three visas issued by the Japanese consul in Lithuania, Chiune Sugihara. They then joined the Mir Yeshiva on the trans-Siberian railway to Vladivostok and from there to Kobe, Japan. From Kobe they traveled with the Mir to Shanghai, China where they remained till 1947. After the war ended and having obtained the necessary visas, the three Levinsons sailed to San Francisco and a new life. They continued to New York and settled on the Lower East Side. Harry was only twelve and had to begin anew in a third country. He enrolled in RJJ (Rabbi Jacob Joseph) Yeshiva, then Brooklyn College and eventually Columbia Law School. Rabbi Levinson continued to learn, forged a friendship with his neighbor Rabbi Moshe Feinstein and also served as the *mashgiach* (kashrut supervisor) in the popular eponymous restaurant of his friend, Shmulke Bernstein.

Deborah Rokowsky Levinson, mother of Aviva Feinman, was born on August 18, 1938 in Basel, Switzerland to Rochelle (née Bollag) and Morris Rokowsky, who was a real estate investor. She had two sisters, Miriam and Ruth and two brothers, Isaac and Yisroel. The family left Switzerland and on May 8, 1941 sailed from Barcelona to New York on the luxury liner SS *Cuidad De Sevilla*. They settled in Boro Park and raised their children there. After attending Bais Yaakov of Boro Park and Brooklyn College, Deborah married Harry Levinson on July 3, 1962. The young couple settled in Brooklyn where they had three daughters, Aviva, Tova and Dina, and they later moved to Monsey, N.Y., where their son Shmuel David was born.

Harry Levinson on lap of his father Rabbi Joseph Pinchas Levinson in Shanghai. c.1942.

Morris and Rachel Rokowsky with their five children. Deborah on extreme right holding sweater. Paris, 1948.

STEVEN FOX

Sam Fuchs, (later Fox), the father of Steven Fox, was born on June 10, 1923 in Dubova, Czechoslovakia, one of the eight children of Freida and Ephraim Fuchs, who was a land-owner/farmer. The family was devout and connected to the Vizhnitz chassidim through a great uncle. During the war Sam fought with partisans but was captured and forced to work as a slave laborer in a German munitions factory where he and his coworkers tried to sabotage as best they could the weapons they were producing. Sam was later sent to Auschwitz and there his parents and five siblings were murdered. Only Sam, a brother, Moishe, and a sister, Leah, survived.

Rose Berkowitz, Steven's mother, was born on September 8, 1929 in Slatina, Czechoslovakia, one of seven children of Chana and Yisroel Ber Berkowitz, who owned a brewery. For a period during the war she and a sister worked as a house-maids in Budapest but eventually the family went into hiding in the woods and Rose fell deathly ill. She recovered, but was ultimately caught and sent to Auschwitz along with her mother and other siblings. Her father and a brother were shot by a firing squad before deportation. In Auschwitz, Rose's twin siblings, Marc and Francesca Berkowitz, were subjected to the sadistic medical experiments of the infamous Dr. Josef Mengele. Marc actually witnessed his own mother's march to the gas chambers.

Dr. Mengele took a special interest in Marc and personally tattooed his number. He gave Marc candy and told Marc to call him "Uncle Pepi." Soon Marc unwillingly become Mengele's messenger relaying important messages from Mengele to other Nazi officials. When he wasn't busy running throughout the camp delivering messages, he and Francesca served as Mengele's guinea pigs in his series of inhumane experiments. Marc recalls, "They put us in freezing baths, smeared chemicals on our skin, but it was the needles we were most afraid of. We were strapped to the marble slabs. I felt a needle digging into my back. My entire body was burning and the next thing I knew I was fighting from fainting. After the first 150 I stopped counting..." Forty years later, Marc still suffers from pains due to these injections.

After liberation Rose and Sam met in a DP camp in Bari, Italy. They were married there on September 13, 1947. The next year, in February 1948, they arrived in the U.S. Because her sponsorship for emigration was being offered to unmarried women only, Rose hid both her marriage and her pregnancy upon arrival and the couple's eldest son, Fred, was born on May 6, 1948 in the ward for unwed mothers at a Staten Island hospital. Soon after the young couple settled on the Lower East Side and opened their home to the surviving twins, Marc and Francesca. A daughter, Helen, was born in 1949 and their youngest, Steven, arrived in 1954. The Foxes eventually moved to Queens where they raised their children and Sam ran a business fabricating and finishing metals in his own factories. He remained a lifelong member of the Marmaris Society and Federation.

Before her death Chana Berkowitz gave her son Marc some advice. "... to love God, to love humanity, and to be a good boy. But should you be bitter and seek vengeance, I will ask God to send you to me."

Child survivors of Auschwitz wearing adult-size prisoner jackets, standing behind a barbed-wire fence. Still photograph from the Soviet film of the liberation of Auschwitz taken by the film unit of the First Ukrainian Front, 1945. Courtesy USHMM

Uncle Marc Berkowitz pointing to his own image in the iconic photo.

55

FRED FRENKEL
George Frenkel

Fred Frenkel was born on October 13, 1927 in Bekescsaba, Hungary, one of the nine children of Lipot (Aryeh) and Regina (Rivkah) Frenkel who ran a successful family business in down and feathers. Yidele, as his friends called him, had seven older siblings, Icu, Chaim Hersh, Mati, Valvish, Hajku (Zora), Edi, Barry (Dov Ber), and one younger brother, Nandor (Nandi). The family was prosperous, closely-knit, and observant. As Hitler's power rose in Germany, anti-Semitism was on the rise in Hungary as well. The Frenkels and their neighbors experienced verbal and physical assaults and by 1943 their business had diminished so that some of the brothers and then the sisters left for Budapest. In May 1944 the family was forced into the town ghetto and Fred into forced labor.

On June 23, 1944 Yidele Frenkel took off his Jewish star and, with the help of his mother, assumed a new identity as Gyorgy Araczki and departed for Budapest. Like his siblings, Gyorgy began to hide in plain sight in Budapest. Only sixteen at the time, he became involved in providing Jews with false papers furnished by the Swedish architect Raoul Wallenberg. With his brothers, he helped countless Jews assume gentile identities and saved them from deportation.

Time and again, through courage and luck, Gyorgy evaded death, even after arrest by the notoriously anti-semitic Nyilas party who were constantly on the lookout for Jews. But by the time the Russians forced a surrender of the city on February 13, 1945, four of the Frenkel siblings and their parents were dead. The remaining Frenkels left Hungary for good. Mati and Valvish went to Germany, Edi to Palestine and Fred and Hajku to America. Settling in Brooklyn, Fred learned the new language and decided to return to the business he knew best, the business of down and feathers. He became a success and married Ann Suranyi, another survivor, in 1959. They had three sons, George, Richard and Kenny, fifteen grandchildren and fourteen great grandchildren. In 2018 he published his memoir, *Chance and Courage*.

It's difficult not to look back and feel some contempt for the Hungarians who enabled Germany to torture and kill Hungarian Jews. But for all of the hate and anger I feel over that time in my life, I have never been sorry I was born Jewish. I'm proud of it. I love Jewish traditions, like the ones our large family kept, all gathered round the table in Bekescsaba.

-- from Chance and Courage
by Fred Frenkel

Regina and Lipot Frenkel with seven children
(Fred and Nandi not yet born). Bekescsaba, Hungary, 1925.

Regina Frenkel

Lipot Frenkel

Fred Frenkel

Edi Frenkel

FRENKEL TESTVÉREK
TOLLKERESKEDŐK
BÉKÉSCSABA
JÓKAI UTCA 62.
TELEFON: 318.
FOLYÓSZÁMLA A BÉKÉSCSABAI TAKARÉKPÉNZTÁR
EGYESÜLETNÉL
EXPORTATION OF FEATHERS
AND DOWNS

Frenkel business sign., Bekescsaba

Chaim Hersh Frenkel and family. All perished.

Nandi, Fred and Icu Frenkel. Bekescsaba

*Edi, Regina and Icu at the railway.
Bekescsaba, c.1940.*

DAVID FRIDMAN

Rabbi Natan Torfstein was the chief rabbi of Stanislawow, located in the heart of Poland. The patriarch of a large and prestigious rabbinic family, he also functioned as the head of the city's rabbinic court. One son, Rabbi Shimon Yehuda Torfstein was the author of the volume *Mitzur Dvash*, a halachic-ethical discourse, which was published in Warsaw in 1931. In 1999 it was reprinted by the Israeli Ariel institute with an impressive introduction written by the chief rabbi of Haifa, Rabbi She'ar Yoshuv Cohen. Another son, Rabbi Israel Elimelech Torfstein, succeeded his father as chief rabbi of Stanislawow and authored many works of Torah scholarship, the majority of which, unfortunately, are lost to us. Rabbi Natan's daughter, Devora, married David Moises Fridman who was a keen observer of the political climate in Poland and who, by 1925, decided that there was no future for Jews in Europe. He convinced his reluctant wife to leave her family and emigrate. The Fridmans settled in Buenos Aires, Argentina where David earned a living in the sweater business. Three children were born and raised in Argentina, Frida, Natalio and Elena. Natalio's son is David Fridman.

Devora's sister Sara, married to Yaakov Rosenberg, remained in Poland with her husband and nine children. All were taken from their home in Poltusk to Auschwitz and only four siblings survived. The Torfstein brothers and their families suffered a similar fate.

Woe! Woe to those who are gone and cannot be replaced.
A pity for the loss of the Torah-Greats of Israel,
who were cut down so mercilessly and their great Torah words are forever lost to us.

*— from Rabbi She'ar Yoshuv Cohen's foreword to the 1999 Ariel edition of **Mitzur Dvash**.*

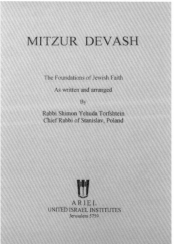

(above) Rabbi Natan Torfstein,
Stanislawow, Poland, late 1920's.

Devora Torfstein Fridman (left),
and her sister Sara Torfstein,
Stanislawow, Poland, late 1920's.

Anne Fridman's mother, Eva Basch was born in Antwerp, Belgium on December 1, 1913, one of two children of Anna Henriette Basch and Benjamin Basch. Benjamin a Lithuanian by birth, worked in the Antwerp diamond business. Eva attended the Tachkimoni school in Antwerp. Her brother Morris immigrated to the United States before the war and served in the U.S. army.

Anne's father, Ignace Oksenberg was born in Warsaw, Poland on March 4, 1901, to Chana and Chaim Juda Oksenberg, who had five other children (Israel, Jack, Salomon, Bela and Ella) and who, after immigrating to Belgium, also worked in the Antwerp diamond trade. Ignace attended cheder in Warsaw as well as public school before leaving Poland. On September 18, 1938 Eva and Ignace wed in Antwerp.

When the Nazis invaded the country, Eva, Ignace and Eva's parents fled the city. They travelled first to Nice where Anna Basch, who had been ill before the war, died. After burying her in France, the Oksenbergs and Benjamin Basch travelled to Spain and then sailed for Havana, Cuba where they remained for approximately one year. Like so many of the other Belgian refugees, Ignace worked in the diamond trade in Havana. In June 1941 the family made its way to Florida and the next month to New York. The Oksenbergs raised their daughter, Anne, on the Upper West Side and Ignace earned a living, once again, in the diamond trade. Chana Oksenberg and her children, Bela and Jack, settled in Brazil, while Solomon and Israel immigrated to the United States. Tragically, shortly before the outbreak of war, Chaim Juda, a Gerrer chasid, traveled with his youngest daughter Ella from Antwerp to Warsaw to visit the Gerrer Rebbe. They never returned to Belgium and perished in the Warsaw ghetto.

Wedding photo of Eva and Ignace Oksenberg. Antwerp, Belgium. September 18, 1938.

Anna Basch

Benjamin Basch

*"What have you done to us, you freedom-loving peoples, guardians of justice,
defenders of the high principles of democracy and of the brotherhood of man?
What have you allowed to be perpetrated against a defenseless people
while you stood aside and let it bleed to death, without offering help or succour,
without calling on the fiends to stop,
in the language of retribution which alone they would understand...."*

David Ben-Gurion, *September 1944*

DANIELLE FRIEDMAN | ERYNNE RENNERT

Marion Freudenberger Freilich, the grandmother of Danielle Friedman and Erynne Rennert, was born on November 9, 1928 in Frankfurt, Germany. Her father, Rudolf Freudenberger, was a physician in Bergen, situated on the outskirts of the city, and her mother, Amalia (née Adler), was a homemaker. The Freudenberger children, Marion, her twin brother Joseph, and their older brother, Joachim, attended the local Bergen public school and went to Hebrew school as well. As Hitler rose to power, life became increasingly more difficult and dangerous for the family. After the adoption of the Nuremberg laws, a camera was placed in the house opposite the doctor's home-office to monitor whether any Aryan patients were being treated. In September 1938 the Freudenbergers, sponsored by an aunt living in America, sailed for the United States on the *S.S. Aquatania* which left from Cherbourg, France. They settled in the Washington Heights section of Manhattan where they lived comfortably amongst other German Jewish refugees. In fact, the caterer of Joseph's Bar Mitzva celebration was none other than the mother of Henry Kissinger. After Kristallnacht, they were joined by Rudolf's mother, Ricka. Tragically, the immigration documents that were prepared for Rudolf's sister, her husband (the Rabbi of Miltenberg) and their two children were stolen, and they were all killed in the Shoah.

Marion's father had to learn English and pass the medical boards before he opened his practice near Yeshiva University and became the physician of some of the great rabbinic luminaries of the time, including Rabbi Joseph Soloveichik. To their chagrin, Marion and her brother, though ten by then, were placed in the second grade of PS 173, but eventually they caught up and entered George Washington High School. Marion met her Yankee husband Gerald Freilich when she was a student at City College and he was a math professor there. They married on June 28, 1953 and settled in Brooklyn where they raised their two children, Sandy and David.

In July 2005 after an absence of sixty-seven years, Marion Freudenberger Freilich returned to Bergen as the guest speaker in her former elementary school. She was presented with a booklet of memorabilia including her old report cards and those of her brothers, dating from 1938. The program was entitled "Gegen Vergessen und Unmenschlichkeit" – Against Forgetting and Inhumanity.

Dr. Rudolf Freudenberger, sixth from left. Red Cross of Bergen, World War I.

The Freudenberger family. Amalia and Rudolf, Joachim and the twins Marion and Joseph. Frankfurt, 1930.

Freudenberger home. Bergen, Germany. Pre-war.

Marion and Joseph Freudenberger. Frankfurt, 1933.

The Bergen elementary school.

Rudolf Freudenberger visa, front and back. Issued in Stuttgart, June 3, 1938.

Nachweisung der noch vorhandenen Anmeldekarten
über früher hier wohnhaft gewesene jüdische Mitbürger.

Name	Vorname	Wohnung	Beruf	Geburtstag	Geburtsort	Familienstand	am		am	verzogen: Nach:
Frank,	Ludwig	Erbsengasse 5	Kultusbeamter	25.10.96	Alsbach, Kreis Bensheim	verh.	17. 8.32	urt/M.	11. 9.59	England
Frank, geb. Röthschild	Ida	Erbsengasse 5		17. 5.95	Neuhof Kr.Fulda	verh.	17. 8.32	"	11. 9.59	England
Frank,	Ruth	Erbsengasse 5		4.11.24	Frankfurt/Main	ledig			4.12.36	Frankfurt, Röderbergweg 87
Frank,	Dagobert	Erbsengasse 5		9. 7.26	" " "	ledig			4.12.36	" " "
Dr.Freudenberger,	Rudolf	Steingasse 30	prakt.Arzt	25. 3.93	Memmelsdorf/Ufr.	verh.	2.12.21	rg	1. 9.38	New York USA
" " ",geb. Adler	Amalie	Steingasse 30		28. 5.95	Reubach /Rhön	verh.	2.12.21	rg	1. 9.38	New York USA
Freudenberger,	Joachim	Steingasse 30		1.11.24	Frankfurt/Main	ledig	10.7.58	rg	10.10.34	Würzburg
Freudenberger,	Joseph	Steingasse 30		9.11.28	" " "	ledig				
Freudenberger,	Bertel Maria	Steingasse 30		9.11.28	" " "	ledig				
Fuld,	Rosa	Offenb.Landstr.1	Verkäuferin	7.12.82	Bergen-Enkheim	ledig			1. 1.41	Ffm.Obermainanlage 26
Grünebaum,	Moritz	Steingasse 28	Taschner	21.8.72	Bergen-Enkheim	verh.			am 29.12.39 verstorben	
Grünebaum,geb. Wetterhahn	Emma	Steingasse 28		23.10.75	Nieder-Weisel	verh.			am 5.9.42 mit Sammeltransport nach unbekannt verzogen.	
Grünebaum,	Bella	Steingasse 28	Verkäuferin	13.11.01	Bergen-Enkheim	ledig			30.5.42 unbekannt verzogen	
Grünebaum,	Sally	Marktstraße 102	Kaufmann	28. 2.91	Bergen-Enkheim	ledig			10. 7.39 Ffm.Quinkostr.13	
Hahn,	Julius	Schwindegasse 2	Handelsmann	12.10.70	Bergen-Enkheim	verwitwet			am 18.2.42 in Ffm.verstorben	
Hahn,	Frieda	Schwindegasse 2	Postbeamtin	22. 7.03	Bergen-Enkheim	ledig			am 30.5.42 nach unbekannt verz.	
Hahn,	Jenny	Schwindegasse 2	ohne Beruf	24. 3.05	Bergen-Enkheim	ledig			am 30.5.42 nach unbekannt verz.	

Proof of Emigration registration of former Jewish citizens of Bergen.

Prescription pad of Dr. Freudenberger. Bergen, 1935.

Dr. med. Rudolf Freudenberger
prakt. Arzt
Telephon: Amt Bergen Nr. 208
Sprechstunden: Mittwoch 8—9, sonst 4—5 nachm.

Bergen, den 3 V 1935
b. Frankfurt/Main

Rp.

ANDREW GASPAR

Steven Gaspar, father of Andrew Gaspar, was born on March 17, 1922 in Kallosemjen, Hungary. He was the youngest of three children born to Joseph and Hermina (née Kronovics) Groszmann. After Joseph, a foreman at a farm, died of appendicitis, the penniless Hermina and her children moved to the nearby city of Nyiregyhaza. When the war broke out Steven was sent into the Carpathian mountains to dig ditches for the Germans. There he remained for several years. He finally escaped from forced labor carrying a backpack which saved his life by absorbing a bullet fired at him as he ran. His mother, brother Larry, Larry's wife Ester and baby Erica were sent to Auschwitz in 1944. Only Larry survived. Their sister Julia managed to remain in Nyiregyhaza throughout the war where she worked as a nurse.

Eva Salamon Gaspar, mother of Andrew Gaspar, was born on August 26, 1925 in Nyiregyhaza, Hungary to Olga (née Diamant) Salamon and Erno Salamon, whose family owned a men's clothing store named Salamon Brothers. She and her sister Vera, along with their parents, were deported to Auschwitz on May 6, 1944. Olga was separated from her daughters on Rosh Hashanah and murdered on Yom Kippur. Eyewitnesses later reported that Erno too was killed. In all, twenty-two members of Olga's family perished in Auschwitz. Eva and Vera were moved on October 6, 1944 to work in a munitions factory in Tauha outside of Liepzig and were liberated by Russian soldiers on May 7, 1945. The sisters returned to their hometown, where Eva met Steven (now) Gaspar and married him in 1947. Their son Andrew was born in 1948. The young family moved to Budapest in 1950 where two years later Eva died after a prolonged illness. Father and son left Hungary with one suitcase and one attaché of watches in October 1956. They settled in Washington Heights where Larry awaited them and Vera and Julia with their families soon followed.

Hermina Groszmann
Joseph Groszmann
Olga Diamant Salamon, Eva Salamon, Veronika Salamon, and Erno Salamon. Nyiregyhaza, c.194(

Eva Salamon Gaspar with a toddler cousin, 1947.
Eva and Steven Gaspar wedding photo. Nyiregyhaza, 1947.
The Gaspars and baby Andrew. Nyiregyhaza, 1949.

NINA GASPAR | SUE TALANSKY

Moty (Marek) Stromer, the father of Nina Gaspar and Sue Talansky, was born on July 5, 1910 in the small town of Kamyonka-Strumilova, just outside of Lvov, Poland. He, his parents, Shaul and Gittel, his two sisters, Zlata and Henia, and a brother, Meyer, were all involved in the family's successful wholesale liquor business. In August 1939, a month before the Nazi invasion, Moty's sister Henia immigrated to America to join her husband. Moty's brother was sent to Siberia shortly thereafter. Moty survived in the Lvov ghetto with his other sister Zlata and her husband and two little boys. One Thursday in 1943, he witnessed the murder of his sister and her two sons. He fasted every Thursday for the next four decades. Moty narrowly escaped being sent to Yanov work camp, but when the Lvov ghetto was finally liquidated, he was put on a train headed to certain death in Belzec. He escaped from the moving train, ran towards Kamyonka and was taken in by a Christian farmer and his wife, Josef and Rosalie Streker. They were former customers of the Stromers. The Strekers hid him in their barnyard attic for over 14 months and thus saved his life. While in hiding, he asked for pencils and paper and succeeded in writing a journal of all his wartime experiences. He entitled it *Memoirs of an Unfortunate Person*. In 2007 the Strekers were inducted as Righteous Amongst the Nations in Yad Vashem and the museum published Moty's translated memoir. In all, 143 members of this once vibrant extended family perished in the Shoah.

In 1947, Rabbi Moshe Steinberg, then chief rabbi of Krakow, officiated at the wedding of Moty Stromer and another survivor from Lvov, Ruth Baumwald (b. 2/22/22). Ruth was a beautiful and intelligent *gymnasium* graduate who had survived the war in hiding with her parents, Sala and Tzvi, and her sister, Lusia. The young couple moved to Belgium and in 1955 sailed on the *Queen Mary* to New York with their two daughters, Nina and Sue. They settled on the Upper West Side and Moty went into the real estate business. Decades after marrying the Stromers in Krakow, Rabbi Steinberg, who had emigrated and become chief justice of the rabbinical court of America, officiated at the weddings of their two daughters in New York.

An eternal optimist, Moty was fond of quoting from Tehilim 126,
"Those who sow in tears will reap in joy." His daughters had the line inscribed on his gravestone.

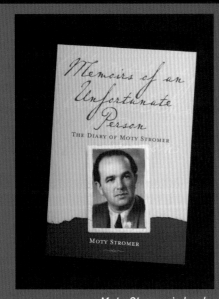

Moty Stromer's book,
"Memoirs of an Unfortunate Person."

Invitation to a Chanukat Ha-Bayit (housewarming)
sent by Reuven and Leah Stromer.
Kamyonka-Strumilova, Poland, August, 1926.

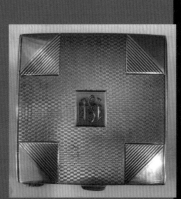

Henia Stromer's gold cosmetic case, pre-war.

Moty Stromer standing, far left with his grandparents, Leah, seated, and Reuven Stromer behind her and five of Leah's brothers. Leah Stromer died in 1937. Of the rest only Moty survived. Kamyonka-Strumilova, Poland, 1930.

Purim gathering at the home of Mechel Eisen and Zlata Stromer Eisen, third and fourth from the left.
Seated, front left, is a young Menachem Begin. Lvov, 1934.
The Eisens and their two boys were killed in 1942.

Bus pass of Ruth Baumwald Stromer. Lvov, 1939.

Ruth Baumwald, left, a friend, and Lusia Baumwald. Lvov, 1930.

Yom Kippur Machzor, printed in Piotrkow. Poland, 1890.

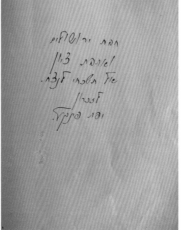

Entry in Henia Stromer's autograph book. Classmate Yaffa Finkle writes in Hebrew, "Never Forget Love of Jerusalem and Zion." Kamyonka, December 17, 1934.

Bankis, or suction cups, used to treat various ailments.

Bridal Trousseau prepared for Henia Stromer Edelstein with her monogram HS. She sailed for the United States in August, 1939

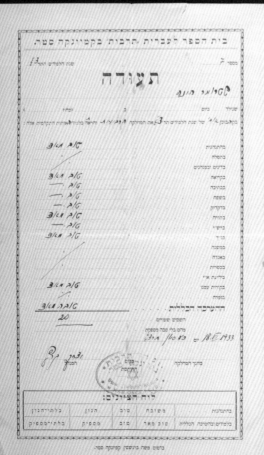

Ruth Baumwald Stromer (left) with friends. c.1935.

(left) Report card of Henia Stromer, the Hebrew Cultural School, Kamyonka-Strumilowa, Poland, June 18, 1933.

BEN GELBTUCH

Moshe Gelbtuch, grandfather of Ben Gelbtuch, was born on the fifth night of Chanukah, December 24, 1878 in Tarnoruda, Galicia (now the Ukraine). His parents Eliezer Lieber and Devora Rothstein Gelbtuch were Chortkover chassidim. Moshe was the eldest of their eight children, of which only four survived infancy. Eliezer Lieber was a spice trader who raised his family in Skalat, a suburb of Tarnopol, which was a center of Chassidism. Moshe in fact was brought by his father to the first Husiatyner Rebbe to lay *tefillin* for his Bar Mitzvah. At the age of seventeen, he married Bryna Yocheved (Bronia) Katz, the daughter of a prominent Husiyatner chassid. Soon after Moshe was asked to become the first chossid of the Kopycznitzer rebbe. Moshe owned a general store and was the *gabbai tzedakah*, (charity administrator) for Skalat.

Moshe lost most of his family in the Shoah. His wife Bronia was gassed in Belzec; his oldest son Yehoshua with wife Gusta and children vanished in Siberia; son Arrin's wife and children were killed; his third son, Michoel with his wife and children were murdered and his daughter Devora was shot on the streets of Skalat. Moshe and his son David survived by hiding in the attic and outdoor pit of his Ukrainian worker, subsisting on nothing more than a sugar cube a day.

When the war ended, Moshe, now 67, and David went to Vienna where they were reunited with Arrin. With the help of the Kopycznitzer rebbe (Rabbi Avraham Yehoshua Heschel) who was already in the States, the three men came to the U.S. and settled on the Lower East Side. There David was reunited with a dear friend from Skalat, Ida Dlugacz (b. 5/20/20), who with her father, was the only survivor of her family. Beaten and scarred by German SS men, Ida survived by hiding in a neighbor's barn, sleeping with the animals and subsisting on scraps of food. When her father David immigrated to Palestine, Ida chose to follow her heart to reunite with David Gelbtuch. They married on November 2, 1947.

True to the prediction of their beloved rebbe, that Moshe Gelbtuch would be blessed with *"chamisha chumshei Torah"* (five Books of Moses) his children David and Ida produced five sons, all pillars of Torah. Ben Gelbruch is the eldest. David opened Gelb Sales on the Lower East Side and their business thrived as did their five boys. Moshe Gelbtuch died in 1975 at the age of 97.

Ida Duglacz parents,
Sara Teomim & David Duglacz.
Skalat, 1910's.

The Gelbtuch home in Skalat.

David Gelbtuch. Skalat, Pre-war.

Ida Dlugacz. Skalat. Pre-war.

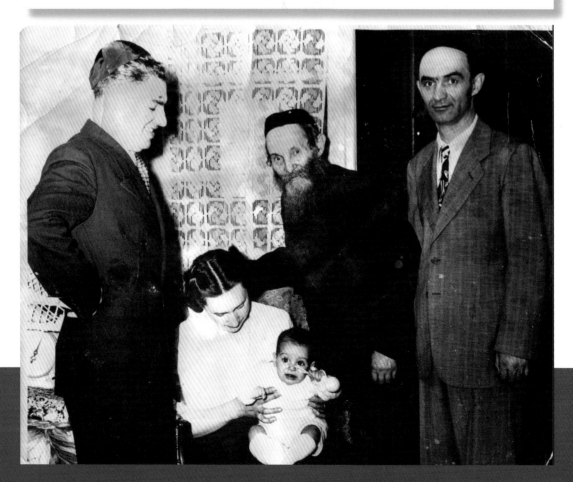

Mr. Moses Gelbtuch
requests the honor of your presence
at the marriage ceremony of his son

David

to

Judith Dlugacz

Sunday evening, November the Second
Nineteen hundred and forty-seven
at six o'clock, sharp
at the Synagogue of
Grand Rabbi Abraham Heschel
132 Henry Street
New York

M. Gelbtuch
282 East Houton Street
New York

Ladies are cordially requested to refrain from low cut dresses.

בעה"ש

קול ששון וקול שמחה
קול חתן וקול כלה

הנני מתכבד בזה להזמין את קרובי וידידי לבא לקחת חבל
בשמחת יום כלולת בני היקר המופלא

כמר דוד נ"י

עב"ג הכלה המהוללה מרת

יהודית תחי'

בת החסיד הנכבד מו"ה יוסף דוד דלאנאשט ע"ה

החופה תהי' בעזה"ש בשטומצ"ל

ביום א' חיי־שרה, י"ט חשון, תש"ח לפ"ק

בשעה 6 בערב בדיוק

בביהכ"נ של כ"ק אדמו"ר הרב הצדיק שליט"א מקיפיטשניץ

132 העניו סטריט, ניו יארק

ידידכם המחכה לקראת בואכם לשלום
וא"ה־ש בשמחת צאצאיכם ישמח לבי גם אני

משה געלבטוך

Top: Invitation to the wedding of David and Ida at the synagogue of the Kopycznitzer Rebbe. New York, November 2, 1947.

(l to r) David, Ida, Moshe and Arrin Gelbtuch with baby Benny. New York, 1948.

Sefer Torah, rescued from the war and dedicated in memory of Moshe Gelbtuch and his wife Bronia.
Chanukiah rescued from the war. Both items buried by Moshe Gelbtuch before he went into hiding.

Ida Gelbtuch once recounted how, during a blizzard that dumped more than a foot and a half of snow in New York City, her father-in-law, Moshe Gelbtuch, who was then well into his 80s, refused to miss minyan and ventured out on his own to the Kopycznitzer shul, over a half mile away. The police, who apparently saw nothing more than a black hat moving in a snow drift, rescued him and brought him back home.
Many people would regularly come to visit Moshe Gelbtuch so that they could receive his blessings and listen to his rich, first-hand knowledge of great chassidic rebbes. He remained sharp and healthy until the last ten days of his life.
Rabbi Moshe Feinstein said of him at his funeral, 'Ki Gamar Chassid Min Haaretz'...
we have lost the ability to see someone who truly exemplified Chassidus.

DASHA GELBTUCH

Chaim Yehuda Aryeh Hakohain Konstam (Leibel), Dasha Gelbtuch's father, was born on April 16, 1912 in Ozorkow, Poland to Chanoch Heinich Konstam and Golda Toronczyk Konstam. Early in their marriage the couple had moved to Ozerkow from Lodz so that Heinich could develop his textile business as his family grew. Leibel and his one brother and four sisters were raised in a home committed to Ger chassidus. Despite only finishing five grades of formal schooling, Leibel trained to become an accountant and when the family was forced into the Lodz ghetto, he worked there in that capacity. He married Devora Frenkel in 1943. When the ghetto was liquidated in 1944, Leibel and the rest of the Konstams were deported to Auschwitz. Devora did not survive. Because of his skills, Leibel was sent to work at the Braunschweig labor camp to help in the manufacture of auto parts, then to Ravensbruck, then Woebellin and finally Bergen-Belsen from where he was liberated on April 15, 1945. In Bergen-Belsen Leibel reunited with his brother Henry and he met an old friend of his late wife, Minja (Mindel) Levin, who also came from Ozorkow. The couple married in a DP camp near Hanover, Germany on May 2, 1946 and before immigrating to the U.S., had two children in Germany, Abie in 1947 and Goldie in 1950. When their visas came through, the young family moved to Cincinnati, Ohio where their daughter Dasha (Rivka) was born in 1951. Leibel began work in dinette sales and then moved on to real estate and nursing homes. The success of his business ventures allowed him to become a lifelong generous supporter of many Jewish causes and, in particular, Gerrer institutions.

Minja Levin Konstam was born on January 31, 1916 in Ozorkow, Poland to Sarah Fraidel and Avram Abba Levin. In 1939 Sarah Fraidel died, leaving Minja and her five siblings, Etta, Faige (Fella), Shimon, Moshe and Yossel motherless. Avram Abba worked in a textile factory and was a rebbe for young boys in the evenings. When the Nazis invaded, father and children endured many humiliations and much suffering. Etta was living with Shimon and his young family when they were all deported to Auschwitz from Zychlin, Poland. Avram was seized from Ozorkow's ghetto. Minja, Fella and Yossel were sent to forced labor in the Lodz ghetto in 1942. Two years later Yossel was separated from his sisters and never heard from again. The two sisters were transported to Auschwitz. There Minja and Fella were miraculously reunited with Etta who, working in the camp kitchen, saved the girls lives by smuggling extra food rations to them. Minja and Fella were then sent to Hambuhren labor camp and finally to Bergen-Belsen, where Minja nursed Fella when she fell ill from typhus. Miraculously all three sisters survived the war and lived to settle near one another in Cincinnati, Ohio.

Opposite page: (clockwise)
Matisyahu Toronczyk, Leibel's maternal grandfather. Ozorkow, 1916.
Chanoch Heinach Hakohen Konstam. Ozorkow, circa 1910
Leibel holding his first-born Abie. Hanover, Germany, 1948.
Leibel and Minja coming to America. 1950.
Leibel and Minja. Hanover, Germany, 1946.
(Group photo) Standing (left to right), Chanoch Heinach, Leibel, Sara Tzirel (Leibel's sister),
Aryeh Rosenbaum (Sara Tzirel's husband). Seated (left to right), Golda, Rosenbaum baby, Tzipra (Leibel's sister). Ozorkow, 1938.

MENDI GERTNER

Elizabeth (Elka Baila) Gertner, mother of Mendi Gertner, was born on December 24th, 1929 in the Alps of Klagenfurt, Austria. Her father, Rabbi Avraham Chanales, was a well-respected rabbi and community leader. He and his wife, Syma, had three daughters who learned Torah and other Jewish subjects with their father at home. The eldest, Chana, made Aliyah to Palestine in 1938 when she was fifteen. The next, Frieda, fled Austria for Paris. The ever-tightening Nazi noose finally led to an arrest warrant for the rabbi as the community records he held were requisitioned. Rabbi Avraham hid himself in the forest, where he was found and beaten to a pulp. It was after this event that the Chanales family knew they had to escape. Avraham and Syma Chanales, along with Elizabeth, left Austria in February/March of 1939 on one of the last ships out, the SS *Konigstein*. The passengers were given visas to enter Trinidad, which was a British colony at the time. England then annulled all the visas and the passengers were denied entry into Trinidad's port. Those on board were terrified that they would be brought back to Germany and almost certain death. However, the captain of the ship, Alfred Leidig, took upon himself the righteous mission of sailing from port to port, begging for different countries to accept his passengers.

In the end, Venezuela opened its doors and gave the 165 souls on the ship a collective visa. When they arrived in Venezuela in 1939, the Chanaleses were able to start their lives again. With few possessions and a language barrier, the family faced many challenges. Initially, they and their fellow refugees lived on a small coffee plantation named "Mampote." The Jewish community in Venezuela generously helped this group and eventually Elizabeth and her family moved to Caracas. The Rabbi never recovered from the beating he had received at the hands of the Nazis. He continued, however, to fulfill rabbinic duties without ever accepting any salary and he home-schooled both Elizabeth and her sister Ada, the daughter who was born in Venezuela. Syma Chanales, breaking all stereotypes, became the family breadwinner and established a very successful linen business. When Elizabeth was seventeen her father took her to New York to find a husband and through his old friend, Rabbi Chazkel Besser, she was introduced to Rabbi Yehuda Gertner, another survivor. The couple married in 1955 and settled in Caracas where they raised three children, Rivky, Moishe and Mendi.

When asked about her father, Elizabeth Gertner said,
"He was a gaon. He always had a sefer under his arm, no matter where he went."

.

(opposite page)
A rare photograph taken of the refugees from the SS Konigstein,
once they had arrived in Venezuela and temporarily settled in
"Mampote," a coffee plantation.
Courtesy of Dr. Celestino Aza Sanchez

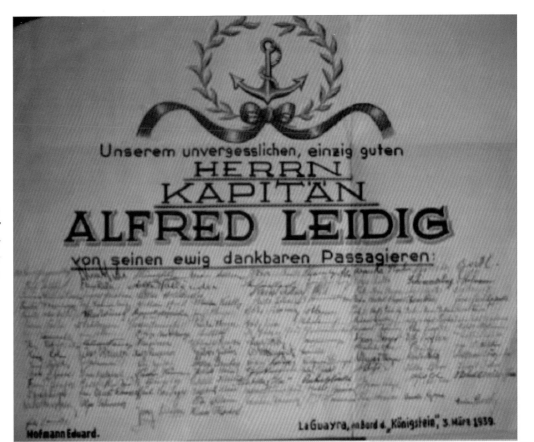

The thank you card inscribed to "our unforgettable and uniquely good" Captain Alfred Leidig and signed by the "eternally grateful" passengers of the SS Konigstein, March 3, 1939.

Rabbi Avraham Chanales & Syma Chanales

Elizabeth Chanales.
Caracas, Venezuela, 1950.

FRANCES GLEITMAN | BARBARA GLEITMAN SAMUELS

Helen Shroda, mother of Frances Gleitman and Barbara Gleitman Samuels, was born in Chrzanow, Poland on January 28, 1927, one of three children, Freydel, Helen (Chayka) and Israel, of Avraham and Rachel Sconhurtz Shroda. Abraham owned the apartment building where the Shrodas lived alongside about one hundred other members of the extended family, from infants to adults. The Shrodas owned a candy factory located adjacent to this apartment building. When the Nazis invaded the town, Helen and her cousin Ben hid in a nearby hole in the ground but Helen was caught and sent to a labor camp which produced textiles for the German war effort. She was fourteen years old and assigned the task of lifting fifty-pound spools of thread onto machinery.

Of the extended Shroda family that had once lived so happily under one roof only Helen and four cousins survived the Shoah. When the war ended Helen returned to Chrzanow, knocked on the door of her family's home and was told by the Polish woman who answered that this was no longer her property. Through the open door, Helen could see familiar remnants of her former life, pictures on the wall, knick-knacks and other reminders of a vanished world. Like so many other survivors, Helen hastily left what was once her hometown and then spent time in a DP camp in Pocking, Germany where she met and married Ben Gleitman in 1946.

Berek (Ben) Gleitman was born in Bedzin, Poland in 1921, one of fivechildren of Beila Frimette and Avraham Moshe Gleitman who was in the glassware business. Ben was the oldest of the Gleitman children (Ben, Sally, Arnold, and twins Yentl and Surale). When the war broke out, Ben initially hid, but when he returned to help his family, he was captured. He was sent to the Gross-Rosen concentration camp, where he remained until he was liberated and assigned to the DP camp in Pocking, Germany.

Ben and Helen immigrated to the U.S. on September 3, 1949. They raised their two daughters, Barbara and Frances, in Brooklyn.

Helen eventually fought for and reclaimed her family's property in Poland. She considered the monies collected as "blood money" and chose to distribute the proceeds to a variety of charities. For many years Helen would visit the Madeleine candy factory, then in Rockaway, for she found it comforting to sit once again surrounded by the aromas that recalled her idyllic early childhood in Chrzanow.

(left to right) Fraidel Shroda, Zaida Shroda (Avraham's father), Avraham Shroda with Israel on his lap, Helen Shroda, Rachel Shroda. Chrzanow, c.1934.

*Ben and Helen Gleitman
Pocking, Germany, 1946.*

*Ben with a friend".
Bedzin, Poland, Pre-war.*

Table top containing postcards

Detail of postcards from Freyde in Freudental to her sister Chayka in Benzdorf

MARC GLEITMAN

Arnold Gleitman, father of Marc Gleitman, was born on March 9, 1923 in Bedzin, Poland to Beila Frimette and Avraham Moshe Gleitman who was a glassware salesman and, on the side, a wedding fiddler. There were five siblings in the family, two older than Arnold, Ben and Sally, and twin girls, Yentl and Surale, twelve years Arnold's junior. As a young man with a seventh-grade education, Arnold worked briefly as an apprentice cabinet maker but the Nazi invasion changed life for good. In the early years of the war he was forced to work in German factories but he received some pay and was eventually sent back to Bedzin. When he returned home after a second round-up, his entire family was gone except for the twin girls, now six, whom he found roaming the streets alone and rummaging in garbage. He placed the girls in someone's care, but sadly Yentl and Surale were never seen again. In 1941 Arnold was deported to Auschwitz and was later transferred to two ruthlessly cruel labor camps at Gross-Rosen and Poking. After liberation he was reunited with his brother Ben and sister Sally and they spent three years together in Germany where both siblings found spouses and immigrated to the U.S. With a promise of Canadian citizenship, Arnold then signed a one-year contract with the Canadian Railroad as a laborer laying track outside of Vancouver. The only Jew on a sixty-man crew, Arnold found the ten months on this project almost as hard on him as the Nazi years. He then moved to Toronto where he met a visiting American girl, Lila Obernick, whom he married in New York on June 20, 1954. The couple first lived in the Bronx, then New Jersey, Brooklyn and finally Long Island, where they raised their two children, Jane (b. 1955) and Marc (b. 1958). Arnold made a living in the lumber business.

Both images are of Arnold Gleitman, post-war

JERRY GOLDBERG

Jerry Goldberg's grandfather, Max Goldberg, was one of twelve children born to Efraim and Krintche Krizelman Goldenberg in Shumsk, Poland on April 6, 1892. Efraim was a successful businessman and accountant who owned a wheat mill. Max, always a bit rebellious, decided to venture out on his own, and left for the United States in 1908 at the age of sixteen. On Ellis Island Goldenberg became Goldberg and Max began working as a textile jobber. One sister, like Max, immigrated to the U.S. and five other siblings left for Palestine between the world wars. Shortly after the arrival of the Red Army in Shumsk, on September 17, 1939, a telegram arrived at the Goldenberg home in New York City with three words of reassurance, "WE ARE ALLRIGHT." The date was December 15, 1939 but the paper is stamped "delayed in the URSS." The town was occupied by Germans on July 3, 1941 and its inhabitants forced into a ghetto. Shumsk, which had about 2000 Jewish inhabitants (90% of its population) was made *Judenrein* one year later. In August 1942 the town's Jews were taken to pits located on the bank of the nearby Viliya river and shot to death by German soldiers aided by Ukrainian auxiliary police. Max Goldberg's mother and five of his sisters and brothers (Zvi Hirsch, Breina, Mika, Tsherni and Leah) and their families, as well as many other Goldenbergs, were killed in the massacre.

The telegram of 1939 was their last communication.

Max Goldberg eventually married a cousin, Gussie Krizelman, whom he had brought over from Europe. They raised their family of three children in Ozone Park, Queens and Max continued in the *"shmata"* (clothing) business.

Max's great-granddaughter, Dara, has tattooed this ancestral telegram onto her arm as a tribute to the family that was so tragically lost.

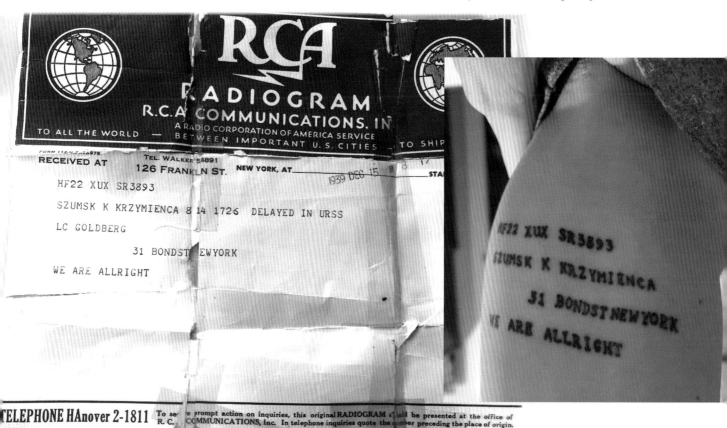

TELEPHONE HAnover 2-1811 To secure prompt action on inquiries, this original RADIOGRAM should be presented at the office of R.C. COMMUNICATIONS, Inc. In telephone inquiries quote the number preceding the place of origin.

SHIRA GOLDEN

Shira Sky Golden, the new administrative director of the Jewish Center of Atlantic Beach, did not know she had any connection to the Holocaust until a few short years ago.

Shira Golden and her husband Rabbi Steven Golden live in Cedarhurst, New York, where he is the rabbi of the Sephardic Temple. Shira was born on September 30, 1966 and was raised by loving, adoptive parents, Zena and Hyman Sky, in Kansas City, Missouri where her father was the cantor in Congregation Beth Shalom of Kansas City, Missouri.

Growing up, Shira was always aware that she was adopted, that she was Jewish and that she was born in Philadelphia. Around 2011 she began to look for her birth parents, an odyssey that was to span almost a decade. She first hired a private investigator who told her the data provided by the adoption agency was completely false. Then, at the suggestion of a cousin, she tried several DNA testing sites including *Family Tree* and *Ancestry.com*. Nothing turned up. Then in 2017, Shira's two grown daughters gave their mother a *23&Me* testing kit for Mother's Day. Success! Shira learned the identity of her birth father Harold but he had died in 2010. Harold's niece identified a woman named Judi who was Harold's girlfriend in 1966 and almost definitely the mother of his child. With the help of a group of volunteers called Search Angels, Shira eventually did connect to her birth mother Judi who was living in New Jersey. Their initial phone conversation was emotional and lengthy. The first question Judi asked Shira was, "Have you had a good life?" Mother and daughter met at a Starbucks in Englewood and have been in close contact ever since. Through Judi, Shira connected with a large, extended and very welcoming new family of half-siblings and cousins. Most touching for Shira was meeting her maternal grandmother, Paula.

Paula was born in Belitza, Poland on November 22, 1923, one of four children of Judis and Chaim Itche who was a salesman for the Singer sewing machine company. After Chaim Itche died, Judis was thirty-seven-year-old widow with four young children. She supported them by working in a bakery. In 1940, while under Soviet occupation, Paula married her neighbor's son, Louis. In June 1941 the nightmare of the German occupation began. She and her husband Louis ran into the woods and left their daughter Osna in the care of a gentile neighbor, but the little girl perished in the war. Paula and Louis survived four years in hiding in the forests of the Polish countryside and then spent several years in DP camps in Germany, where two daughters were born, Judi in 1946 in Berlin and Ruth a few years later in Konstanz. The family then immigrated to the U.S. and attempted to settle in St. Louis, Missouri, where Louis worked long hours in a supermarket. Hearing of opportunities for survivors back east, they eventually moved to Vineland, New Jersey, where Louis began as a chicken farmer and then built a successful lumber business. Another child, Izzy, was born in 1956.

When Paula met her newly discovered granddaughter, Shira, she unclasped a gold necklace that was around her neck and placed it on Shira's. The necklace had been given to her by her late husband during their early years in the United States. "I want you to have it," she insisted. Paula passed away on September 30, 2020, which was also Shira's birthday.

Louis and Paula, Berlin, 1948.

Louis, Judi and Paula, New Year's card, Berlin, 1947.

Louis, first row, second from right. Belitza, Poland, 1932.

Necklace given to Shira Golden by her grandmother Paula.

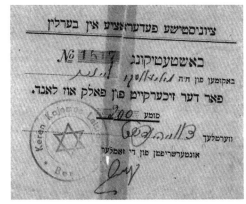

Receipt for donation Louis made for Jewish refugees in Israel, Berlin, 1948.

SARAH GOLDMAN
Charlene Khaghan

Esther and Hirsch Zev Magids lived in Werynia, Poland, a town of about 3000 Jews not far from Vilna. Esther and her mother-in-law operated a fabric store and Hirsch was in the lumber business, felling trees in the nearby forests and sending lumber to Germany. They had three children, Molly born in 1929, Dinah in 1932 and Robert (Baruch) born in 1933. When the Germans marched into town in 1939 they established a ghetto and the Magids were forced to welcome three other families into their home. Shortly thereafter Hirsch and the family were sent to Zalpaniki where he was made a supervisor over about eighteen young lumberjacks. During their months in this outpost Esther and her husband built with their own hands a small bunker and when they were certain that a transport to their death was near they retreated to the bunker and remained there for two and a half years. Their challenges were great. The children foraged for berries and mushrooms in summer and Hirsch stole potatoes from nearby fields. A kindly priest knew of their whereabouts and brought them bread and milk. A plastic tarp kept rain water and melting snow out and the dim light of a kerosene lamp was their only illumination. The children were permitted to venture out for airings only in the dead of night. In 1944 Esther became pregnant with her fourth child and Hirsch bribed a farmer to allow her to give birth, with Molly's help, on a straw mat in his chicken coop. Their daughter Sarah was born on April 9, 1945.

When the war ended, the Magids returned briefly to their hometown, where they found that only one other family had survived. They continued on to Lodz, where they stayed a year, earning money by selling used clothing at the market. They were smuggled into Germany and successfully crossed over form the Russian zone, to the American zone where they found shelter in the Schlochtensei DP camp. The three older children went to Munich to attend school and finally, after a five year wait, the entire family immigrated to the U.S. in 1950 on a cargo ship. They settled in Williamsburg, N.Y. and began a new life. Hirsch worked in a laundromat and Esther in a hat factory, while six-year-old Sarah entered school, speaking only Yiddish. She attended Bais Yaakov, a local elementary school and then Eastern District High School. In 1964 she married Martin Goldman, another survivor from Poland.

*Robert, Hirsch Zev holding baby Sarah, Dinah.
Lodz, 1946.*

*Hirsch Zev and Esther
Werynia, Poland. pre-war.*

*Robert and Dinah Magids.
Date unknown.*

*"… we are first commanded to survive as Jews, lest the Jewish people perish.
We are commanded, secondly,*
to remember in our very guts and bones
the martyrs of the Holocaust, lest their memory perish.
*We are forbidden, thirdly, to deny or despair of God,
however much we may have to contend with him or with belief in him, lest Judaism perish.
We are forbidden, finally, to despair of the world
as the place which is to become the kingdom of God,
lest we make it a meaningless place in which God is dead
or irrelevant and everything is permitted.
To abandon any of these imperatives, in response to Hitler's victory at Auschwitz,
would be to hand him yet other, posthumous victories.*

Emil Fackenheim,
To Mend the World
Foundations of Post-Holocaust Jewish Thought, 1982

HOWARD GOLDSCHMIDT

Helen Warisch Goldschmidt, Howard Goldschmidt's mother, was born on November 6, 1930 in Hamburg, Germany, the youngest of the three children (Natan, Miriam and Helen) of Herman and Kathe (née Kessler) Warisch. The Warisch family had arrived in Germany from Poland in the early 1600's and during World War I Herman was a groom for the Kaiser's army horses, which led to a business importing animal hair for brush manufacture. By 1935, with Naziism on the rise, the family decided to flee to Antwerp. In 1941 they fled again, like many of Antwerp's Jews, and passed through Paris, then Montpelier, a backwater of Vichy France. Herman, his brother, and his son Natan were interned at the Gurs detention camp but managed to escape. Affidavits from a business partner now living in the U.S. allowed the family to board the *SS Navemar* in Seville on August 6, 1941. The ship, filthy and overcrowded, was privately chartered by the American Joint Distribution Committee to hastily carry over a thousand refugees to safety. The seven-week transatlantic crossing was a torturous one, with many passengers contracting typhus and six dying during the voyage. The Warisches entered the U.S. on September 12, 1941, two weeks before Rosh Hashanah. They settled on the Upper West Side of Manhattan and Herman continued his import business from an office on Beaver Street near the docks. He attended weekly shiurim by Rabbi Joseph Soloveichik. There he met his future *mechutan*, Dr. Karl Goldschmidt.

Helen was only eleven when she arrived in New York. She attended Joan of Arc High School and earned a Masters in Early Childhood Education from NYU. Helen married Eric Goldschmidt on July 1, 1954. They lived in Baltimore, Newark, and Philadelphia and finally settled in Kew Garden Hills, Queens, where they raised their three children, Daniel, Howard and Judy.

Eric Nathan Goldschmidt, Howard's father, was born on November 25, 1927 in Berlin, the son of Dr. Karl Goldschmidt and Ina Feuchtwanger Goldschmidt (née Posen). Ina's first husband, Hans Feuchtwanger, died of the Spanish flu when she was pregnant with Eric's half-brother, Hans. The Goldschmidt and Posen families had lived in Frankfurt from at least the 1600's when a Posen ancestor served as a *dayan* (judge) there. Ina's father, Herman Naftali Posen, had owned and operated a very prominent jewelry shop in Berlin. Karl had served in the Kaiser's army in World War I and then attended law school in Heidelberg and Munich. He relocated to Berlin after receiving his law degree and worked for his brother-in-law, the financier and industrialist, Jakob Michael. In 1932 the family fled Frankfurt for The Hague, where Eric and his brother spent an idyllic childhood by the North Sea. As Dutch citizens they were allowed to move to Dutch Guyana while they waited for visas to the U.S. The Goldschmidts arrived in New York via Paramaribo and Trinidad on May 6, 1940 and they settled in Riverdale. Eric attended the Bronx High School of Science, Brooklyn College and then Harvard, earning a Ph.D. in chemistry.

Helen's grandparents had died of natural causes before the war. Eric's grandmothers had lived together in Amsterdam. One died of natural causes before the war. The other, Esther Posen, age 69, was deported via the notorious Westerbork transit camp to Sobibor. She either died on the train or was gassed upon arrival in April 1943.

Herman and Kathe Warisch. Norderney Island, North Sea. Summer, 1928.

Ina and Karl Goldschmidt on their honeymoon.
Taormina, Sicily. February, 1924.

Ina Posen Goldschmidt with baby Eric and brother Hans. Berlin, 1927.

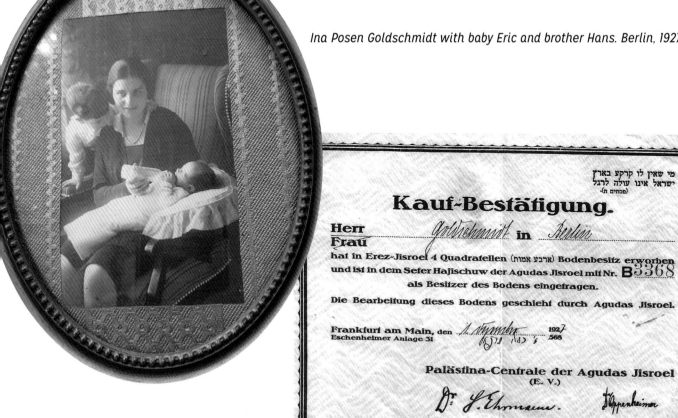

מי שאין לו קרקע בארץ
ישראל אינו עולה לרגל
(פסחים ח.)

Kauf-Bestätigung.

Herr _Goldschmidt_ in _Berlin_
Frau

hat in Erez-Jisroel 4 Quadratellen (ארבע אמות) Bodenbesitz erworben
und ist in dem Sefer Hajischuw der Agudas Jisroel mit Nr. B3368
als Besitzer des Bodens eingetragen.

Die Bearbeitung dieses Bodens geschieht durch Agudas Jisroel.

Frankfurt am Main, den _1. November_ 1927
Eschenheimer Anlage 31 _____ 568

Palästina-Centrale der Agudas Jisroel
(E. V.)

Dr. S. Ehrmann.   J. Oppenheimer

Purchase of "Arba Amot" in Palestine for Karl Goldschmidt. Berlin. November, 1927.

Kathe Warisch with her children Miriam, Helen, and Natan. Hamburg, 1935.

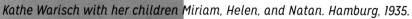

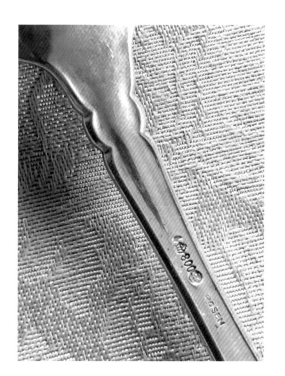

Imprint on Posen silverware. Posen Jewelry and Silverware Shop on Unter den Linden Strasse, Berlin.
Goldschmidt family in Holland. Karl and Ina, far right. Early 1930's.

Revoked citizenship from Berlin

Revocation of German citizenship. Berlin, 1938.

Shipping label fragment from the same voyage.

Steamer trunk KIG (Karl and Ina Goldschmidt) on the SS Cottice bound for Curacao, December 4, 1940.

GEORGIE GROSS

Nathan Kleinhaus, the father of Georgie Gross, was born on September 25, 1912 in Galicia, Poland. He was next to the youngest of six children (Simcha, Tzilla, Wolf, Yidel, Nathan and Lily) born to Chaim and Fayge Kleinhaus. By the 1930's the entire family had moved to Belgium where they worked in the busy Antwerp diamond trade. In the spring of 1939 Nathan traveled to Brazil on a business trip and, as a result, he ended up spending the war years there. The rest of the family managed to survive the war and emigrate through the agency of the Portuguese consul in Bordeaux, France, Aristides de Sousa Mendes. By 1946, when Nathan came to New York, his family had already settled there. Nathan met Ruth Jassy, another survivor, and two weeks later they were engaged. After a brief stay in Brazil, the couple began their family in 1947 with the birth of their daughter, Georgie, followed by two other children, Faye and Murray. In New York Nathan earned his living as a diamond merchant.

Ruth Jassy, was born on May 26, 1924 in Berlin, the second of two daughters of Moshe and Bertha Jassy. The two Jassy girls, Anita and Ruth, spent their formative years in a Germany that was growing evermore threatening to Jews. On Kristallnacht, Moshe was picked up by the German police and sent to Dachau. He was released a few months later and by then Bertha and the two girls had already left for Switzerland. By 1939 they had reached the U.S. Moshe joined them soon after, but died of cancer in 1942. Ruth was a teenager when she came to New York and she attended high school there. In 1946 she was working on 47th Street where she met Nathan.

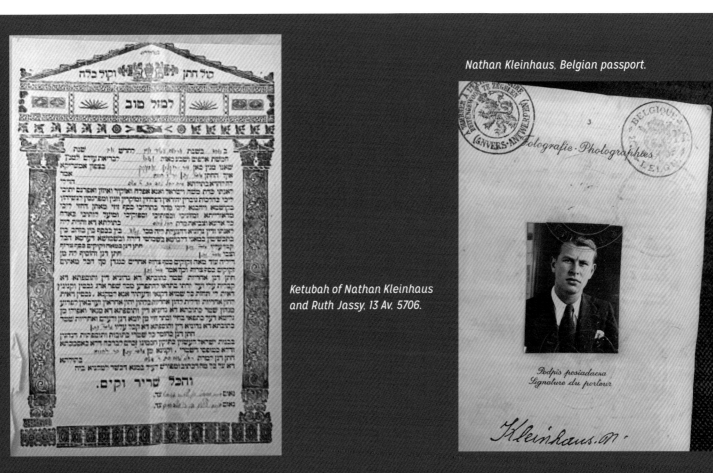

Ketubah of Nathan Kleinhaus and Ruth Jassy, 13 Av. 5706.

Nathan Kleinhaus, Belgian passport.

STEVEN GROSS

Steven Gross' father, Alexander Gross, was born on May 16, 1898, one of nine children of Anna and Shimon Gross who was a baker in the Polish town of Skawina, outside of Krakow. (Several sons of Alexander's eldest brother, Akiva, took part in the first Maccabiah games in 1932, and eventually founded the largest bakery in Tel Aviv, *Maafia Gross*. Two brothers immigrated to the U.S. in the 1920's and one of their sons was killed in the Battle of the Bulge.) Alexander left home at an early age and he moved to Vienna where he started a very successful business. His first marriage produced a child, Ilse, but ended in divorce after which Alexander moved to Berlin where once again his business ventures prospered. An acquaintance who happened to be a member of the Nazi party warned him in early 1933 that his name appeared on a blacklist of German industrialists and that he would be wise to flee. Alexander left Germany that very night and traveled to Prague. In 1937 the sister of one of his closest employees, Lola Mandelbaum, came to Prague. The couple married on July 3, 1937.

Lola Mandelbaum was born on June 20, 1907 in Trzebinia, a shtetl west of Krakow. Her parents, Israel and Raizel (Rosalie) Mandelbaum had seven children, Mendel, Manya, Steven, Lola, Esther, Daniel and Emil. Israel was in the steel business and owned a small farm. Most impressive was that Israel Mandelbaum also served as the mayor of Trzebinia which was a town with a mixed population of Jews and non-Jews. In the mid- 1920's Lola fled an arranged marriage and moved to Palestine where she worked as a seamstress. A visit to her brother in Prague resulted in marriage to Alexander Gross.

In 1938 Alexander and Lola came to New York but in March 1939 they returned to Poland in order for Alexander to liquidate his businesses. On the voyage to Poland the Grosses met a Polish couple from Warsaw, the Abreys, who became friends. It was clear in early summer that Hitler's armies were drawing nearer to Poland, and at Alexander's insistence, Abrey purchased the position of British Honduras consul to Poland thereby obtaining a visa for Lola. Once the war began, Lola, now equipped with the necessary papers, traveled to the Balkans, then Italy, and eventually she arrived back in the U.S. Alexander, in the meantime, walked eastward, where he met the U.S. consul to the Soviet Union, Angus Ward. Ward, during the Soviet invasion, was busy helping American citizens who needed to flee. Eventually, after many months of doing errands for Ward, Alexander, as yet not a citizen, persuaded the consul to take him back with him to the States in early 1940.

Lola's mother Rosalie and sister Manya, together with her husband and children, were murdered in Treblinka. Her sister Esther, married to a communist, was shot dead in the doorway of her house in September 1939. Her brother Steven lost his wife and child. Several of Alexander's siblings and their children were murdered in the camps as well. Israel and his sons Mendel, Steven, Daniel and Emil all survived and all but Mendel were eventually brought to the U.S.

Alexander and Lola settled on Manhattan's Upper East Side, where they raised their two children, Alice and Steven, and Alexander earned a living in real estate.

The Abreys and the Grosses remained lifelong friends.

AUSWEIS

ichtbild
he Ausweis
1234767

/.

Eigenhändige
Unterschrift

Lya Gross

Herr ... Lya Gross
Frau
geboren am 20 Juni 1907 ...... in ... Trebinia
wohnhaft ... Warschau Bagatela 15.

wünscht von Warschau nach ... Amerika über J.
über Katsowik, Wien, ...

zu reisen.

Gegen die Reise bestehen in polizeilicher Hins
Bedenken.

Warschau, den ...... 31. Okt. 19

Der Polizeipräsident 57
Abt. II 4000 Nr. ...... /

I.A.

*Lola Gross, exit papers from Poland
Warsaw, Poland, 1939.*

Israel Mandelbaum, late 1930's.

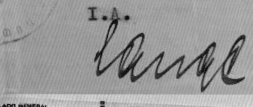

CONSULADO GENERAL
DEL HONDURAS
EN POLONA

GROSS - Lya

Visa to Honduras, for Lola Gross, 1940

keine

* A BERLITZ TRANSLATION *

Dr. Isidor Rapaport, Counsel for Defense in Criminal Matters, in Krakau,
Podwale 3, sworn legal interpreter for the German, English, French, and
Italian languages.

Translation from the Polish

Ref. No. 113/1936
Office of the Rabbi in Krakau, F. 66, No. 263

CERTIFICATE OF MARRIAGE BANNS

It is hereby certified that the marriage banns of the coming marriage
of Mr. Aleksander Moses Gross, born in Skawina, divorced, residing in Vienna,
son of Simon and Alta, née Eisen, to Mrs. Laja, née Mandelbaum, Araten,
divorced, born in Trubinia, residing in Krakau, daughter of Isser Hirsch and
Reizla, née Mandelbaum, were pronounced according to law in the local synagogue once during the solemn divine service on July 4, 1936, and that no legal
objection to this marriage has been shown. The dispensation from the other
two marriage banns was granted by the Municipality of the city of Krakau on
July 3, 1936, Adm. Ref. No. ZA/2.

Krakau, July 5, 1936

S. Kornitzer, own signature

I hereby attest the agreement of the above translation with the at-
tached original.

Krakau, July 6, 1936
(Signature): Dr. Rapaport

Stamp of Dr. Rapaport

_____

CERTIFICATION

*Lola Mandelbaum and Alexander Gross,
translation of certificate of marriage,
July 6, 1936.*

Mandelbaum cousin, killed in Treblinka.

JAY GRUENFELD

Jacob (Jack) Gruenfeld, father of Jay Gruenfeld, was born on March 25, 1930 in Negresti, Hungary, the fifth of the nine children of Margot and Isaac Gruenfeld who was a butcher. When Jack was thirteen, in the spring of 1944, his entire family was ordered by the Hungarian police to the town's main synagogue from where they were transported to the ghetto in Satmar. There the Gruenfelds crowded into a single room for two weeks after which German soldiers marched them all to the Satmar train station to board cattle cars headed to Auschwitz. After the torturous five-day journey, the infamous selection process sent Jacob and two older brothers, Mordechai (16) and Chaim Dovid (22) to the right and the rest of the family to the left. That was the last time Jack ever saw his parents or his four younger siblings, Yisroel Yosef (2), Shifra (4), Eliezer (6) and Shmuel (9). Jack was then sent with his brothers to hard labor in Mathaussen where the oldest perished. In April 1945 Jack and Mordechai took part in a death march to Gonskirchen labor camp. They were liberated by American soldiers on May 4, 1945 shortly before the Germans were to set the camp on fire. Jack, now only 15, and his brother then spent four months in a DP camp in Wels, Austria, after which they traveled by foot and train to the Hungarian/Romanian border. When they registered their names on the refugee list, they discovered the names of their two older sisters, Feige and Devorah. The siblings were reunited in Negresti. Jack continued on to Germany to find work and remained there till 1950 when he immigrated to the U.S. He lived in the Bronx and married an American girl, Miriam Hass, on May 2, 1954. The young family moved to Des Moines, Iowa where Jack purchased a kosher butcher shop. They had four children, Margie, Sheila, Jay and Barry. In 1963 the Gruenfelds moved back to New York, and Jack bought a supermarket in Huntington, Long Island. In 1966 the Gruenfelds moved permanently to Long Beach.

Back row, right to left, Jack Gruenfeld, his sister Vera and her husband Leon Kornfeld. Front row, left to right, Martin Gruenfeld, sister Vally and her husband Nathan Berko - late 1940s.

Miriam and Jack Gruenfeld, engagement photo, 1953.

HILDA HELLER
Jonathan Heller, Carrie Hirschfeld

Hilda Heller's mother, Chaya Sarah Gutkind, was born on March 15, 1915 in Warsaw, Poland. She was the second of the eight children born to Zipporah and Moshe Baruch Gutkind who were poor Jews and ardent followers of Gerrer Chasidus. Though details are missing, it is believed that, through a connection with the Gerrer Rebbe, six of the Gutkind children, including Chaya Sarah, were able to sneak out of the Warsaw ghetto and head east. They ended up finding a haven of sorts in a labor commune in Tashkent, though the youngest, a fourteen-year-old boy, died there after falling off a horse. Chaya Sarah's parents, a little sister, and an older married brother with his family were all left behind in the Warsaw ghetto. They either met their end there or in the Treblinka death camp. When the war ended, the five in Tashkent were the sole survivors of the Gutkind family.

Hilda Heller's father, Yisroel Shabtai Gross, was born on September 11, 1909 in Tarnow, Poland. He and his three sisters, Hannah, Regina, and Esther, were the children of Mattel and Yitzhak Isaac Gross, who was the well-to-do owner of a leather factory. Before the war broke out, Yisroel was married and the father of two children, Dora and Pinny. Believing that only the men were in danger, Yisroel, his wife's brother, a physician, and his sister's husband, a wealthy landowner, all fled east, across the border to Russia where they ended up working in a slave labor camp in Siberia. Though very strong and with the features of a native Pole, Yisroel suffered in the harsh camp conditions. Afraid of displaying any weakness, he labored in the frigid weather, even, at one point, with a broken leg. When the war ended, Yisroel returned to Tarnow only to find his home was taken over and his family murdered. A massacre in Tarnow had preceded the deportations. Yisroel learned that both his parents, his wife, his two children, his sister Esther, and his sister Hannah's three children had all perished in Auschwitz. It was believed that Hannah's baby was actually shot before her eyes. Only Hannah and Regina survived.

After the war, Chaya Sarah Gutkind and Yisroel Shabtai Gross met and were married in a DP camp in Augsberg, Germany. On January 12, 1949 their only child Hilda was born in the camp. Eight months later, the young family immigrated to the U.S., docking in New Orleans. They eventually settled in Brooklyn where Hilda was raised and Yisroel opened a fruit business and later, a business as a diamond broker.

Hannah and Esther Gross, Tarnow, pre-war.
Yisroel Gross holding one of his children, Tarnow, pre-war.
Mattel Gross, Tarnow, pre-war.

DWIGHT HERSHMAN

Paula Baum Hershman, mother of Dwight Hershman, was born on October 3, 1922 in Belchatov, Poland one of two children of Esther Malka and Dovid Baum, a Talmud scholar who learned full time. The Baums were a Chassidic family and were supported by Dovid's brother who owned a lumberyard. It was a true *Yissoschar-Zevulun* relationship (the earner supporting the learner). When the Germans arrived in Belchatov, Esther Malka and Dovid were taken to Chelmno where they were loaded onto trucks and gassed with carbon monoxide and then thrown into mass graves and burned. Only a teenager when the war began, and now orphaned, Paula spent some time in the Lodz ghetto and then was transported to a series of concentration camps including Bergen-Belsen, Dachau and Auschwitz from where she was ultimately liberated. Her brother, Yisroel, also survived the war. Paula was assigned to a DP camp in Zalsheim, Germany where she met Georg Hershman.

Georg Hershman was born in Lodz, Poland in 1919, the son of Baila and Eliezer Hershman who also had two daughters. Georg spent most of the war in the Lodz ghetto, somehow surviving until he was put on the very last transport to Auschwitz, along with Chaim Mordechai Rumkowski, the Jewish head of the ghetto. Rumkowski, who thought he would get special treatment from the Nazis, was burned alive on his way into Auschwitz. Georg Hershman was a witness to this. Only one of Georg's sisters, Tecia, survived the war.

Georg and Paula were married in Zalsheim on January 20, 1948. The next year they immigrated to the U.S., and settled in Brooklyn, where they raised their three sons, Dwight (Ike), Ezra and Ronnie. Georg at first supported the family as a piece worker in a factory, then worked as a butcher, then drove a taxi. When his children were grown, he moved to the Bronx and opened a luncheonette.

For Georg and Paula education was of paramount importance.
What was in your head could be transported anywhere and it could never be taken from you.

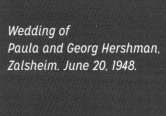

*Wedding of
Paula and Georg Hershman,
Zalsheim. June 20, 1948.*

BARRY HOLLANDER

Fay Jakubovits, Barry Hollander's mother, was born on March 9, 1925 in Irshava, Czechoslovakia, one of the four children of Draizel and David Jakubovits, who was a landowner and farmer and who died in 1933 in a farming accident. Still a teenager when the Germans invaded Hungary in 1944, Fay and her family were forced into the Munkacz ghetto in April and then she was deported to Auschwitz with her mother and two sisters, Irene and Olga. Draizel was killed that very day. The three girls were transferred to other concentration camps including Essen and Gelsenkirchen until they were ultimately liberated from Bergen-Belsen. Their brother Moshe was imprisoned in Dachau and tragically trampled to death on the day of liberation as starving prisoners stormed the camp kitchen. Now orphans, Fay and Olga were sent to Malmo, Sweden by the Red Cross. They lived there for two years before immigrating to the U.S. in 1948. Irene remained in Czechoslovakia. Fay worked for a time at the *Barton's* candy factory which was owned by the Klein family, to whom she was related. On May 29, 1950 she married Ernest Hollander, another survivor.

Ernest Hollander was born on October 1, 1914 in Kivyasht, Czechoslovakia, the second youngest of the eight children of Sheindel and Yosef Hollander, who died before the war.

Two of the Hollander daughters had moved to Brazil in the 1930's eager to accept Baron Hirsch's offer of free land to Jews who were willing to emigrate. Three siblings perished in concentration camps. Another sister remained in Hungary where her husband enjoyed a high rank due to his radio engineering skills. The youngest brother immigrated to Palestine.

Ernest himself was drafted into the Czech army in 1936 and then forced into a labor camp by the invading Hungarians. He succeeded in escaping and joined the underground as a partisan. After the war ended, he went to Presburg, and then, in late 1947, was sent to the U.S. to train volunteers in hand- to- hand combat in preparation for Israel's war of independence.

Fay and Ernest settled in Brooklyn and raised their two sons, David and Barry, there. After succeeding in many endeavors, Ernest settled into a propserous nursing home business.

Ernest Hollander in the Czech army, 1936.

Ernest Hollander, left, in the Czech army, 1936.

Ernest's nephew, also name Ernest, settled in Oakland, California and spoke frequently about the Holocaust in neighborhood high schools. In 1992 he appeared on the Montel Williams show in order to debate two Holocaust deniers. Sitting at home in Brooklyn, a Serbian émigré watching the program was struck by the survivor's uncanny resemblance to his old neighbor, Zoltan Hollander, back in his hometown. That neighbor was in fact Ernest's brother, who was believed dead. In truth, though eyewitnesses had reported his death by hanging, Zoltan had survived, settled in Serbia and lived there also believing that all his family had perished. Montel Williams orchestrated an emotional reunion on network TV, fifty-two years after the brothers had last seen each other.

Ernest Hollander, of Oakland, on the Montel Williams show in 1992 holding a sign in tribute to his relatives who died in the Shoah, one of whom was about to appear on stage.

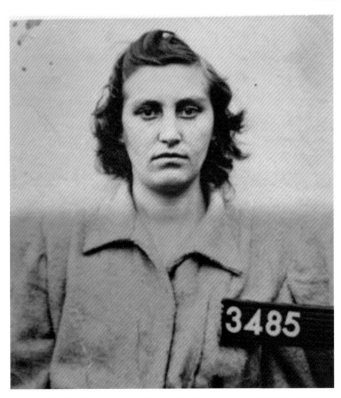

Fay Hollander after liberation from Bergen-Belsen, 1945.

Ernest and Fay Hollander wedding portrait. New York, May 29, 1950.

ESTIE HOLLANDER

Estie Hollander's father, Naftali (Nat) Trauring was born on December 28, 1920 in Rzeszow, Poland, the youngest of three sons (Sam, Jack and Nat) of Sala and Moshe (Morris) Trauring. Moshe himself was born in the United States but returned to Poland in the early part of the century and married Sala who was from Tarnow. The family eventually moved to Antwerp, Belgium where Moshe owned a jewelry shop. He died in 1929. His status as a U.S. citizen, however, saved the lives of the rest of his family as it enabled Sala and her three sons to immigrate in 1940. Once in the States, Nat worked for a while in Philadelphia but eventually moved to Manhattan where he met another Belgian, Annie Kacenelenbogen. The couple married on March 22, 1947.

Annie Kacenelenbogen was born in Antwerp, Belgium on February 7, 1927 to Bela and Szlama Kacenelenbogen, who was a tailor and maker of women's coats. She had an older brother who died in a car accident before the war and a younger brother, Alex. When the Nazis invaded Belgium, the family, along with an uncle and his son, traveled south through France and stopped in Marseilles for a time before a friendly chief of police warned them of an imminent round-up. Left alone by their parents for the night, Annie and Alex were almost arrested, but Annie's quick tongue and fluency in French saved them. Returning the next day, the Kacenelenbogens and their children continued their journey through Spain, then Portugal, where they awaited their visas. With the help of HIAS, Annie was able to leave first and she sailed alone to New York, where she lived with an aunt in Brooklyn, and then a relative in Detroit. Eventually she reunited with her parents and brother and settled on the Upper West Side of New York. She began life again and attended Haaren High School. At twenty she married Nat Trauring.

Nat and Annie raised their three daughters, Shirley, Helen and Estie, on the Upper West Side. The three Trauring brothers worked together in the diamond business.

Nat beside the Trauring Jewelry shop. Antwerp, pre-war.

Left to right: Morris, Joseph, Esther, Katie, Francis with baby Arno. New York, 1899.

Isaac Trauring with sons and sons-in-law. Morris, standing center. Rzeszow, Poland, 1913.

Sala, Jack, Nat, Sam and Morris Trauring Rzeszow, Poland, 1926.

Bela and Szlama Kacenelenbogen. Belgium, pre-war.

Annie with her father Szlama, wedding day. New York. March 22, 1947.

Trauring brothers, Sam, Jack and Nat, Rzeszow, Poland, 1938.

Szlama's father., Menachem Mendel Kacenelenbogen

MARCEL JUNGER

Marcel Junger was born on October 15, 1933 in Antwerp, Belgium, the youngest of the three children, Helen, Betty and Marcel, of Jolan (née Lazarovic) and Sam Junger. Jolan, originally from Romania, and Sam, originally from Poland, had immigrated to Belgium seeking a better life. Sam worked as a tailor and the family lived comfortably on Van Meir street in the heart of the city.

When war broke out, the Jungers sent their girls to safety in Switzerland and proceeded with young Marcel, to the south of France. They placed their son in the care of nuns at the monastery in Draguignan and they themselves went into hiding in a cloister in Nice. Marcel was given a new name – Marcel Dupuy – and a new birthplace – Tunisia. These years were very difficult for the young Marcel who had to endure wartime deprivations, separation from his loving parents and, worst of all, the isolation of living as the only Jewish child of the fifty at the monastery. He was terrified by the frequent Nazi raids, in which uniformed and armed soldiers looked for Jews in hiding. He wrote many letters to his parents, begging for food, but the nuns intercepted them, fearing detection by the Nazis. Two and a half years later, his parents retrieved him from the monastery and attempted to flee, but the Jungers were captured and held in the Fremont, Gurs and Rivesaltes internment camps. Samuel's skills as a tailor helped keep the family from deportation to Auschwitz. They fled again and were again nearly captured, with little Marcel jumping from the second floor of a building and breaking his arm in the process. Ultimately the Jungers went into hiding in an abandoned villa in Nice with five other families, subsisting oftentimes on little more than chestnuts.

When the war ended, Marcel returned to Antwerp with his family and began school. Re-entry was filled with firsts – like the first time he tasted milk and had to ask his mother to identify this unfamiliar white liquid. While still a teen, Marcel left for Brussels to study diamond cutting and marking under the tutelage of his brother-in-law, Morris, Betty's husband. Jolan and Sam immigrated to the U.S. in 1961 to join their daughter Helen and Marcel followed in 1963. He continued in the diamond trade and while working for the jeweler Harry Winston, he met and fell in love with a co-worker, Susan Kaufman. The couple married on December 9, 1967 and Marcel soon started his own diamond business. The Jungers raised their three daughters, Shani, Jolie and Linda, in Atlantic Beach.

Marcel Junger tearfully recalls "The nuns wanted to convert me but I told them I was a Jewish boy and would remain a Jewish boy." To this day the sound of firecrackers on July 4th reminds Marcel of the gunfire he heard as a young child in Antwerp.

Sam Junger's parents

Jolan Lazarovic, standing, and her parents

Jolan and Sam with their daughters, Betty and Helen.
Antwerp, c. 1930.

Helen and Betty in Switzerland, 1942.

Junger family. Marcel, Betty, Jolan, Sam and Helen.
Antwerp, 1946.

DANNA KALTER | JILL WILENSKY

Esther (Anna) Farber Givner, paternal great-grandmother of Danna Kalter and Jill Wilensky, was born in 1891 in Tambov, Russia, and came to the United States in 1929, settling in Brooklyn. Her sister in the Soviet Union (Govorova, formerly Poland) in the years immediately following World War II kept up a correspondence with her on postcards. An incredible collection of these postcards was discovered in a supermarket shopping bag in the cellar of the textile store that Anna's son, Morris Givner, owned in Brooklyn. They are filled with the everyday details of life in the Soviet Union in these post-war years: the birth of a child, the need for medications, and the aches and pains that were the legacy of the labor camps.

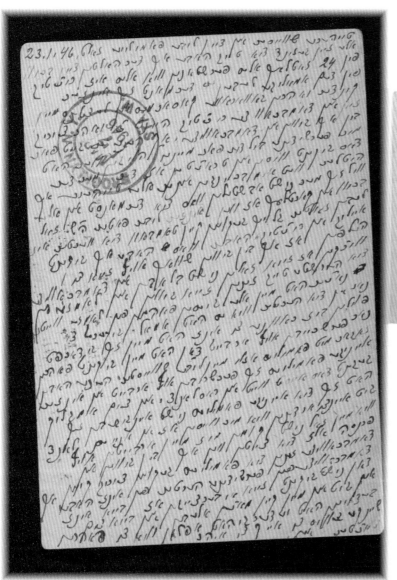

Postcards from the U.S.S.R. to Anna Farber Givner.

(above) Givner family. Left to right: Morris Givner, Leiba Rochel and Avram with their mother Esther Farber Givner.
Goworowo, Poland, c.1922

(above, right) Esther Farber Givner standing with her children, Leiba Rochel, Avram and Morris, seated on chair.
Goworowo, Poland, August 8, 1925.

JESSICA KAPLAN | AMY LANDY

Colman Steuer (Kalman Sztajer) was born on December 24, 1920, in Sosnowiec, Poland. His parents, Nachum and Leah (née Berlinsky) Sztajer, had four children, Julia, Kalman, Henry and Aaron. The children were raised in a Zionist home and were active in *Hanoar Hatzioni*. Colman attended public school and daily cheder. Shortly after the Nazi invasion, in November 1939, he was sent to a labor camp, from which he escaped with a group of other Jews, and made his way east. After a brief stay in Russia, he returned to Sosnowiec to help his family. In 1942, concerned that their parents would not survive to see them married, he and his childhood sweetheart, Jean Eckstein, were secretly married, breaking Nazi law. They lived in the Sosnowiec ghetto until June 1943, when he was sent to the Annaberg concentration camp. He and Jean were separated for the next two years. Colman was imprisoned in several concentration camps, including Gross-Rosen and Buchenwald. His sister Julia escaped to Russia, where she married Jean's older brother and survived the war. His parents and brothers were killed in Auschwitz in August 1943. A few days before the American army liberated Buchenwald, Colman escaped. He hid in a nearby farmhouse attic until he saw a column of American tanks driving past. Colman then returned to Buchenwald, where the American army was offering assistance to survivors. At Buchenwald, he found Jean's name on a list of survivors of Bergen-Belsen. They were reunited at Bergen-Belsen after Colman rode an old bicycle all the way there from Buchenwald.

Although he spoke no English, he approached the first American soldier he saw, who handed him a pen and paper. Colman drew a Jewish star and the soldier gave him everything in his pockets, including money and candy.

Jean Steuer (Genia Eckstein) was born on February 23, 1923 in Gleiwitz, Germany. She was the youngest child and only daughter of Yitzchak and Shprintza Eckstein. She had three older brothers, Sol, Henry, and Max Eckstein. Jean was raised in Sosnowiec, Poland, in a traditional Jewish home amongst extended family. In November 1939, her brothers left Poland and escaped to Russia, where they survived the war. Still a young bride in 1943, Jean was separated from her new husband, and sent to Gross-Rosen, then Mauthausen, and then Bergen-Belsen. Both her parents were killed in Auschwitz in August 1943. When the British army liberated Bergen-Belsen, they found Jean sick with typhus, and treated her until she recovered.

A few weeks after the liberation, she received a letter from Colman, that read "I am alive and coming for you. Stay where you are."

The young couple decided to immigrate to the United States, and arrived in New York on May 24, 1946 aboard the *SS Marine Perch*. They first moved to the Lower East Side, and then to Bensonhurst. In 1954 Kalman and Genia Sztajer officially became Colman and Jean Steuer. That same year they bought land in Plainfield, Connecticut, and built a chicken farm, where they worked and lived until 1980. Their son Neil was born in 1952 and their daughter Sherry in 1954. Tragically, Neil was killed by a hit-and-run driver when he was eleven.

The Berlinskys, Kalman Sztajer's maternal grandparents.

Nachum Sztajer's mother.

Nachum and Leah Sztajer.

The Sztajers – Nachum and Leah
with Julia, Henry and Aaron.
Kalman seated at center.
Milowka, Poland, 1932.

Friends in the countryside. Genia Eckstein
(middle row, second from right). Sosnowiec, 1937.

Genia & Kalman
Sosnowiec, 1939.

The Bund, Kalman and Genia (front, second and third from right). 1945.

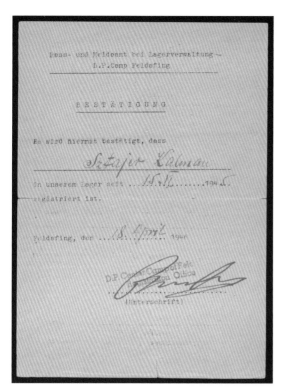

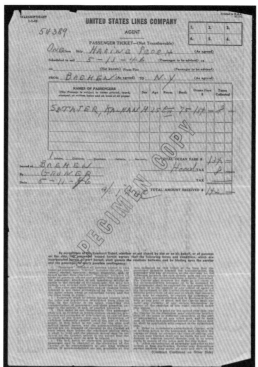

(far left)
Registration card for Kalman Sztajer for Feldafing DP camp attesting to his arrival on June 15, 1945. Feldafing, April 18, 1946.

(left)
Ticket for passage on the Marine Perch, embarking from Bremen, Germany to New York. May 13, 1946.

Genia Sztajer registration card issued in Funk-Caserne, a transit and resettlement camp established by the Allies near Munich.

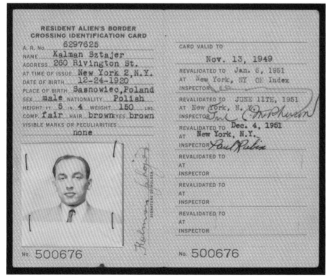

Kalman Sztajer resident alien ID card.

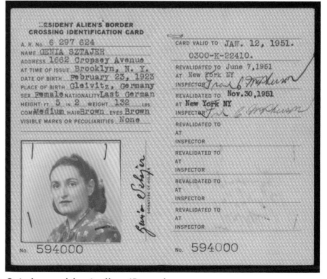

Genia Sztajer resident alien ID card.

Photographs and documents courtesy USHMM, United States Holocaust Memorial Museum

BEN KEST

Sol Kest, father of Ben Kest, was born on March 10, 1922 in Vilchovitz, a small town in the Carpathian mountains in Czechoslovakia. He was the second of nine children born to Freida Lebowitz Kest and Yitzchok Elimelech Kest, who earned a living in the hide business as well as selling apples grown in his orchards. Freida, the daughter of a poor rabbi, was so beautiful that Yitzchok Elimelech married her even without a dowry. The children grew up in a happy, loving household though they slept four to a bed and the bread that was baked on Thursday had to last them the entire week. Showing great promise in Torah study, Sol was sent to a yeshiva in Munkacs at the age of twelve and he boarded there with local townsfolk. When the Hungarians invaded in 1938, Sol returned home for good and helped transport apples for his father who, because of his long beard, was afraid to venture out. The oldest son, Velvel, was sent to the front and died there. In April 1943 the entire town was crowded into the ghetto in Munkacs and by Shavuot they were all deported to Auschwitz, where all the rest of the Kest family perished. Sol who claimed to be a builder was sent to Buchenwald to help in the building of barracks, and then to build tunnels for the Germans in Dora and then Ellrich, two of the cruelest subcamps of Buchenwald. After ten months of hard labor with minimal rations Sol was sent to Bergen-Belsen from where he was liberated by the British on April 15, 1945.

Twenty-three years old, weighing only eighty pounds and terribly weak, he was unable to partake in the frenzied eating that took place immediately after liberation. According to Sol, this saved his life, as so many fell ill from their ravenous consumption. After recuperating in the Bergen-Belsen DP camp, Sol went to Prague and then to his hometown where he reunited with Clara Adler, the daughter of an old family friend, a butcher from a neighboring town. They married in 1945, and for the next four years Sol ran a successful grocery store in a nearby village. In 1949 the couple and their young daughter immigrated to Israel and remained there till 1955, when, with two children in tow, they immigrated again, this time to the United States. The Kests settled in Los Angeles and two more sons were born.

In his early days in Los Angeles, at a time when he would collect bottles at the construction site where he worked in order to afford drinks for his children, Sol Kest still managed to send money from every pay check to less fortunate relatives in Israel. Years later, the Kests became world renowned philanthropists, building and supporting yeshivas and other Jewish institutions in Los Angeles and around the world.

(left to right)
Velvel, Sara Golda, and Sol Kest in front of the family home, Vilchovitz, Czechoslovakia, c.1943.
It is unclear if the two little boys at right are their younger brothers, Asher-Zelig and Moishe, or a neighbor's children.

Clara Adler Kest, mother of Ben Kest, was born on November 21, 1921 in Dubová, Czechoslovakia to Herschel and Basya Adler. The Adlers owned a cattle farm and a dairy and made a prosperous living selling meat and distributing apples to nearby towns. The three Adler children, Shlomo, Tzila and Clara, were raised in a religious, loving household with ties to Vizhnitzer chassidim and to Bnei Akiva.

When the Hungarians invaded, Shlomo was sent into slave labor and life for all of the town's Jews was forever changed. Rumors of horrific events in Poland filled the air and Polish refugees flooded the neighborhood. By 1944 all of Dubová's Jews were sent to a nearby ghetto and a few weeks later deported to Auschwitz where Clara, Tzila and a cousin named Fay were separated from the rest of the Adlers. The three young women worked in a factory weaving belts for machine guns and later in hard labor outdoors in the freezing cold. Joe Simon, a relative from their hometown, worked in the kitchen and was able to provide the girls with some extra food and clothing. On January 1, 1945 they were transported to forced labor in Bergen-Belsen and in April, to factory work in Kraslice. From Kraslice they went on a torturous death march which they miraculously survived. After the war ended the three girls wanted to find a way back home from Carlsbad to Prague and then to Zilina where their joy knew no bounds as they were reunited with their father, uncle, and soon after, brother.

Marriage to Sol Kest, the son of an old friend and business connection, soon followed. The Kests and Joe Simon remained close for the remainder of their lives.

At the time of the invasion, Clara was given the opportunity to flee and find safe haven with a distant relative. But, though her parents urged her to save herself, she simply would not abandon them at a time of peril. That kind of "kibud av v'aim," respect for one's parents, is the family's inspiration and legacy.

Sol Kest, center, with friend. David Sokol,
left, and Joe Simon, waving.
Clara at the window.
Shortly after the war.

(left to right)
Zirel, Clara and a relative,
Devora Schlesinger.
post-war.

JERRY KESTENBAUM

Zachary Kestenbaum, Jesse Scherban and Erica Zuckerman

David Kestenbaum, grandfather of Jerry Kestenbaum, was born on March 8, 1895, in Tarnow, Poland, the son of Rabbi Eliyahu and Leah Rachel Kestenbaum. In 1914 the couple and their six children moved to Leipzig, Germany where the rabbi and his sons opened a fur business. David married Gisella Goldman in 1918 and they had seven sons. After escaping imprisonment by the Nazis in 1933, David and Gisella moved first to Holland, then to Paris and finally to the United States in 1936. Settling in Brooklyn, David joined his brother Jacob in establishing a successful fur business and all the boys were enrolled in Yeshiva Torah Vodaath.

When the plight of the Jews of Europe became known, the brothers realized that there was no mitzvah more urgent than saving Jewish lives. The brothers were asked by Rabbi Kalmanowitz of the Vaad Hatzoloh to assist the Mir Yeshiva students stranded in Europe. Together the Kestenbaums filed over 800 affidavits for relatives, friends, rabbis, yeshiva students and scholars. These affidavits represented an enormous commitment, as they guaranteed undertaking financial responsibilities for the immigrants – all now labeled "cousins." The Kestenbaum brothers worked with the U.S. government and contacts in neutral Switzerland as well as in England and Scandinavia. At least one full-time employee was hired solely to move the mountains of paperwork through the State Department to secure visas. As a result of their efforts, hundreds of Jewish lives were saved.

Speaking at David Kestenbaum's funeral in 1957, a tearful Rabbi Aharon Kotler uttered only five words: "He was a great tsaddik."

David Kestenbaum as a young man. Leipzig.

David Kestenbaum tombstone, Israel.
One line reads: "He saved souls from their oppressors."

David and Gisella Kestenbaum and their seven sons aboard the SS Washington en route to the U.S. in 1936.
(left to right) Joseph, Binyamin, Leonard, David, Menashe, Ray (top center)
Gisella, Ephraim (Menashe's twin) and Bernard.

Letter from Rabbi Aharon Kotler, dean of the Yeshiva in Kletzk, to the Kestenbaum brothers, requesting assistance. February, 1940.

Letter from Hersh Tzvi Kanarek of Leipzig to David Kestenbaum, asking for assistance after being driven out of Germany to Krakow, Poland. 1938.

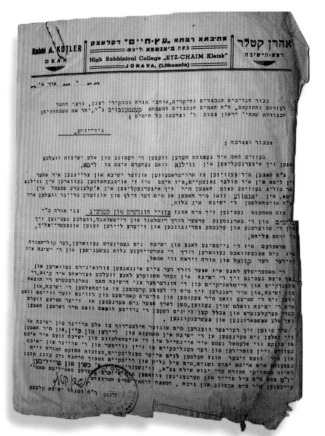

Letter from the Mirrer Yeshiva Association thanking David Kestenbaum for executing nine affidavits on behalf of students of the Mir Yeshiva. New York. March 11, 1941.

Mirrer Yeshivah Association, Inc.

ועד העזרה בעד

ישיבת מיר

Office: 109 EAST BROADWAY
New York, N. Y.

Phone COrtlandt 7-1742

ב״ה

March 11, 1941

Mr. David Kestenbaum
243 West 30th Street
New York City.

Dear Mr. Kestenbaum,

We thank you very much for your willingness to execute ten affidavits for ten of the Mirrer Yeshiva students now in Japan.

The names follow. The address of all is

% JEWCOM
KOBE JAPAN

Name	Affidavit to be sent
Pruszanski, Chaim	Kobe Japan (American Consul)
Kunda, Zalmon	Kobe Japan
Edeltuch, Szmuel	Kobe Japan
Baranowicz, Lejba	Yokohoma Japan (American Consul)
Bryskman, Pinchus	Yokohoma Japan
Rojtenberg, Tuwia	Yokohoma Japan
Kaplan, Mowsza	Tokyo, Japan (American Consul)
Bursztejn, Szloma	Tokyo, Japan
Samulewicz, Szloma	Tokyo, Japan

Please send one set of three to the various consuls designated, another set of three to the students on the Jewcom Kobe address, and one set for Washington please forward to our office in a sealed packet which we shall turn over to the State Department.

With sincere thanks,

Very truly yours,

[signature]

Executive Sec'y

RINA KESTENBAUM | DEBBIE KAMINER FURST | TOMMY FURST

Aryeh (Arie) Eliezer Kaminer, maternal grandfather of Rina Kestenbaum, was born in Kielce, Poland on April 15, 1912, the son of Chaya and Yizhak Tzvi Kaminer, who was in the leather business. Aryeh was one of seven children (Yehuda, Myer, Haenoch, Rakhel, Sarah and Hadassah) in this prestigious and learned family. Aryeh was a direct descendant of the Magen Avraham, the great 17th-century Talmudist and leading religious authority for Jews to this day. Aryeh's great-aunt was married to the Torah giant, the Sfas Emes. Another relative, Meshulum Kaminer, was the editor of the *Warsaw Yud* and later was appointed the head of the *chevra kaddisha* (burial society) in the Warsaw ghetto. Aryeh had already joined his father in the leather trade and the family remained in Kielce for the first two years following the Nazi invasion. Aryeh Kaminer married Dora Tenenbaum in January 1940 in Kielce.

Dora Tenenbaum was born on August 16, 1918 in Starachowice, Poland, the daughter of Dobra and Berel Tenenbaum, who was in the egg business. The couple also had two sons, Herschel and Mendel. Berel Tenenbaum, according to many accounts, was a man of deep religious convictions. Berel later stood out in the Starachowice ghetto as one of the Jews who not only remained devout himself, but encouraged others with his prayers and his devotion to Yiddishkeit.

In March 1941 the Kaminers were transported to the Starachowice ghetto, where most Jews were assigned to work in the nearby Hermann Goering factory, manufacturers of heavy steel products. This labor camp was nicknamed "The Shooting Camp" because of the random fatal shootings of inmates by the sadistic head of security, Willy Althoff. Conditions improved somewhat when Althoff was relieved of his duties due to the fact that his superiors felt his murderous conduct impeded production. When the Staracho-wice ghetto was liquidated in August 1944, Aryeh and Dora, having survived countless atrocities and deprivations, were transported to Auschwitz. Most of the Jews entering the camp at that time did so without undergoing the routine selections and, as a result, miraculously, most survived.

By the end of the war Aryeh had lost both parents and five of his six siblings. One sister, Sarah, had made aliya before the war. Dora, whose mother had died prior to the war, had lost her father, her stepmother and their baby. Various accounts exist about the discovery and subsequent horrific murder of this mother and child.

The young couple, along with Dora's brothers, spent the next few years in the Fohrenwald DP camp (where a new *ketubah* was issued) and then in Munich proper. Their daughter Debra was born in Munich in 1948. On February 28, 1951, the Kaminers sailed on the SS *Queen Elizabeth* to New York City where they lived until they settled in Toronto, Canada in the 1960's. Another daughter, Hindy, was born in Toronto. Aryeh earned a living from real estate and the residential washing machine business. Their children and grandchildren remained true to their legacy of piety and lovingkindness.

> About the Jews of the Starachowice ghetto, Rabbi Yosef Friedenson wrote,
> "Whenever we would sit together, we would hear a word of encouragement,
> a dvar Torah, a story about tzaddikim. How they would speak with such longing of times
> in the past when they were able to serve Hashem with happiness and without worry."
> -- Faith Amid the Flames: The Story of Reb Yosef Friedenson by Rabbi Yosef C. Golding

(above)
Yehuda Kaminer, Aryeh's brother.
Perished in the Shoah.
Berel Tenenbaum, Dora's father.
Perished in the Shoah.

(left, top photo)
The girls third grade class in the Bais Yakov of Starachowice.
Dora is top row fourth from left. c. 1926

(left middle photo)
The boys cheder of Hershel Tenenbaum,
Dora's brother. He is second boy standing from left.
Their father, Berel Tennebaum is top row, extreme right.
Starachowice, c.1926.

(left photo)
Bride and female guests. Pre-war wedding in Kielce.
Girl directly above the bride is Yehuda Kaminer's daughter,
Sarah. Yehuda's wife, Ruth, is third seated from right.
Yehuda, Ruth and Sarah were killed in the Shoah.

Aryeh Kaminer holding his daughter
Debbie. Munich, 1948.

A check for 4200 DEUTSCHE MARKS for the March of Dimes presented by Hershel
Tenenbaum, center , on behalf of the Jewish displaced persons in the Munich area.
Receiving the check is Brigadier General Edmund B. Sebree, commanding general of
the Munich military post. To his right is the Jewish Chaplain, Captain Hersh Litvazer.
To Hershel Tenenbaum's left are Israel Zweig and Benjamin Lapin.
Munich, February 5, 1951.

Seated Dora and Aryeh Kaminer. Standing, left
to right Mendel and Hershel Tenenbaum.
Munich, post-war.

The Kaminer ketuba. Though they were married in Kielce in 1940 this
ketubah was written for them in the Fohrenwald DP camp in 1946.

Gita Ament, paternal grandmother of Rina Kestenbaum, was born on March 1, 1926 in Kosice, Czechoslovakia to Yehuda and Eidel Ament. Gita was the middle Ament child, with two older brothers, Mendel (Jan) and Sam, and two younger sisters, Erika and Helen. In the summer of 1944, Nazis marched into town and commanded all Jews to gather in a brick factory. Gita, eighteen at the time, and her two brothers, sensing danger, had already scattered to different towns. Eidel bribed a farmer to smuggle herself and her two young daughters out of the factory and she spent the rest of the war years in hiding. Yehuda, who chose to remain in the factory, was in one of the first transports to depart for Auschwitz, where he was murdered. Gita meanwhile, having run from Kosice, connected with another young family and took charge of their two children when the father fell ill. Beautiful and brave, blonde-haired, blue-eyed Gita managed to charm her way out of many dangerous confrontations with enemy soldiers and was thus able to save the lives of her two young charges. They would forever refer to her as their second mother. After the war Gita met Harry Furst, and they married in 1947.

Harry Furst was born on July 11, 1917 in Trnava, Czechoslovakia, the son of Chana and Yosef Furst, who were wealthy wine merchants and descendants of the Chasam Sofer. They also had the distinction of owning Trnava's first automobile. Three of Harry's siblings (Hedy, Sari and Rose) survived the war but the Furst parents and their son, Moshe, perished. Harry himself spent the war years in hiding.

Gita and Harry's son, Thomas, was born in Bratislava in 1948. In 1949 the Fursts left Czechoslovakia and waited in Paris for visas to emigrate. In 1950 they arrived in Canada and settled in Montreal where their daughter Annette was born that year.

Harry became a manufacturer of leather goods and, upon retirement in 1986, became a full-time bikur cholim volunteer in nursing homes. He learned calligraphy and to play the mandolin in order to better entertain the residents on his daily visits. His exemplary dedication to this volunteer work earned him an award from the Canadian government.

Left to right: Sam, Gita, Eidel and Mendel Ament. Kosice, Czechoslovakia, 1928.

Gita and Harry Furst. Czechoslovakia. c. 1946-7.

Front row, left to right: Gita, Eidel, Helen and Erika. Back row, left to right, Mendel and Sam. Kosice, Czechoslovakia, post-War.

"Whoever saves one life, saves an entire world"

-- Talmud Bavli

P. Wintner & Sons textile business was so important for the Nazi war effort that Pinchas Wintner and his entire family were granted the privilege of staying on in Kosice to keep it running. When Gita Ament found herself all alone in 1944, she appealed to Irene and Andre (Avraham) Wintner for help. Irene mercifully obliged. As she herself needed a hand with her two small children while she nursed her ailing husband, the arrangement was mutually beneficial. Klari (Zipi) Wintner, age six, and her brother Shaya, age two, thus remained in the care of Gita Ament for the remainder of the war. The Wintners knew their reprieve would be short lived so they had prepared bunkers in the mountainous terrain outside the city. For a time they all hid in these bunkers in the mountains. Later it seemed safest to send Gita out of the bunker with the children. Posing as a Christian peasant woman, Gita fabricated a story about a dead sister and the orphaned niece and nephew accompanying her, and then she brazenly asked an SS officer to give her and the children a lift to a neighboring town. Once there, she rented a small room and again, with her beauty and charm, successfully requisitioned a ration card in order to feed herself and her charges. Days were spent hiding in a cowshed. Sundays they went to church with their devout landlady. When the Wintner parents eventually emerged from their hideout they paid someone to find their children. Finally reunited, the family and Gita again went into hiding and suffered that winter of 1944-45 riddled with lice, freezing cold and starving.

After they were liberated by the Romanian army in April 1945 the Wintners emerged as a rare unit – an entire extended Czech family that survived the war intact, apparently the only one. Only Avraham had died of natural causes in a primitive hospital in Rimovska Sobota on April 12, 1945, the same day as Franklin Delano Roosevelt. For a time, the Wintners resumed their textile business but with the advent of communism they made another daring escape, traveling to Prague, then Paris and, in 1948, making aliya to Israel. Klari was ten and entered school for the first time. Shaya was six. Irene, widowed at thirty-three, never re-married. Klari at eighteen married an officer in the Israeli air force and Shaya got smicha from Yeshivas Chevron and worked as a teacher and an advocate in the religious court. The two siblings produced six children and eighteen grandchildren and many, many great-grandchildren. An entire world -- all through the courage, the ingenuity and the chesed of one woman - Gita Ament Furst.

Gita and Klari reconnected in the 1970's. Gita's son Tommy and Klari connected in 2021.

She [Gita] was as smart as she was beautiful. No matter what the situation was she knew exactly what to do. She was our second mother. And she herself always said she had four children – two in America and two in Israel.
– Klari Wintner Harsit

Klari and Shaya Wintner. Kosice, Czechoslovakia, 1944.

*"Now in the light of past and present events the bitter truth must be spoken.
We feared too little and we hoped too much.
We underestimated the bestiality of the enemy; we overestimated the humanity,
the wisdom, the sense of justice of our friends."*

Chaim Weizmann, *Address to 22nd Zionist Congress, December 1946*

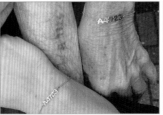

FAYE KLAUSNER

Faye's mother, Susan Wahrman was born on March 11, 1938 in Vienna, Austria the very day that the Nazi army marched into the city. Her parents, Sophie and Jacob Wahrman, also had a son, Jonah, born in 1933. Jacob was a well-regarded chazzan and also very involved in the cultural life of the city – its operas, plays and concerts. He was the rare combination of a yeshiva boy who grew up to attend the Vienna Conservatory of Music. Sophie, Susan's mother, was originally from Poland where her father, Yonah Mehr, had been the estate manager for a Polish baron. When he died, Sophie was only four and her mother Ruth was left a widow with eleven children. At the urging of one of the older Mehr children who was already living in Vienna, the family moved to Austria. Sophie and Jacob married in Vienna on March 20, 1932. Ruth Mehr died a few years later. By the late 1930's some Mehr brothers had moved to New York and were working in the fur business. After the Anschluss, they urged their younger sister Sophie to emigrate and they managed to procure visas for her family. Originally, they sent three visas since they had not yet learned of the arrival of the new baby. Eventually, a fourth visa arrived. Departure was set for late 1938 when newborn Susan would be old enough to travel.

Jacob's chance encounter with a stranger that summer luckily overturned the family's plan. The man advised that they delay no further and then he insisted on trading his voyage tickets with theirs. Heeding his warnings, the Wahrmans packed up and sailed the very next week. Two days after their hasty departure, armed SS officers knocked on the door of the abandoned Wahrman apartment. A guardian angel had saved them. His identity remains a mystery.

The Wahrmans landed in New York in the summer of 1938 and briefly stayed with relatives in Boro Park. They then moved to Pittsburgh where Jacob found work as a chazzan in the Poale Zedek shul. The city's pollution proved too unbearable for Jonah's health so the family again relocated, this time to Baltimore, where Jacob became the chazzan of the famous Shaare Tfiloh Synagogue, listed today in the National Register of Historic Places. Sophie, too, immersed herself in communal work and founded the Bais Yaakov school of Baltimore. Susan, still so young, learned English quickly after having been taunted as a "Nazi" in the playground, and she soon shed all traces of her German accent for good. She attended Forest Park Senior High School, graduated from Baltimore College *magna cum laude* and moved to New York where she found work on 47th Street. She soon met Saul Klausner.

Saul Klausner, was born in Williamsburg, Brooklyn on July 31, 1930, to Aaron and Rose Klausner who already had a toddler daughter, Judith. Aaron's parents, Feyga and Moshe Klausner were hoteliers in Poland and owned a kosher hotel in the resort town of Krynica as well as a few other properties. Rose's parents, the Greenfields, originally from Poland, had settled in Palestine in 1935 where the revered Rabbi Baruch Greenfield was the *Av Beit Din* of Jerusalem. Aaron, always a staunch Zionist, tried for three years (1933-36) to make a life for his young family in Palestine but he returned to the States where economic opportunities were more plentiful and he began working for the Metropolitan Life Insurance Company until his retirement decades later. With the Zionist dream still in his heart, Aaron Klausner finally made aliya in 1971 at the age of 70. Young Saul spent his early years visiting both sets of grandparents, one in Poland, the other in Palestine. After the Nazi invasion of Poland, however, the visits to the Klausners stopped. Tragically, Feyga and Moshe were fatally shot by Polish police in front of one of their hotels. Faye is named after this grandmother.

Susan Wahrman and Saul Klausner married on September 7, 1959, and raised their children, Faye and David, in Brooklyn.

Store on the ground floor of the Wahrman home in Vienna. Sophie Wahrman on the right. Her sister Clara Schiff on the left and niece Jennie, center.

Today this a delicatessen and Kosher grocery store.

Wedding invitation for Sophie Mehr and Jacob Wahrman. Vienna. March 20, 1932.

FRAU RACHEL MEHR

ERBITTET SICH DIE EHRE IHRER GEGENWART, ZUR TRAUUNG

IHRER TOCHTER

SOPHIE

MIT HERRN

OBERKANTOR JAKOB WAHRMANN

HERR DAVID MOSES WAHRMANN

ERBITTET SICH DIE EHRE IHRER GEGENWART, ZUR TRAUUNG

SEINES SOHNES

JAKOB

MIT FRÄULEIN

SOPHIE MEHR

WELCHE SONNTAG, DEN 20. MÄRZ 1932 UM 3 UHR NACHMITTAG IM POLNISCHEN TEMPEL, WIEN, II., LEOPOLDSGASSE 29

STATTFINDET.

WIEN, IM MÄRZ 1932.

TELEGRAMM-ADRESSE: MEHR WAHRMANN, WIEN, II., HOLLANDSTRASSE NR. 10/28

Rabbi Baruch Greenfield (1872-1956) known as the Hermanshtater Rebbe and author of the Ohel Baruch.

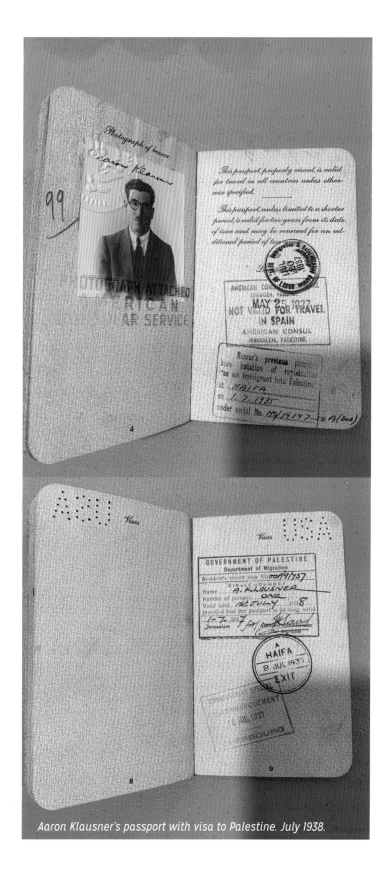

Aaron Klausner's passport with visa to Palestine. July 1938.

Sophie and Jacob Wahrman. Wedding photo. Vienna. March 20, 1932.

HELEN & ARNOLD KLEIN

Adolf Moskovic, father of Helen Klein, was born on February 2, 1912 in Porubka, Czechoslovakia to Chaim and Chaya Moskovic, who were farmers. There were five children, Sara, Moshe, Isidore, Adolf, and Binyamin, who died before the war. As a young man Adolf worked as a roofer's apprentice and during the war he was sent to a forced labor camp in Hungary. His sister Sara and his parents perished in Auschwitz. Adolf returned to Porubka after the war and started his own roofing business there. He married Lenka Naftulovic in 1946. They raised three daughters, Magdalena (b.1946) Helen (b.1952) Silvia (b.1954) and moved to Kosice in Eastern Slovakia in 1961.

Lenka Naftulovic, mother of Helen Klein, was born in Porubka on January 10, 1927 to Mariam and Moshe Yitzhak Naftulovic, who was farmer. She was a teenager when she and the rest of her family were sent to a ghetto in Uzhorod in the Ukraine and later they were all transported to Auschwitz where Lenka and her sister Berta were assigned the task of sorting the clothes of the murdered victims. There their parents, their sister, Sara, and their brother, Mayer, all met their end. From Auschwitz, Lenka and Berta were transferred to Ravensbruk from which they were liberated in April 1945. Returning to Porubka the two young women were taken in by Adolf Moskovic.

Helen Moskovic, raised and educated in Kosice, married Arnold Klein in 1972. The couple had two children, Eva, born in 1976, and Tibor, born in 1973. In Kosice, Helen worked as a comptroller and Arnold as an engineer. In 1984 the young family made a daring escape from Czechoslovakia to Yugoslavia, and then with the help of the United Nations, they arrived in the United States. The Kleins settled in Brooklyn and Helen once again found work as a comptroller and Arnold as a business entrepreneur.

Arnold Klein is also the son of two survivors. Arnold's mother, Edith was born on June 18, 1929 in Rad, Czechoslovakia, one of three children born to Gisela and Maximilian Klein who was a farmer. She had two brothers Arnold (b. 1931) and Pavel (b. 1934). Maximilian was taken into the Hungarian labor brigade in 1938 and was never seen again. It is believed he died of typhus in a concentration camp. Edith's mother, Gisela, left alone to support her family, worked hard doing errands with her horse and wagon. In 1944, Edith, her paternal grandmother, her mother and her two little brothers were deported to Auschwitz. All but Edith perished there. Number A1256, Edith Klein became very sick in the camp but was protected by fellow inmates. Eventually she was transported to Leipzig and then marched to Terezin from where she was liberated by Soviets on May 9, 1945. After the war she married a cousin, William Klein, on February 15, 1948 in Kralovsky Chlmec. Unable to emigrate, the Kleins did agricultural work on a collectivized farm in Pavelova and had two sons, Arnold, born in 1950, followed by his brother Paul (Pavel) in 1952.

Of her experience after the war, Edith Klein says, "...those of us from Slovakia were told to report to an office. We were put in wagons and I went to Bratislava. I was given an ID and 500 crowns. The only document I have about myself is this Auschwitz tattoo. Nothing else.... I went to Rad but there was a woman living in our house. I can't talk about it."

Emlek - Memorial Yahrzeit calendar for Chaim Moskovic.

Lenka and Adolf, wedding portrait. Porubka, 1946.

Moshe Yitzhak Naftulovic (b.1899) with his parents. Porubka, 1905.

Challah cover made before Chaya Moskovic was married. Turn of the last century

Edith and William Klein wedding photo. Kralovsky Chlmec, Slovakia. February 15, 1948.

Left to right:
Paul, Edith, William and Arnold Klein. Pavlova, c. 1960.

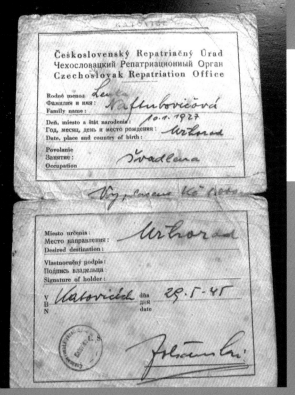

Lenka Moskovic and her three daughters. Porubka. c.1958.
Adolf Moskovic, Identification card, issued by Organization of Hungarian Jews. Budapest, 1945.
Lenka Naftulovic. Czech registration card for repatriation. 1945.

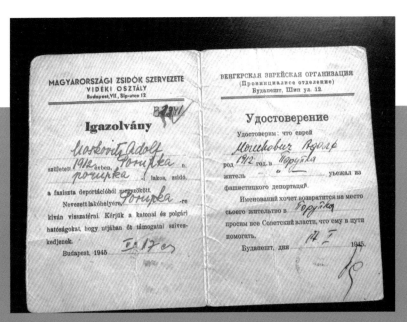

HARRY KLEINHAUS

Poriah Gradom Kleinhaus was born on September 9, 1915 in Scheveningen, Holland to Pauline and Moses Gradom. She and her three siblings were raised in Antwerp, Belgium where Moses worked as a diamond merchant. After graduating high school, Poriah married Jehuda Kleinhaus on June 28, 1936 in Antwerp. Jehuda Kleinhaus was born on December 23, 1908 in Rzeszow, Poland, the fourth of the six children of Feiga (née Bodner) and Chaim Kleinhaus. By 1925 the entire family had relocated to Antwerp, where Jehuda learned the art of diamond sawing.

Like many of Antwerp's Jews, Jehuda and Poriah left for France as soon as Hitler invaded Belgium. They arrived in Bayonne just as the Portuguese consul, Sousa Mendes was issuing visas to Portugal to thousands of Jews lining up in front of the embassy there. As a result of the heroism of Sousa Mendes, who was acting against the official orders of the Portuguese government, the Kleinhauses drove into Portugal and, after ten months, were able to come to United States under the Polish quota.

Jehuda's extended family survived by finding a safe haven in North Africa via Portugal. Tragically, Poriah's parents and two younger sisters remained in Belgium and were deported to Auschwitz, where they and most of their extended family perished in the autumn of 1943. One brother survived by living as a gentile in southern France from 1942-1945.

Jehuda and Poriah arrived in New York City on April 25, 1941. They settled on the Upper West Side of Manhattan where they raised their three children, Albert, Harry and Paulette. Jehuda began again and established a successful diamond sawing factory and later a diamond trading company in New York.

Between 1940-1943 Pauline Gradom in Antwerp wrote letters and postcards to her daughter Poriah Kleinhaus in Portugal and New York. The letters were filled with family news, gratitude for packages sent, anxiety about the paucity of communications and some veiled references to economic hardship. "Uncle Parnosse no longer comes to us anymore, because he has been ill for a very long time now." The mother also expresses encouragement and hope for the future. "Have courage and patience my dear children. God help us so we will be able to see each other again soon in good health." The last letter was dated August 20, 1943. Pauline and Moses were taken two weeks later.

Aristides de Sousa Mendes (1885-1954)

Jehuda Kleinhaus passport/Visa signed by Sousa Mendez assistant in Bayonne, France on June 22, 1940. and admission to Portugal.

Pauline & Moses Gradom

The Gradom children, left to right, Willy, Ida, Poriah and Matilda. Antwerp, 1928.
The two younger girls were killed in Auschwitz in 1943.

The extended Gradom family at the wedding of Poriah and Jehuda Kleinhaus.
Antwerp, June 28, 1936.

Most of those in this photograph perished in the Shoah.

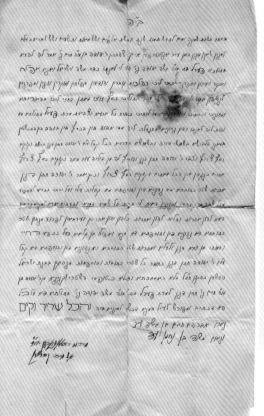

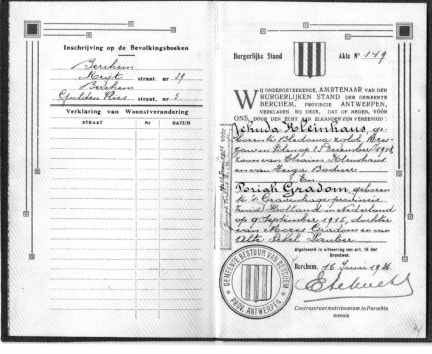

The Ketubah of Jehuda Kleinhaus and Poriah Gradom, 8 Tamuz 5696.
The Flemish Trouwboek or marriage certificate, Antwerp, June 28, 1936.

Kleinhaus and Gradom family papers, courtesy of
United States Holocaust Memorial Museum Archives,
Washington, DC.

Poriah Gradom's ID card,
issued by the Belgian Department
of Health for recipients of
restitution payments,
November 14, 1958

Poriah & Jehuda Kleinhaus
New York, 1950.

Poriah Gradom identity card November 16, 1939.

Poriah Gradom's sister Ida.
Ida was killed in 1943.

Willy Gradom, Poriah's brother. Immediately
after his wedding in the summer of 1942 he
fled to Vichy, France and lived there as a
gentile with his bride.

20/8 1943.

Meine Liebste!
Wir haben Eueren l Brief empfangen und Ihr könnt sich garnicht unsere Freude vorstellen, Wie geht es Euch meine Teuere, und was macht der süßer Alberike? Bei uns ist gs.d alles in Ordnung, Ruth und Mann wohnen bei Minka, und befinden sich gut, Die Eltern von Malvine und die meinste von unsere Bekannte besuchen Oft AndGus Mutter, Wir nicht auch nicht Onkel und familie, Wir können die nicht leiden, Von Regina und Mann haben wir kein Neues seit einem Jahre, wir sind sehr unruhig, denn sie müsste ein Kind bekommen, Golda lässt Euch schön grüßen, sie fühlt sich gsd gut, Sie wohnt nicht mehr bei Ida den anders hätte sie die Geschwister von Arno müssen sehen, Ihr könnt ruhig Tante Julia danken für alle Sorge die Sie uns überlassen hat, Papa und Kinder befinden sich gut, Wir denken viel an Euch und möchten Euch mit dem Teueren Alberike schon gerne gesehen. Ich hoffe das es wird nicht mehr lang

"Bei uns is gsd alles in ordnung." By us, all is (gott sei dank), thank G-d all ok.

Postcards from Willy in Antwerp to Poriah
in Portugal. In another card dated March
1942 Willy begs for Matzos because Passover
is approaching. Willy, unlike his mother,
writes in French rather than German.

ROSALIE KLEINHAUS

Rosalie Kleinhaus' mother, Sara Fruma Altschuler, was born in Suwalki, Poland on December 6, 1920 to Chana Fryda (née Mirkis) and Avraham Altschuler, who were in the shoe business. Avraham died in 1928, leaving Chana responsible for Sara and her little brother Mordecai. Sara eventually graduated gymnasium in Suwalki in 1937, a notable achievement, and she began university studies until the extreme antisemitism on campus forced her to withdraw. When the German planes flew over Poland at the start of WWII, Sara, age 19, her mother, and Mordecai fled from Suwalki, very close to the German border, to Volkovysk, near the Soviet border. Within a few weeks the area came under Soviet rule. The Soviets forced them to declare whether they wanted to leave or stay and become Soviet citizens. Because they chose the former, they were rounded up in the middle of the night in June 1940 and put into cattle cars headed to a Siberian labor camp. There they chopped down trees and sawed lumber in the bitter cold. If you didn't work you didn't eat. There was very little food to go around and many people died of starvation and disease. Sara herself fell ill with typhus but survived. Possessions were sold in exchange for bread. For the remainder of her life, Sara considered bread her favorite and most important food.

After the agreement between Soviet Russia and Poland was signed, the Polish citizens began to leave the labor camps. Chana, Sara and Mordecai went to Dzhambul, Kazakhstan, where there were many Polish Jews. In Dzhambul, Sara fell ill again, this time with malaria. Recovered, she walked two hours each day to work, but had a good job as a bookkeeper and was able to get extra loaves of bread for her family. Despite all her years of struggle in Soviet Russia, Sara used to say that the Russian people were good to them. Her brother went to school and she was allowed to work. Nobody had much, but they shared what little they had.

In 1946 the family was permitted to return to Poland. Upon their return, they were greeted with suspicion and contempt. However, when they arrived in Suwalki, their hometown, their former housekeeper, Rozalia, who had been very devoted to their family from the time Sara was a child, looked for them. She was a devout Catholic whose priest had told her to bury the religious items from the Altschuler home so the Germans wouldn't take them. She dug up the Altschuler candlesticks and kiddush cup and presented them to Chana when she returned after the war.

While in Dzhambul, Sara met Emil Mandelbaum. Emil Mandelbaum was born on January 21, 1914 in Trzebinia, Poland to Reizel (née Gutter) and Yisroel Tzvi (Isser) Mandelbaum who was in the steel business and owned a farm. Notably he was the first Jewish mayor of Trzebinia. Emil had six siblings, Mendel, Manya, Stephen, Lola, Esther and Daniel. During the war, Emil was imprisoned in a small concentration camp in Poland from which he escaped. He also fought against the Germans in the Polish army and in a resistance group. He was shot in the head and remained unconscious for many weeks. The trauma caused him to have seizures for several years and as a result he was never allowed to drive. He was evacuated by the Soviets and eventually came to Dzhambul, Kazakhstan where he was a leader of the Polish Jewish community and where he met Sara.

Yisroel Zvi and two of his sons, Mendel and Daniel, fled toward the Soviet border as soon as the war began. Emil, his father and two brothers ended up together in Kazakhstan. Reizel and Manya and Manya's two children stayed behind, believing that Hitler would leave women alone. They were killed in Treblinka in 1942. Esther, another sister, was shot in September 1939. Emil's brother Stephen fought with the Polish brigade of the British army. He survived the war, but his wife and son were killed in the concentration camps.

Sara and Emil were married on August 12, 1946 on the street in Krakow. A trip to Suwalki, in northern Poland, was dangerous because Jewish men were being pulled out of trains and shot. Yisroel Tzvi therefore organized a minyan in the street for the marriage. The small wedding party had to disperse quickly because it was dangerous for Jews to congregate. The young couple left Poland after they were married and went to Stockholm, Sweden, where they waited for a visa to the United States. They arrived in the United States in May 1947. Emil had declared himself a farmer so the family was assigned to a chicken farm in Lakewood, New Jersey. After a few months they settled in Brooklyn, where their only child, Rosalie, was born and raised. Emil began work as a porter in a candy factory and quickly worked his way up to management level. Eventually he partnered in a very successful business manufacturing Salton hot trays and he prospered. Emil Mandelbaum always said that the streets of America were paved with gold.

"There once was a city with fine and good Jews. Where has it all gone?... It is difficult to describe the pain I felt when I came to Suwalk on 20th May, 1946. The city had not suffered much during the war. There stood the same Jewish houses, but there were no Jews in them. Strangers had taken over everything. "Our inheritance has gone to strangers, our houses to foreigners." Our brothers and sisters perished in the gas chambers and concentration camps, and blood enemies occupied their property. There was not the same movement in town. No Jewish children with their beautiful sparkling eyes playing in the streets. No Jewish youth in the streets. As we walked by the Jewish houses, it seemed as though we heard a voice demanding justice and calling for vengeance for the spilling of Jewish blood." From Chana Altschuler's contribution to the Suwalki Yizkor book.*
Eicha 5:2

Yisroel Tzvi Mandelbaum c.1950.

Reizel Mandelbaum, Trzebinia, c.1935.

Chana Fryda & Avraham Altschuler

Judaica buried during the war by a faithful housekeeper in Suwalki and unearthed in 1946.

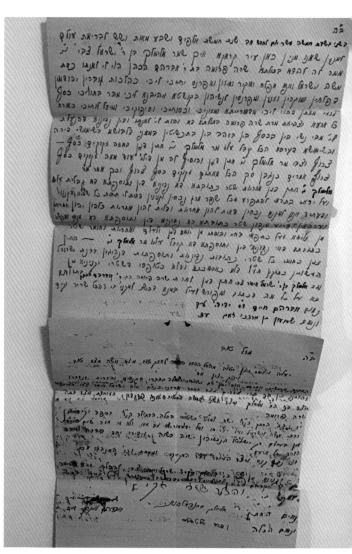

The ketubah and tenaim documents of Emil and Sara Mandelbaum. Married in Krakow, August 12, 1946.

Silver spoons buried by the family's housekeeper and then unearthed after the war.

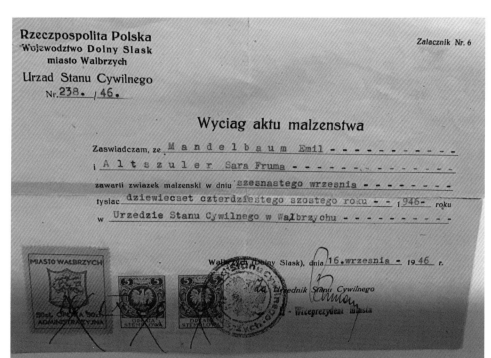

Emil and Sara. Krakow, c.1946

Polish marriage certificate - Walbrzych, Poland, September 16, 1946.

Sara Altschuler, front row center, sitting for a written German exam, Suwalki, May 14, 1937.
Note proctors standing in the rear.
White collars were mandatory for all girls.

Gymnasium diploma of Sara Altschuler. Suwalki. June 1937.

RENA KOHN

Yechiel (Chiel) Melon, father of Rena Kohn was born on the first day of Rosh Hashana, 1910 in Lancut, Poland. He was one of nine children born to Eliyahu Melon, who owned a cobblestone business and his wife Rechama, who was an inn keeper. Chiel was raised in a religious home, attended cheder and was tutored by rebbeim. As a young man he went into the cobblestone business with his father and then managed a stone quarry owned by his brother. After the invasion of Poland in 1939, he survived in the nearby Sieniawa ghetto until he was sent to a forced labor camp, where he worked as a blacksmith. Saved from deportation many times, hidden in makeshift bunkers, overpowering would-be collaborators, Chiel Melon managed to survive. He would later tell his children that a *malach*, an angel, carried him throughout. Chiel spent the last eighteen months of the war hidden in the hay loft of a barn on the property of a Polish woman, Josefa Dudek, who, with her children, was honored at Yad Vashem as one of the Righteous Among the Nations. What also helped keep him alive was his ability to daven and say tehillim with the leather-bound siddur that he had managed to keep with him throughout. When the war ended, Chiel was the only survivor of his large, closely-knit family. He was placed in a DP camp in Castel Gondolfo, outside Rome, and finally immigrated to the United States. He arrived in New York City on the SS *Marine Jumper* (the first U.S. DP ship from an Italian port) in November 1949. Settling on the Lower East side with a cousin, Chiel went into the used-clothing business. In 1953 he met an American girl, Leah Delman, and he married her in 1954. The Melons settled in Brooklyn and raised their two daughters, Suri and Rena, there.

Forever sorry that he had not taken his tefillin along with him when he left the ghetto, Chiel Melon made it a lifelong mission to buy tefillin for anyone who was in need but could not afford the purchase of a pair.

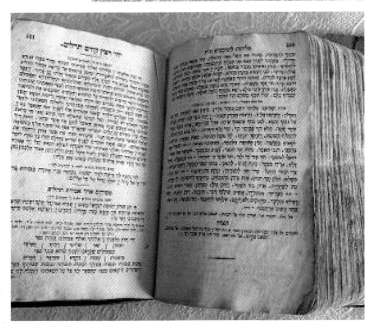

Chiel Melon's precious siddur, with his notations. While he was in hiding this siddur fell into a pail of water and Chiel painstakingly preserved and dried each waterlogged page with pieces of straw.

(opposite page)
The Melon family.
Lancut, c. 1915-1920.
Chiel, furthest left,
the only survivor.

*Baila Melon Rubinfeld,
Chiel's older sister. Pre-war.
She and her two children
were taken from the
Rzeszow ghetto and killed.*

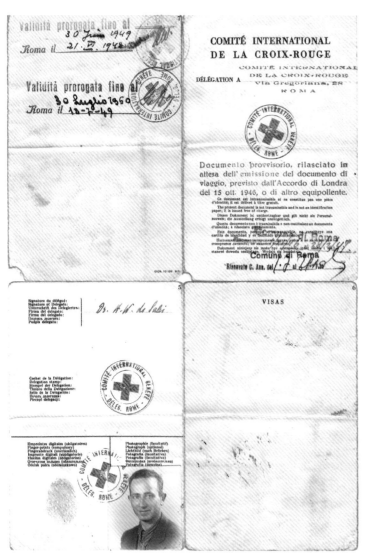

Luggage tag from the voyage, front & back.

Temporary ID issued by the Red Cross.
Rome, May 27, 1946.

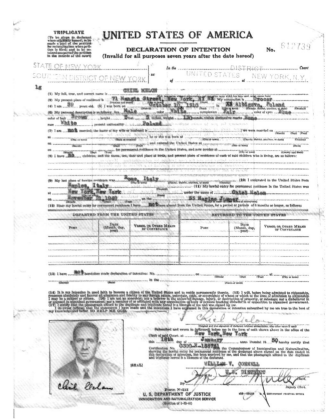

Certificate of Intent to become a U.S. citizen.
Issued January 18, 1950.

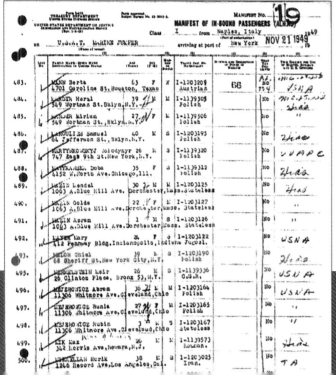

Ship's manifest from the SS Marine Jumper. Chiel Melon is #493.

   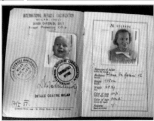  

*"The story of the survivors is one of courage and strength,
of people who are living proof of the indomitable will of human beings
to survive and of their tremendous capacity of hope.
It is not the story of a remarkable people.
It is a story of just how remarkable people can be."*

William Helmreich,
Against All Odds
*- Holocaust Survivors
and the Successful Lives
They Made in America, 1992*

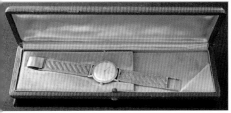   

ESTHER KREMER

William Bernstein, grandfather of Esther Kremer, was born in Hamburg, Germany on September 13, 1910, one of five sons (Rubin, William, David and twins Marcus and Leon) of Ethel and Nathan Bernstein, who had moved to Germany from Poland in 1907. Nathan owned and operated a shop that sold cigars, eggs and cheese. William attended the Jewish day school in Hamburg – the Talmud Tora Realschule and eventually he became a commodities trader on the Hamburg exchange. On August 16, 1936 he married Bertha Rubin in Warsaw. Her parents, Moshe and Celia, had moved back to Poland in 1932 after the Nazis had requisitioned their leather factory in Frankfurt.

William Bernstein was arrested at 5:00 AM, on November 10, 1938, the morning after Kristallnacht. He was shoved into a gestapo car while his wife watched in horror. For six weeks she lived with the terror of not knowing his fate. She feared being left a widow. with her 18 month-old daughter Henny and her elderly in-laws. Luckily, William's boss in the commodities trade was a truly righteous gentile named Richard Moser, a German who was so anti-Nazi that he sent his teenage son to Peru to avoid being enlisted in the Nazi youth movement. After six weeks, Moser, with his government connections, was able to track William to Sachsenhausen concentration camp, outside of Berlin. Moser claimed that Herr Bernstein was an essential worker necessary for the war effort. During the six weeks that William was interned, Moser was able to secure affidavits for him, Bertha and little Henny to leave Germany, a task made possible because an uncle in Crown Heights, Brooklyn, Israel Bernfeld, had already agreed to sponsor the young family. The Bernsteins arrived in New York on May 1, 1939 aboard the *Queen Mary*. William and Bertha settled in Brooklyn and William began work as an international trader in spices and herbs. The couple had three more children, Evelyn in 1942, Nathan in 1945 and Celia in 1947.

William worked tirelessly, but in vain, to get his parents out of Germany. When the war ended, he tried desperately to learn their fates. He wrote dozens of letters and sent countless telegrams, but ultimately he received word from the American Red Cross that both his parents had perished. Both were sent to Theresienstadt, where Nathan Bernstein died of typhoid. Ethel Bernstein was sent from there to Auschwitz, in one of the last death transports.

In 2002, after trying for seven years, Henny Bernstein Brener, then living in Venezuela, was able to secure Richard Moser's legacy as one of Yad Vashem's Righteous Among the Nations. Not only had he saved William, Bertha and Henny, but he had sent food to the elder Bernsteins when they were starving in their ghetto. He was honored in Hamburg by the Bernstein family in a formal dinner attended by both Moser's and William's descendants. The next day there was a formal presentation. The Israeli ambassador in Germany presented to Peter Hans Moser, Moser's son, a posthumous Yad Vashem award honoring his father. Three generations of descendants of the Moser and Bernstein families remain connected to this day.

(above, right)
William Bernstein, front row center, a short distance runner in the first Maccabee games. Palestine, 1932.

(above, left)
Ethel Bernstein with her five sons. Top row, left to right: William, Rubin, Ethel. Bottom row, left to right: David, twins Leon and Marcus, Hamburg, 1914.

David, Ethel and Nathan Bernstein in their store in Hamburg. pre-war.

On the following pages:
A mother's desperate letters to her children and a son's desperate search for his parents.

June 30,1941

All my dear ones,

our hopes have fallen into the water.
meanwhile, to travel,there is nothing to think
about. all is in vain.
I went to the joint today,there is nothing else
to be done. the consulate is closed. we must
  see how we will survive here. we await mail
from dear willy.
papa has written everything-
stay well and we hope everything is going well
with you all

                    MAMA

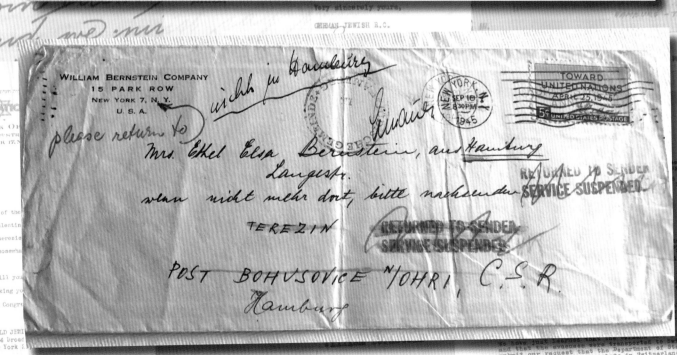

RCA RADIOGRAM
R.C.A. COMMUNICATIONS, INC.
A SERVICE OF RADIO CORPORATION OF AMERICA
TO ALL THE WORLD – BETWEEN IMPORTANT U.S. CITIES – TO SHIPS AT SEA

DIRECT

TO OBTAIN THE BENEFIT OF RCA DIRECT SERVICE THE VIA "RCA" **MUST** BE INSERTED BY THE **SENDER** OF THE MESSAGE

...wing Radiogram subject to the conditions, regulations and rates as set forth in the ...ff of R.C. Communications, Inc., and on file with the regulatory authorities.

August 8. 1945

"Via RCA"

Rp 25 words-NLT

NLT Martha Glass - Hauptstrasse 15 - Theresienstadt (CSR)

reference your cable Ingeedgar as their good freends kindly help me finding my mother deported from Hamburg last heard December 1944 address Langestrasse Theresienstadt please cable whether she is still there mmm or what happened to her many thanks - William Bernstein - 15Parkrow - Newyork -

FULL-RATE MESSAGE UNLESS MARKED OTHERWISE

Address ...tted}

Cable Address: CONGRESS, NEW YORK

GERMAN JEWISH REPRESENTATIVE COMMITTEE
Affiliated with the
WORLD JEWISH CONGRESS
1834 Broadway   New York 23, N.Y.
Circle 6-1900

July 23, 1945

Mr. William Bernstein
899 Montgomery Street
Brooklyn 15, N.Y.

Dear Mr. Bernstein :

    In reply to your letter of July 15, we wish to inform you that just to-day we received a list of the liberated Theresienstadt internees. We are sorry, the name of your mother does not appear therein. However, we cannot assume any responsibility for the completeness of this list.

    Kindly fill out the enclosed inquiry form. We shall try to trace the whereabouts of your mother. There is no possibility to cable to Germany so far; but you could try by yourself to locate your mother in sending a cable to the administration of Teresin .

    As to the application for getting a visa for your mother to immigrate to the United States there is nothing what could be done right now. If you have located your mother, please, inform our Immigration Department; they will give you further advise.

    We will be glad to be of assistance whenever possible.

Very sincerely yours,

GERMAN JEWISH R.C.

by _____
Secretary

IX:xy

ARMAND AMIEL LINDENBAUM

Bennett David Lindenbaum | Ariel Lindenbaum Sebag | Abigail Masha Tambor

Ghity Amiel Lindenbaum Stern was born in Swinzian, Lithuania on April 2, 1907. She was the second of eight children born to Rabbi Moshe Avigdor Amiel and Masha Neviaski. Rabbi Amiel became chief rabbi of Antwerp in 1920 and was one of the leading ideologists of religious Zionism and the founder of the Tachkemoni day school, a school that became the paradigm of modern yeshiva day schools worldwide. In 1927 Ghity married Nathan Lindenbaum in Antwerp where the couple settled and had four children, Marcel (1930), Maidy (1932), Henry (1937) and Armand (1938).

Nathan Lindenbaum was born in Lancut, Poland in 1901, one of four children born to Mordechai Lindenbaum and Rachel Ingber. The Lindenbaums moved to Antwerp in 1907, lived briefly in Holland during World War I, and then returned to Antwerp in 1918. As a teenager in Antwerp, Nathan became a member of the Mizrachi youth movement which held its meetings in Rabbi Amiel's home. By 1927 he had married one of Rabbi Amiel's seven daughters, Ghity, and soon made a name for himself as a leader in the diamond trade in Antwerp. Well-respected, resourceful and quick-thinking, he managed to procure a bus to get almost his entire family out of Belgium the very day after the Nazis invaded, May 10, 1940. The Lindenbaums drove first to La Panne and then to Bordeaux where the Portuguese consul, Aristides de Sousa Mendes, furnished them with visas to Portugal. After a harrowing journey through Spain which included Nathan's brief arrest, the family sailed from Lisbon to New York on the SS *Siboney*, arriving on December 3, 1940. A bill was introduced in Congress for their relief in January 1941 but it was not passed and they sailed on to Havana, Cuba, where they stayed a month, returning to New York on April 1, 1941 aboard the SS *Oriente*. Ghity and Nathan with their four children settled on the Upper West Side of Manhattan. Tragically, Nathan died in a plane crash in Gander, Newfoundland in 1946. Ghity married Max Stern in 1950.

Bill introduced in Congress to aid the Lindenbaum family. January 8, 1941.

77TH CONGRESS
1ST SESSION

H. R. 1737

IN THE HOUSE OF REPRESENTATIVES

JANUARY 8, 1941

Mr. SOMERS of New York introduced the following bill; which was referred to the Committee on Immigration and Naturalization

A BILL

For the relief of Nathan Lindenbaum, his wife Debora Gita Amiel Lindenbaum, and their four children, Marcus Lindenbaum, son, Fanny Lindenbaum, daughter, Henri Lindenbaum, son, and Armand Lindenbaum, son.

1   *Be it enacted by the Senate and House of Representa-*
2   *tives of the United States of America in Congress assembled,*
3   That in the administration of the immigration and naturali-
4   zation laws, the Attorney General be, and he is hereby,
5   authorized and directed to record the lawful admission for
6   permanent residence of Nathan Lindenbaum, his wife Debora
7   Gita Amiel Lindenbaum, and their four children, Marcus
8   Lindenbaum, son, Fanny Lindenbaum, daughter, Henri
9   Lindenbaum, son, and Armand Lindenbaum, son, as of
10 December 3, 1940, the date on which they were admitted
11 to the United States, if they are found to be otherwise

Ghity and Nathan (center) with Nathan's mother, Rachel. New York, c.1945

Maidy and Marcel Lindenbaum. Antwerp, 1935.

The Lindenbaum children at Marcel's Bar Mitzvah. (l to r) Armand, Maidy, Marcel and Henry. New York, October, 1943.

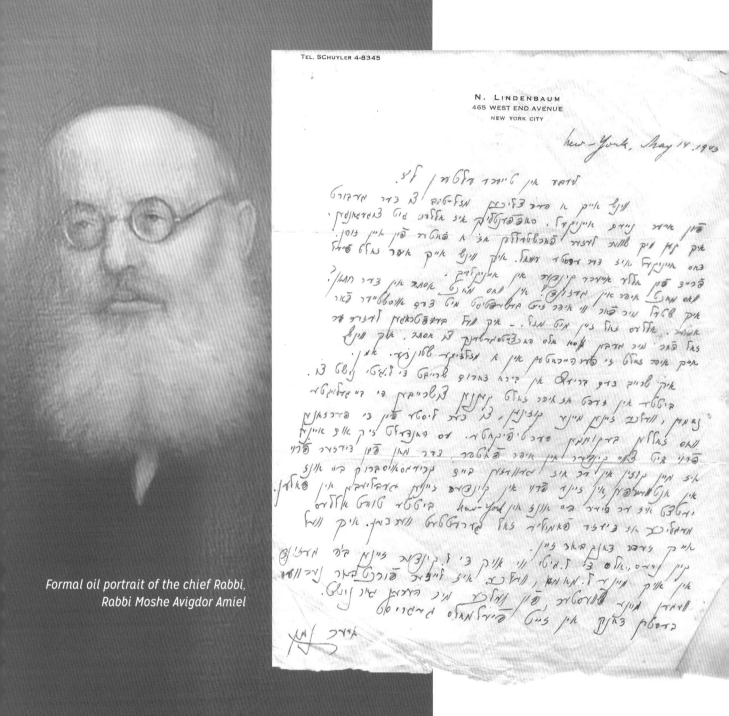

new-York, May 14. 1943

Formal oil portrait of the chief Rabbi,
Rabbi Moshe Avigdor Amiel

Letter from Nathan Lindenbaum in New York to his father-in-law in Palestine, asking for help for a visiting cousin whose wife was trapped with their children in Poland, and thanking him for the certificates already procured. May 14, 1943.

Nathan closes by expressing his mother's anxiety about the fate of her daughter Paula and her family who were unable to leave Antwerp with the rest of the group. As it turned out, Paula, her husband, their three children and her in-laws were killed in Auschwitz around the time this letter was written.

Rabbi Amiel and his family at the seaside.
Knokke, Belgium. c.1920.

Rabbi Moshe Avigdor Amiel. Palestine, 1940's.

LINDA MARSHAK

Linda Capp Marshak was born on July 11, 1938 in Ostrog, Poland. She was the youngest child of Blanche (Bronia) and Joseph Capp. Joseph was a leather merchant by trade but also a great fan of theater and music. When the Germans invaded Ostrog in 1941, Linda was three, her sister Rivka (Lala), ten, and her brother Efraim (Fima), twelve. Storm troopers surrounded their house and Linda's two siblings were rounded up and later marched into the nearby forest and killed along with hundreds of others. Joseph had died of a heart attack during a Nazi raid the previous year, so Blanche and her baby were left alone to fend for themselves. They first went to the Ostrog ghetto, then escaped to hide in the barn of a farmer for a year and ultimately joined some partisans in the forest till the war ended. Blanche and Linda spent two years in a DP camp in Bari, Italy where the camp's school put an emphasis on Hebrew language and the arts. Mother and child finally sailed for America, departing from Naples on the SS *Vulcania* and arriving in February 1948.

Linda was only ten and the two new arrivals had to quickly learn the language and adjust to their new life. They settled in Brooklyn and, at the advice of a friend, Blanche Capp enrolled her daughter in the Yeshiva of Flatbush. Blanche, having had some nursing training in Poland, supported herself and her daughter in that manner. She never remarried, despite many opportunities, and remained all her life completely and steadfastly devoted to her surviving child. Linda, at 20, married Albert Marshak on March 30, 1958 and, after earning a BA, she became an elementary school Hebrew teacher. The Marshaks raised their two children, Craig and Diana, in Atlantic Beach where they have lived for 56 years.

After the war Blanche remembers thinking,
"Maybe I'll find the children. Maybe they are alive. It was easier for me to live with
that belief. In the back of my mind I knew they were not alive but I thought,
maybe, maybe. Even today..."

Excerpted from an interview in the Fortunoff Video Archive for Holocaust Testimonies, Yale University, 1982.

Linda Marshak's granddaughter, an ordained rabbi, recently added the Capp name
to her own, becoming Ariana Capp Tauber, in order to memorialize
all her Capp family relatives who perished in the Shoah.

Capp family at dinner.
Joseph & Blanche Capp (center),
Ostrog, Poland. c.1936

Polish school portrait. Lala, center with flowers. Fima lower right with poster. Ostrog, c.1937

Capp family. Joseph and Blanche with Lala and Fima. Ostrog, Poland. c.1937

*Fima holding
baby Linda.
Ostrog, Poland. 1939.*

*(clockwise), A friend, Blanche, Fima and Lala.
Ostrog, Poland. c.1938*

Linda's sketch "Nest for a Bird." Age 8. Bari, Italy. 1946.

Linda Capp, center with bow, in DP camp. Bari, Italy. 1947.
Linda performing in a Yiddish play at the DP camp. Bari, Italy. 1947.

JONAH MEER

Abram Meer, father of Jonah Meer, was born in Chelm, Poland on December 25, 1924. He was one of four children born to Yechiel Mechel Meer and Chana Rasha Hochman Meer, who owned and operated a grocery store in the town. When the Germans invaded Poland, Abram was only fifteen. Chana Rasha, by then a young widow, was afraid that her son would be rounded up with other young able-bodied Jews so she sent him into Russian-occupied territory to stay with relatives. Abram then joined the Russian Polish army and also spent a period of time in hiding in church roofs. Back in Chelm, the Meer grocery was seized by the Germans and the entire family, mother, sisters and brother, were murdered in Sobibor.

After the war, Abram, the lone survivor, lived in Paris while awaiting a visa either to the U.S. or Israel. On April 21, 1949 he arrived in New York City. Shortly thereafter he met an American girl, Helen Greenberg, and they married on March 26, 1950. They raised their three children, Michael, Jonah and Rashi, on the Lower East Side of New York. After working at some odd jobs, Abram opened a zipper factory in New York and worked there until his retirement. Not comfortable being idle, he then became a salesman in the notions business and retired at age 90. Abram Meer remained devout his whole life, going to shul and attending shiurim. This is the legacy he left to his nine grandchildren and two dozen great-grandchildren.

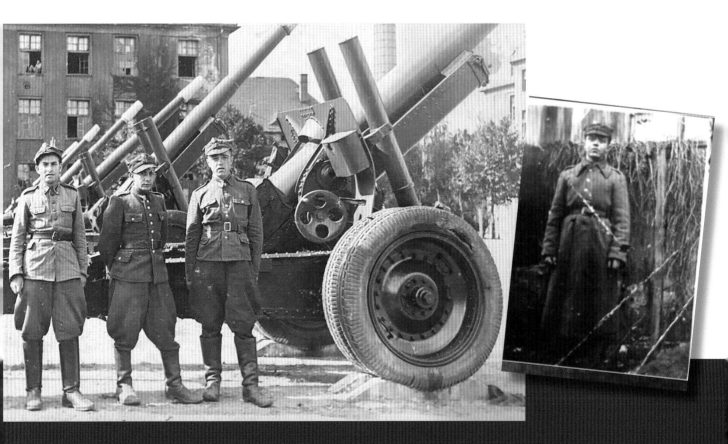

Abram Meer, right, with two comrades in Russian army. Early 1940's.

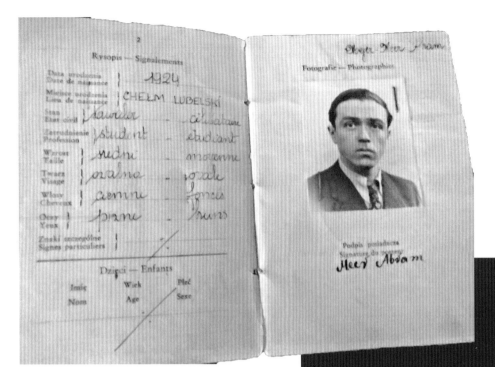

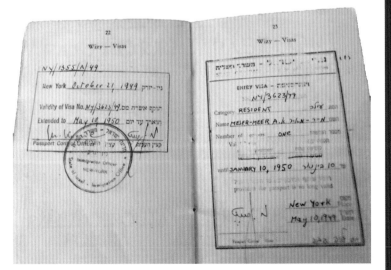

Abram Meer Polish Passport
Visa to Israel, issued in New York, October 21, 1949.

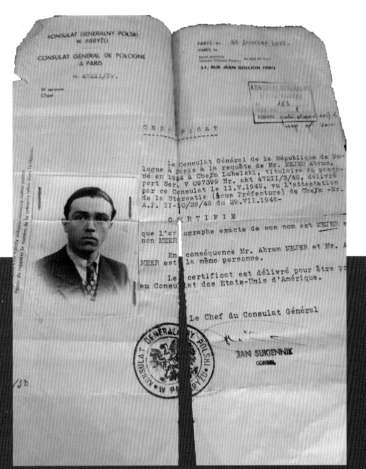

Certification from the Polish consul in Paris that Abram Mejer and Abram Meer were one and the same person.

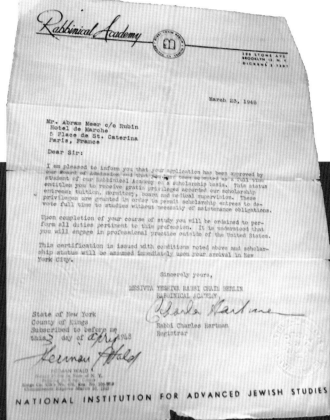

Letter of acceptance as a scholarship student at Mesivta Yeshiva Rabbi Chaim Berlin Rabbinical Academy sent from Brooklyn, New York to Abram Meer's temporary Paris address. April 3, 1948.

Passenger ticket on the merchant ship MS Sobieski for voyage from Cannes to New York, April 21, 1949. Ticket was purchased on April 12 for $188. or the equivalent of $2,000 in 2020.

JOEL NESSIM

Sophie Rozen Nessim, mother of Joel Nessim, was born on October 18, 1936 in Brussels, Belgium, the only child of Anna and Elia Joel Rozen. The Rozens were an Orthodox Jewish family and lived adjacent to a furniture factory and store that they owned. Anna had moved from Russia to Belgium with her parents, Sophie and Jankiel (Jacob) Polonski, and an older brother, Isaac, when she was a baby. Two other brothers, Morris and David, were already living in Brussels by the time they arrived. Sophie's father was born in Poland and moved to Belgium in his 20's to avoid joining the Polish army. His parents remained in Poland with his four sisters. The Nazis invaded Belgium on May 10, 1940. Just 18 days later, the Belgian army surrendered and Germany occupied the country. By 1942, Elia decided that the family should flee. Although he encouraged his brother-in-law, Isaac Polonski, to do the same, the Polonskis remained and were among the approximately 25,000 Jews from Belgium who were rounded up in the summer of 1942. They were never heard from again, and were likely taken to the Mechelen detention camp before deportation to the Auschwitz-Birkenau extermination camp.

Sophie and her parents survived by paying an older Christian couple to hide them at their farm in Waterloo, approximately 10 miles south of Brussels. They packed as many possessions as they could into their suitcases and made their way on foot to the farm. For nearly three years, Sophie lived openly with the couple, who told people they were taking care of her because her parents were sick. During the day, Sophie helped milk the cows and bake bread. Her parents lived in the basement which they entered through a hidden trap door in the floor. At night, they walked outside but stayed close to the house. The arrival of American and British soldiers in September 1945 signaled the end of the war and the family's freedom. They returned to Brussels to find that the Germans had destroyed the factory, the store and their home. Elia resumed his furniture business but became sick and died approximately one and a half years later.

In 1955, when Sophie was almost nineteen years old, she and her mother left Belgium for the United States, sponsored by her uncles Morris and David, who had immigrated to New York as teenagers. Sophie and her mother sailed from Rotterdam, Belgium on October 4, 1955 aboard the SS *Ryndam* as passengers 9012024153965 and 9012024557318, respectively. Ten days later, on October 14th, the ship, carrying 14,935 passengers, arrived at Ellis Island. They lived with Sophie's Uncle Morris in Brooklyn for a few months before renting their own apartment in Brooklyn. Neither Sophie nor her mother spoke any English but found jobs in a factory, gluing fabric swatches on sample sheets. They did this for approximately one year and then Sophie began attending night school to learn English. She saw a "Help Wanted" ad for a bookkeeper at a clothing factory and managed to get hired despite having no bookkeeping experience. Soon after, she found a new bookkeeping position at *Leslie Fay*, a leading women's clothing manufacturer, where she worked many years. During this time, her cousin introduced her to Abraham Salim Nessim, originally from Baghdad, Iraq, and they married on September 14, 1957. Abraham passed away in 1977 and Sophie in 2018, leaving behind three children, Joel, Daniel and Michael, and eight grandchildren.

Nom et prénoms du père Familienaam en voornamen van de vader	Palonski Jankiel
Nom et prénoms de la mère Familienaam en voornamen van de moeder	Eberowitz Sophie
Résidence actuelle en Belgique Huidige verblijfplaats in België	Schaerbeek 81, rue Royale Ste Marie
Profession	garnisseuse

PERSOONSBESCHRIJVING

	grisonnants
	gris
	droit
	ovale
Gestalte	1.52

Sophie in Spa, Belgium. c.1946
Spa was a resort town known for its mineral-rich thermal waters.

Souvenir de Spa

2

NUMMER DER AKTE	VOORNAMEN DER KINDEREN	GEBOORTEN Plaats	GEBOORTEN Datum	Plaats
1248	Sofi	Etterbeek	18 october 1936	

Kinderen uit dit Huwelijk gesproten

Birth record for Sofi Rozen in the Etterbeek municipality of Brussels, Belgium. October 18, 1936. The other documents are pages from the Belgian passport of Anna Rozen. February, 1955.

Ce titre de voyage contient 32 pages.
Deze reistitel bevat 32 bladzijden.

ROYAUME DE BELGIQUE
KONINKRIJK BELGIË

MINISTERE DES AFFAIRES ETRANGERES
Ministerie van Buitenlandse Zaken

TITRE DE VOYAGE — REISBEWIJS

pour les étrangers qui ne sont pas des réfugiés politiques (1).
voor vreemdelingen, die geen politieke vluchtelingen zijn (1).

Nº d'ordre B. 135/8 · Nº de série : 39598
Volgnummer : Serienummer :

Nom et prénoms du porteur POLONSKI
Naam en voornamen van de Vve Anna E
houder Rozen. E
Alexoten

Lieu et date de naissance
Plaats en datum van geboorte 31. 12. 1909.

nationalité d'origine
polonaise van oorsprong

(1) Ce titre de voyage est délivré uniquement pour donner au porteur qui n'est pas un réfugié politique la possibilité d'effectuer des déplacements à l'étranger. Il n'implique en faveur du titulaire aucune protection du Gouvernement belge.
Il est interdit, sous peine de lui faire perdre sa validité, de rallonger ce titre de voyage qui doit être renvoyé au Ministère des Affaires Etrangères, à Bruxelles, dès que sa validité est expirée.

(1) Deze reispas wordt alleenlijk afgeleverd om aan de houder die geen politieke vluchteling is, de mogelijkheid te verschaffen naar het buitenland te reizen. Hij geeft geen recht op bescherming vanwege de Belgische Regering.
Het is verboden op gevaar af hem zijn geldigheid te doen verliezen, een verlengstuk te hechten aan deze reispas, die aan het Ministerie van Buitenlandse Zaken te Brussel, moet worden teruggezonden zodra zijn geldigheidstermijn vertreken is.

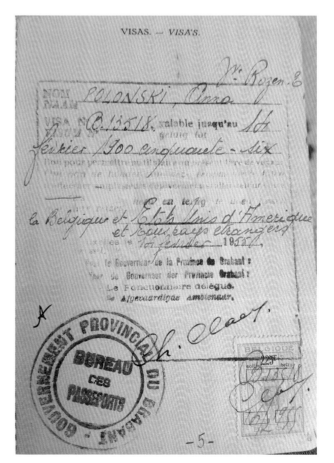

VISAS. — VISA'S.

NOM POLONSKI, Anna
NAAM

VISA Nº B. 135/8 valable jusqu'au 1er
VISUM geldig tot

février 1900 cinquante - six

la Belgique et Etats Unis d'Amérique
et tous pays étrangers

Bruxelles le 1er février 1955

Pour le Gouverneur de la Province de Brabant :
Voor de Gouverneur der Provincie Brabant :
Le Fonctionnaire délégué.
De Afgevaardigde Ambtenaar.

GOUVERNEMENT PROVINCIAL - BRABANT
BUREAU DES PASSEPORTS

-5-

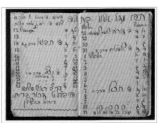

Prayer in Memory of the Six Million

*May God remember the souls of our six million
brothers and sisters of the House of Israel
who gave their lives in sanctification of His name
during the Holocaust.
May God remember their sacrifices
among those
of the holy martyrs and heroes of Israel.
May their souls be rewarded in Gan Eden,
joined in the bonds of everlasting life.
You are their heritage.
May they rest in eternal peace.
Amen.*

DAVID OHAYON
Bari Erber

Esther Lender Ohayon, mother of David Ohayon, was born on December 12, 1925 in Rozavlea, Romania near the town of Sighet. Her parents, Herman and Pesi Lender, lived in a comfortable home surrounded by fruit and nut trees and Herman was a successful business man who dealt with both laymen and government officials. The Lenders had eight children, Morris, Joe, Yakov, Faygie, Leah (Lily), Esther, Leib and Allen. They attended secular school during the day and then, in the late afternoon, a *cheder* in Sighet run by their maternal grandfather, David Tuvel. At this *cheder* Esther made friends with another child, a young boy named Elie Wiesel. When Hungarians occupied the town of Rozavlea in 1939 the atmosphere changed overnight. Former Christian friends hurled anti-Semitic taunts at the Lender children and one by one they left for Budapest. Esther left in 1939, traveling alone by train, and at the age of fourteen she lodged with a doctor and his wife and worked as a seamstress for a furrier. Traveling home for Passover in 1944 proved to be a dreadful mistake. With the rest of her family, Esther was sent to the ghetto in Dragomir where they were crammed ten in a room and then a few weeks later they were all deported to Auschwitz in cattle cars. Clinging to her mother during the selection process she was pushed by another more knowledgeable prisoner to the right, thereby avoiding the fate of most of the rest of her family. Given the number A7547 Esther was assigned the job of bringing food to hospitalized prisoners. In this capacity she was an eyewitness to some of the horrific medical experiments conducted by Dr. Josef Mengele and his associates. The job also gave her access to extra rations which she shared generously with fellow inmates. From Auschwitz Esther was sent to Bergen-Belsen and then to Braunschweig where she cleaned bricks found in the bombed rubble and then to Bendorf where she worked in an ammunition factory. After a brief time in Buchenwald Esther was liberated and like many of the young women who needed to physically recuperate from injuries and illness she was sent to Malmo, Sweden where her healing began. Eventually Esther joined an uncle in Paris and in 1947 got her visa and immigrated to the United States. Her brother Morris had survived in Russia, her brother Joe and sisters Lily and Faygie survived various camps. The rest of the Lenders and Tuvels were gone.

In New York Esther married Morris Eliezer Sklar in 1948 and with him she had a daughter Pauline (b.1949) but the marriage was an unhappy one and the couple divorced. On February 29, 1956 she married Eli Ohayon, a Moroccan-born former-member of the Haganah and with him she had two sons, David in 1956 and Jacques in 1960. The Ohayons raised their children on the Upper West Side of Manhattan and worked in the real estate business.

Esther remembers her grandfather's words:
"Life is a front and you must know when to surrender."
But Esther was a fighter and she saw herself as a descendant of the Biblical Joseph.
Like him, she would survive. When she was being wheeled in to her last surgery she
held up her fist revealing her number A7547 and said to her granddaughter Bari,
"I will fight this but if I can't, you give them hell!"

Esther and a friend in Malmo, Sweden 1946.

Pesi Tuvel Lender, Budapest. c.1919

Esther, 2nd from right & friends
Malmo, Sweden, 1946.

Esther Lender's Romanian passport, bearing her mother's maiden name, Tuvel.

DANIEL OTTENSOSER

Ruth Israel Ottensoser, paternal grandmother of Daniel Ottensoser, was born in Karlsruhe, Germany on June 9, 1920, along with her twin brother Joachim. Karlsruhe was a city near the Black Forest known for its art and culture. Her parents were Friedrich, a WW I officer in the German army, and Eva Loewe Israel. Her childhood was a happy one up until 1935 when she was forced out of her school which was filled with anti-Semitic propaganda.

By 1937, she was engaged to Max Ottensoser (b. 1915 in Markelsheim, a small village in Germany), the youth sports coach and teacher in Karlsruhe. On Kristallnacht, the Loewe's department store was shattered and Max and Friedrich were taken to Dachau. Upon release they were ordered to leave Germany immediately but securing immigration papers was incredibly difficult. Ruth (who was only eighteen) went to the Gestapo office repeatedly to try to obtain the needed papers to leave Germany. Max and his future father-in-law got visas to Trinidad, later followed by Eva who acquired papers by bartering her ivory-keyed piano to a Gestapo officer. After a brief sojourn in New York, Ruth joined the group in Trinidad and married Max there on October 8, 1939.

Ruth's grandparents, Julius and Rosa Loewe, were unable to leave Germany due to old age and illness. Julius died and shortly thereafter, Rosa Loewe was deported to Camp de Gurs in France, where she perished.

In 1940 Ruth and Max left Trinidad to begin their life in America. Friedrich and Eva were interned in Trinidad by the English as *"enemy aliens."* They were treated very badly and accused of being spies for Germany. They too eventually left Trinidad in 1941. Max's mother, Rika Ottensoser arrived in New York, from Camp de Gurs in 1941. In total, thirty-two members of the family died at the hands of the Nazis.

Ruth and Max began their life in America working as the live-in maid and butler of a family in Croton-on-Hudson. They then moved to Washington Heights where Max earned a living as a truck driver and two sons, Samuel and Milton, were born. Eventually they made a life in Elizabeth, New Jersey, where their daughter, Aviva, was born and Max worked as a merchant in partnership with his father-in-law.

Wedding of Ruth Israel and Max Ottensoser. Trinidad, October 8, 1939.

Julius and Rosa Loewe. Karlsruhe, Germany 1890.

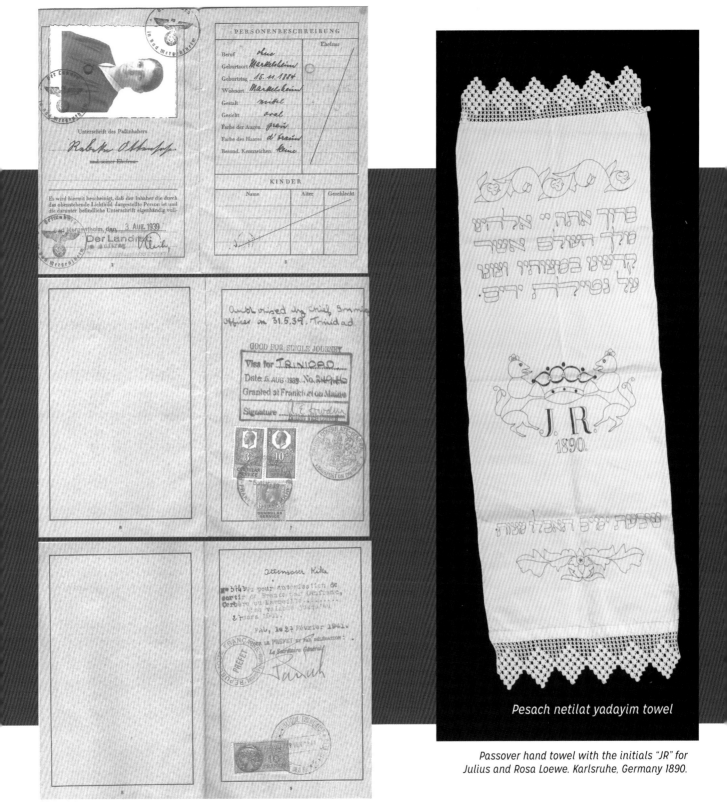

Pesach netilat yadayim towel

Passover hand towel with the initials "JR" for
Julius and Rosa Loewe. Karlsruhe, Germany 1890.

*Pages from the passport of Rika Ottensoser, Max's mother, issued by the Nazis on August 3, 1939
in Bad Mergentheim, a town near Markelsheim.. (top)*

A visa issued on August 5, 1939 by the British consulate in Franfurt for travel to Trinidad, which, at that time, was a British colony. (center)

*When war broke out on September 1, 1939, Rika could no longer travel and she was deported to Gurs, a concentration camp in the Pyrenees.
In early 1941, remarkably, her children in New York procured documents allowing her to come to the United States. An exit visa (bottom) was
issued by the Vichy French government in Marseilles allowing her to leave France. She proceeded to Lisbon and sailed to New York in 1941.*

JOSEPH PACKIN

Ronit Packin-Ymar | **Natan Packin**

Alexandra Gittelsohn Packin, mother of Joseph Packin, was born in Riga, Latvia on May 16, 1922, one of three daughters of Joseph Gittelsohn, a furrier and his wife Eugenia, a dentist. Joseph died before the war and one of the children, Miriam, died at age three of typhus. A teenage student in gymnasium at the outset of the war, Alexandra fled Riga and went behind Russian lines where she worked as a nurse caring for wounded Russian soldiers. Her mother and sister Rachel were killed at the Kaiserwald concentration camp in Riga. After the war, Alexandra returned to her hometown, where she reunited with a distant relative, David Packin. They were married on February 9, 1946 in Riga by Rabbi Leib Spitz and together the newlyweds traveled to a DP camp in Munich, Germany, where they awaited paperwork to immigrate to the U.S.

David (Dov-Ber) Packin was born near the town of Mogilev, Belarus on December 27, 1912, part of the large family of Shaul and Malka Gurevitch Packin. Dovid went to *cheder* as a child and by the 1930's he was a busy lumber merchant with a wife and child. When the Nazis occupied Riga, David was sent to a labor camp, where he was wounded on the job. A friend named Gregor Shelkan warned him that death was the inevitable fate of those who could no longer work, so David escaped the camp and eventually hid in the cloakroom of Christ the King Church whose priest was beholden to him for a past favor. This church was located directly across the street from the Kaiserwald camp. When the cloakroom became too dangerous David found another hiding place in a shed on church property. The priest, Father Kazimir Vilnis, at great personal risk, provided him with shelter and food for eleven months. When the Russian victory seemed imminent, David repaid the priest's kindness by advising him to flee before the anti-clerical Soviets reached Riga. When the city was liberated, David emerged and began life anew with Alexandra at his side. Before leaving Riga for Germany, he helped rebuild the synagogue that was destroyed during the war. Once in Germany, David testified at the Nuremberg trials. He had lost his parents, most of his siblings, his wife and his young child.

David and Alexandra arrived in New York in 1947. They settled on the Upper West Side and raised their children Joseph (b. 1948) and Eugene (b. 1954) there. David tried to earn a living at several jobs - snow sweeper, produce seller and at a lumber yard making coffins. He eventually partnered with a friend and founded D & M Lumber which his sons and grandsons run today.

In 1954 David Packin appeared on national TV as part of a " This is Your Life" segment featuring his wartime friend Gregor Shelkan. David and Father Kazimir Vilnis were reunited in 1986 in New York and David presented the priest with a gold watch inscribed with the words "To Father Vilnis for saving my life."
Interviewed at Yale University in 1985 David said
"I fought every day to stay alive just to see what the world would do. That's what kept me alive."

Above:
David Packin. Riga, pre-war. This photo of a handsome young man sporting a jaunty hat was displayed in the window of a photographer's shop which David passed twice daily on his way to and from the labor camp.

Alexandra Gittelsohn. Riga, pre-war.

Yellow star worn by David Packin during his years in hard labor.

Below:
David Packin and Father Kazimir Vilnis at their emotional reunion. New York, December 11, 1986. David's grandson Tamir presents the priest with a bouquet. Courtesy: Catholic New York, December 18th, 1986.

—Odette Lupis

Tefillin, siddur and talis belonging to David Packin and kept with him throughout the war.

Labor camp ID number.

Fragments of matzohs baked by David Packin while in the Riga ghetto in 1942-43 and the Riga church in 1944. Some were baked during Aktions in the German ghetto when thousands of Jews were murdered. Each fragment is labeled in Yiddish.

David Packin wrote about Passover 1944.
*"I even managed to bake some matzos on the stove.....
Of course I didn't have the wine to drink four cups for a seder,
but I shed more than enough tears to fill the required four cups."*

Shreds of a towel from Alexandra's home in Riga.
She felt that it brought her good luck and she gave each of
her boys a piece.

BEA PEYSER
Miriam Goldberg | Ruthie Kestenbaum | Josh Peyser

Beate (Bea) Peyser was born on July 20, 1931 in Kiel, Germany. Her mother, Rose Brachfeld, was pregnant with Beate when her husband, Beryl Munz, died suddenly. Beate was lovingly raised by Rose and her second husband, Avram Galanty. The young family moved from Kiel to Berlin where another daughter, Rita, was born in 1934. Avram was successful in the piece goods business but as Hitler's rise to power became ever more threatening, he made arrangements for his family to emigrate. When some of his savings were embezzled by an acquaintance, the family, already equipped with visas, hastily left Berlin and followed the culprit all the way to Rotterdam and aboard the Holland America ship, the SS *Statendam*. The Galantys arrived in the U.S. in late June of 1938 and, after a brief time with family in Newark, they settled in the Washington Heights section of Manhattan. Avram Galanty died in 1943 and Rose, now widowed for the second time and alone in a foreign country, bravely started anew. For many years she supported her young daughters by working in the millinery trimmings business. Beate celebrated her seventh birthday in a new country with a new language to learn. She went on to attend the prestigious Bronx High School of Science and then City College. She married Irwin Peyser on January 9, 1954 and the couple raised four happy children, Renée, Miriam, Ruthie and Joshua, in Oceanside, New York.

The Galantys always believed that by hastening their exit, the notorious embezzler inadvertently saved their lives. The stolen monies, in fact, were also returned.

Tova Brachfeld.
Beate's maternal grandmother.

Rose and Beryl Munz.

Beate Galanty at 2 in Kiel, 1933.

Rose Galanty.

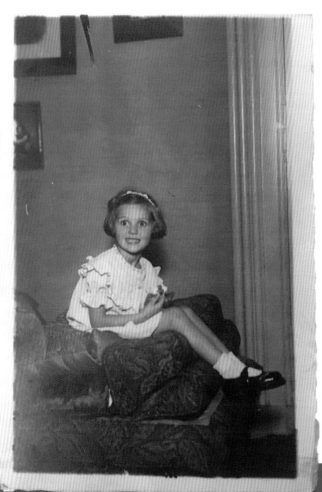

Beate Galanty at 5 in Berlin, 1936.

ALLEN PILEVSKY

Ephraim (Fred) Pilevsky, father of Allen Pilevsky, was born on October 24, 1925 in Musteika, a small town in Lithuania. He and his sister, Sara, were the children of Chana and Chaim Shlomo Pilevsky. An older brother, Yonkel, went to live with Chana's family, the Boyarskys, in Belarus. By 1931 the Pilevskys had moved to nearby Marchinkonys and begun trading in mushrooms for a living. Life changed for the family under the Russian occupation between 1939 and 1941. However, the true horrors only began with the German takeover when the Jews of the town were crowded into ghettos, four families to a room, and then transported to death camps with the help of the Lithuanian police. On November 2, 1942 the Pilevskys were ordered to gather at the town's gate, but when an attempted uprising resulted in a chaotic confrontation, seventeen-year-old Ephraim ran into the woods and hid there for months. Alone and afraid, he was desperate to learn about the fate of his family. After hearing many rumors of their death, he was miraculously reunited with his parents and sister in early 1943. This part of Lithuania was liberated by the Russians on July 12, 1944. Shortly thereafter Ephraim was wounded during an attack by some drunkards and he was hospitalized in Grodno. He met and fell in love with a girl from his hometown named Pola (Paula) Kartzmer and the couple married on February 22, 1945 in a shul in Vilna.

Pola (Pesha) Kartzmer was born on May 20, 1926 in Rudniya, Lithuania. Her parents, Tzvia (née Rabinovitch) and Feivel Kartzmer, owned a general store and a restaurant that was established by Pola's grandfather. After the family was forced into the town's ghetto, they managed to run into the woods and the parents, Pola, her uncle and her cousin Batya hid in a bunker. Her father was murdered one night while out foraging for food. Pola and Batya's mothers, two sisters, were also killed during the war. The cousins were separated but later reunited when they fortuitously met at the house of a sympathetic Pole.

After their marriage, Pola and Fred went to the Foehrenwald DP camp in Germany. En route to the camp, their first son, Philip (Feivel), was born in Lithuania. The young family was able to obtain visas to the United States by 1949. They settled in Brooklyn where another son, Allen, was born in 1951 and a daughter, Sheila, in 1957. Fred worked as a laborer for a time, then as a skilled carpenter before he began a very successful career as a builder.

The greatest legacy of Ephraim and Pola Pilevsky is that their grandchildren and great-grandchildren, including now many little Ephraims and Peshas, and spanning the spectrum from Lakewood to Englewood, carry on the tradition of Torah observance and chesed passed down from their great-grandparents in Lithuania.

Fred & Pola Pilevsky

SHOSHANA PILEVSKY

Genia Link Fluss, mother of Shoshana Pilevsky, was born in 1922 in Poland, the daughter of Sarah and Mordechai Link, who had six children – Yoel, Yisroel, Charna, Hinda, Genia and one other. Genia spent the war years in a labor camp in Siberia and the post-war years in a DP camp in Italy where she met and married Yeshayahu Fluss in 1947. The couple then immigrated to Israel in 1949 and settled in a suburb of Haifa. Their son Michael was born that year and their daughter Shoshana in 1954.

Yeshayahu Fluss, father of Shoshana Pilevsky, was born in 1922 in Poland to Chaya and Yisroel Fluss who worked as a tailor while Chaya tended to their home and their five children – David, Heshu, Shlomo, Tova and Yeshayahu. He too spent the war years in a labor camp in Siberia and then after the war was in a DP camp in Italy.

In 1959 the Fluss family immigrated to the United States and settled in Brooklyn. Yeshayahu earned his living as a tailor, or as the family said, a "clothing engineer." Sadly, Genia died in 1966 at the age of forty-four.

Sarah Link. Poland, pre-war.
Mordechai Link. Poland, pre-war.

Yeshayahu Fluss, left, with friends.
Italy or Palestine, post-war.

Michael and Shoshana Fluss. Israel,
Purim, 1957.

ALAN PINES
Michael Pinewski

Eli (Hillel) Pinewski, father of Alan Pines, was born in Pultusk, Poland on November 3, 1917 to Esther Raiza (née Stajfman) and Moshe Pinewski who owned and operated a flour mill. Eli was one of eight children, Sarah, Eli, Ella, Harry, Zelig, Henia, Steve and Jack. When Eli graduated high school he went to work with his father in the flour mill. Eli's grandfather, Rabbi Avraham Yakov lived in nearby Serock.

In the fall 1939, the Germans entered Serock and Rabbi Avraham Yakov was murdered. Eli hid the family's valuables in the ground and urged his family to flee towards Russia. The Germans arrived suddenly in Pultusk and ordered the Pinewskis and everyone else in town to run over a bridge. Whoever could not run fast enough, was pushed into the river by the Nazis. Miraculously, Eli and his entire family made it over the bridge. Before fleeing from Pultusk to Bialystok, Eli traveled the 23 km to Nasielsk to try to convince his older sister, Sarah and her husband to join them. They refused and sadly, they perished in the Warsaw Ghetto.

The family then traveled by train and stopped in Bialystok for a few days, where Eli met his future wife, Hilda Rotbard, and her family. From there, the Pinewskis made their way to Grajewo (under Soviet rule). In Grajewo, Eli's father, Moshe, received grain from Soviet peasants to bake bread. Since all the synagogues had been destroyed, Eli and his father established a secret daily minyan, prohibited under Soviet rule. From May 1941 to the end of the war, Eli and his brother Harry spent time in Turkistan and worked making bricks in a labor camp in Siberia.

After the war ended, Eli bravely traveled back to Pultusk to recover the family's valuables. In 1946, he was sent to the Traunstein DP Camp in southeastern Germany. He later ran a textile business in Munich before immigrating to the United States on the SS *Liberte* in August 1951. Waiting for him at the New York harbor was Hilda Rotbard. Eli and Hilda married on February 9, 1952 and raised two sons, Seymour and Alan, in Brooklyn, where Eli owned a dry goods store.

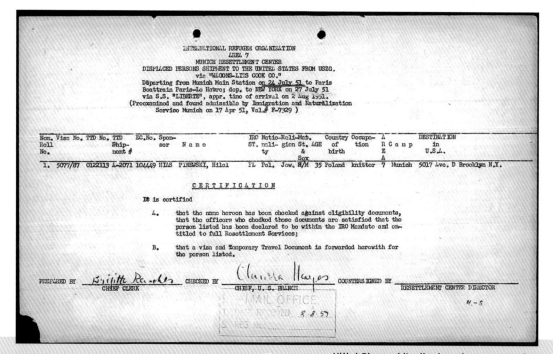

Hillel Pinewski's displaced person card.

Wedding of Hilda and Eli Pinewski. New York, February 9, 1952.

*At the grave of Hilda's maternal grandmother, Chana Katz,
who died on the 17th of Shevat, 1937.
, top to bottom, Simcha Rotbard, his friend, the stonecutter, Hilda, seated.
Right, top to bottom, Dora (Devoira), Esther and Yankel.*

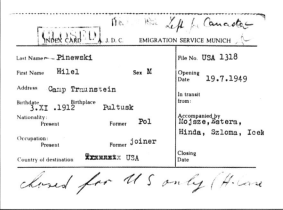

*Hillel Pinewski's International Refugee Organization
travel certification, sponsored by HIAS.
Munich, 1951.*

*At Traunstein DP camp a Pinewski family gathering. Front, from third from left:
Harry Pinewski, Moshe Pinewski, Henia Pinewski Pilchik, Eli Pinewski,
Esther Pinewki. Top row, left: Steven Pines. 1948.*

Hilda Rotbard Pinewski, mother of Alan Pines, was born on March 2, 1929 in Brok nad Bugiem, Poland, the daughter of Simcha Dovid Rotbard, who owned flour mills and his wife Dora Katz Rotbard, who ran a small general store selling staples like bread and milk. Hilda had six siblings, Shmuel Ersh, Moishe Haim (Martin), Ita Roisa, Yankel, Esther and Alter (Arthur). She grew up in Brok, surrounded by grandparents and cousins. Her extended family of Katz and Rotbards lived side by side. Hilda's maternal grandfather, Israel Alter was a very righteous man known far and wide for his Torah learning. Brok was a haven for children, a town with no cars, and with friendly neighbors who knew each child by name. The Jews in Brok strictly observed Shabbos and holidays.

When the Germans arrived in September 1939, Hilda was ten years old and in third grade. The invaders destroyed Brok by setting fire to the houses. Hilda's family's home was burned to the ground while Jews were attacked in shul. All the Jews were rounded into the town church. Days later, displaced from their home, the Rotbard family left for Ostrow. They then went to Bialystok, where Shmuel and Yankel, Hilda's two brothers, were sent to Yeshiva in Vilna. This was the last time the family saw them. The rest of the Rotbards were transported to Northern Russia. One of Hilda's brothers, Martin, had left for New York prior to the war. He tried hard but unsuccessfully to procure visas for the family. From Archangel, Russia, they went to Turkestan where Hilda remembers the family suffered from hard work in forced labor camps, from sickness and starvation. This is where the Rotbard family story overlapped with Hilda's future husband's family, the Pinewskis. Sadly, this is also where Hilda's father Simcha Dovid died of typhus disease in February 1942.

In September 1945, after the war ended, her mother Dora left Turkestan with Hilda, her older sister, Ida, and her younger siblings, Esther and Arthur. They traveled by train to Moscow and then another train to Lvov, Poland. From Poland, they travelled to the DP Camp Feldafing in Germany. Dora and Arthur arrived in New York in August 1947. Hilda and her sister Esther left Bremen for the U.S. on the SS *Marine Tiger* on January 12, 1948 and arrived in New York harbor on January 24, 1948.

When Eli Pinewski's shipped docked in New York harbor in 1951, Hilda was waiting for him.
They married on February 9, 1952 in Brooklyn.

The Rotbard family home in Brok.
At the door, Dora and Simcha, Hilda and Yankel.

ELISA PINES

Murray Pantirer, father of Elisa Pines, was born on June 15, 1925 in Krakow, Poland, the son of Sara Bella and Eliezer Pinchas Pantirer, who owned a store selling milk and eggs and who was also a *baal tefilla* (cantor). Murray was the second of their seven children, Herschel Zvi (1923), Murray, Chaim Yosef (1927), Mordecai Yehuda (1929), Ester Rochel (1931), Israel David Tuvia (1933), and Chaya Rachel (1935). On September 1, 1939, the day the Nazis invaded Poland, Murray Pantirer was fourteen years old and on that day his childhood came to an end. The Pantirers lived behind the walls of the Krakow ghetto from 1941-1942 wearing their white armbands with blue Jewish stars and scrounging for food. Murray, with his light hair and blue eyes, was sometimes able to cast off his armband, sneak out of the ghetto and procure food and other supplies for the rest of the family. In 1942, Murray and his older brother Herschel were deported to Plaszow concentration camp, built on top of a Jewish cemetery. At Plaszow, Murray, young and able bodied, was assigned to the crews building barracks and sidewalks. The camp's commandant, Amon Goeth, was notorious for his barbaric, sadistic cruelty. In 1943, Murray was assigned kitchen duty which enabled him to have access to more food for himself and for the other inmates whom he helped. That same year, in May, Herschel was transported to Auschwitz where he was murdered and thus Murray lost his last surviving relative. In October 1944 Murray was transported to Gross-Rosen, a camp known to be especially horrendous and where most inmates survived only a few days. On his fourth day there, the name Murray Pantirer was called out as #205 on Oscar Schindler's now-famous list. Murray spent the remaining years of the war as a sheet-metal worker in the Schindler factory in Brünnlitz.

After liberation in 1945, his family's sole survivor, Murray went to the Bindermichel DP camp in Austria where he met another survivor, Lucy Lorber. Lucy and Murray wed in the DP camp on January 5, 1947, a day he cherished. Not only did he marry his *eshet chayil*, he was no longer an orphan. Lucy's mother, Ethel, welcomed him as a son and lived with them until she passed away in her 80's. Two years later, in January 1949, the Pantirers arrived in the United States and settled in New Jersey where they raised their three children, Larry, Betty and Elisa. Murray went on to build a real estate business.

Murray Pantirer never learned how his name had suddenly appeared on Oscar Schindler's list, but he firmly believed that an angel had placed it there to ensure the survival of the family name. As Murray Pantirer's real estate business grew he frequently named streets in his developments after his angelic savior and as a result the New Jersey landscape is dotted with many a Schindler Drive and Schindler Way.

Murray Pantirer at the Bindermichel DP camp. Linz, Austria, 1946.

Lucy Lorber Pantirer, mother of Elisa Pines, was born in Rozwadow, Poland on February 6, 1928. Lucy and her sister Jane grew up in the loving home of Ethel and Leon Lorber, surrounded by extended family and friends, including maternal grandparents who lived with them. They attended public school by day and afternoon Hebrew school. Life was pleasant and safe in this shtetl of about 2000 mostly Orthodox Jews on the river San. In 1939 Germany invaded and the Lorbers were sent to Russian occupied Kolonia where the Lorber grandparents lived. Lucy needed to learn Russian and begin a new school as she and her family coped with living with eight people under one roof. The extended family was then sent by train towards Siberia in June 1940. Leon Lorber died during their time in Siberia at a labor camp. The rest of the family was then sent along the Volga river to Tashkent, Uzbekistan. Famine and cold continued to plague Ethel and her daughters as they continued on foot to Uzgen, Kyrgyzstan where other relatives were found. There they remained until 1946. Lucy attended various underground schools and emerged from her seven-year odyssey speaking fluent Russian, Polish, Hebrew, Yiddish and Uzbek.

The end of war did not bring about an end to the wanderings of the three women. They went first to Moscow and then, afraid of pogroms in Rozwadow, they came to Krakow. Eventually the *Bricha* (organization that helped survivors reach Palestine) placed them in the Bindermichel DP camp in Linz, Austria where Lucy met and married Murray Pantirer.

Murray & Lucy Pantirer, DP Camp Linz, Austria, 1946.

Murray and Lucy Pantirer wedding photo, Linz, Austria. January 5, 1947.

Dancing with Oscar Schindler, lifted on chair, at the 25th wedding anniversary party of Murray and Lucy Pantirer.
Murray Pantirer is at right with cufflinks.
New Jersey, January 1972.

Steven Spielberg, on behalf of the United States Holocaust Memorial Museum, accepting the violin played by survivor Henry Rosner in the Plaszow concentration camp.
Violin was donated by Murray Pantirer and Abraham Zuckerman. Murray Pantirer in photograph with Steven Spielberg.

TALI GOLDBERG PINES

Aryeh Goldberg, Tali Pine's grandfather, was born in 1909 in the town of Piaski and grew up in Krasnik, Poland. Aryeh was one of ten children of Hinda and Itzhak Goldberg, a Ger chasid who owned a successful kasha grain mill. When the Nazis invaded, Aryeh was taken to the Budzin labor camp near Lublin where he successfully feigned work as a carpenter. When the camp was liquidated in May 1944 the prisoners were marched to Majdanek but at a curve on the trail Aryeh jumped into a ditch, escaping inevitable death. He joined the partisans in the forest where he fought the rest of the war. At war's end, Aryeh's parents, grandparents and seven siblings had all been murdered. Aryeh was sent to the Zalzheim DP camp in Germany and subsequently met Penina Tofler at the Eschwege DP camp.

Penina Tofler was born in Tarnegród, Poland in 1922, the daughter of Margalit and Yechezkel Tofler. She and her nuclear family survived the war in Siberia and Uzbekistan.

Penina and Aryeh were married in the Eschwege DP camp in 1947 and immigrated to Israel that year. Soon after arriving, Aryeh was drafted into the newly-formed Israeli army where he served as a Davidka mortar operator in the War of Independence. Settling in Haifa, Aryeh toiled in the wholesale fruit business and, with Penina, raised two children, Itzhak and Shoshana. Hard times were followed by a measure of prosperity and though Aryeh spoke often and proudly of his battles in Israel he rarely mentioned his experiences in the Shoah.

When Aryeh Goldberg died in 1995, his son was gifted his father's gold Patek Philippe watch as inheritance. Hidden under the box's lining Itzhak found a small photo of two young women. Sensing that his father wanted to keep this photo a secret, Itzhak did not investigate the identity of these women until his mother passed away in 2008. Utilizing the newly uploaded online Yad Vashem database, Itzhak learned of the existence of one Chaya Holzberg Goldberg. Reaching out to a Holzberg cousin Itzhak discovered that one of the women in the photo was, in fact, Aryeh Goldberg's first wife, Chaya. She and their two daughters, one seven years old and one newborn, were murdered in the Shoah. The newborn was inadvertently smothered as the Germans searched their hiding place and Chaya and her other daughter were gassed in Majdanek. Aryeh Goldberg had kept this secret for his entire lifetime.

In 2012, Itzhak's daughter named her newborn baby Chaya in honor of the tragic woman in the hidden photograph.

Aryeh Goldberg. Munich. c.1946.

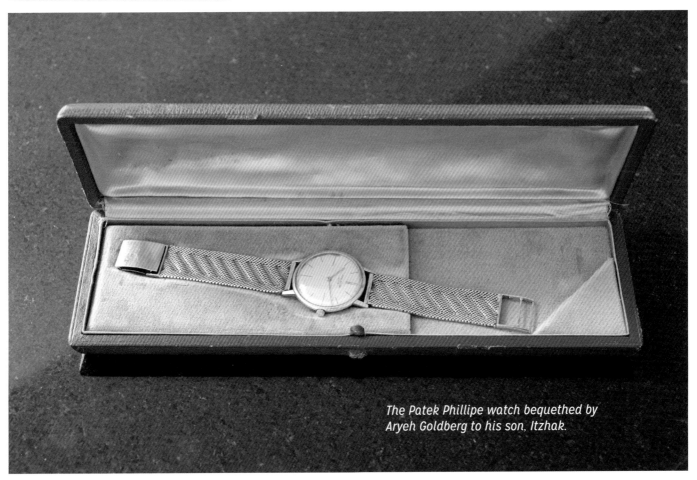

*The Patek Phillipe watch bequethed by
Aryeh Goldberg to his son, Itzhak.*

ELIZABETH PINEWSKI

Max Berger, maternal grandfather of Elizabeth Pinewski, was born on August 1, 1921 in Chorzele, Poland to Miriam and Faibol Berger who owned a large farm and was a money lender and a tailor. The Bergers had seven children, Chiel, Mendel (Max), Abie, Bayla, Joe, Rifka and Harry. There were also three half-siblings from Faibol's first marriage, Leonard, Chaim and Devora. After about eight years of schooling, Max began working on the farm with his father.

Faibol Berger died a year before the Nazi invasion and since his oldest son Chiel was away studying at the Mir yeshiva, eighteen-year-old Max became the head of the family. He suspected there was going to be an invasion of Poland, so he sent his family off to his older half-sister, Devora, while he stayed back to sell off the animals and produce from the family farm. Reunited in Warsaw, the Bergers traveled East towards Russia (Bialystok). They became prisoners of war several months later in Russia and were then sent to Siberia to labor camps.

They were released in late 1941 and went South to Kyrgyzstan where it was warmer. Max spoke many languages, including Russian and was a great chess player. In 1942, he manipulated his way into the Russian army through various connections and played chess against commanding officers. This led to his promotion to sergeant and he was put in charge of replenishing food and supplies to many of the outposts around the country. He peddled and bartered some of the merchandise on the black market and thus provided for Jews who needed aid. He remained in the Russian army, disguised as a gentile, until the war ended.

In the summer of 1945 Max met his future father-in-law in a marketplace. Nissan Kohn could not believe that this blonde-haired, blue-eyed man dressed as a Russian soldier could possibly be a Jew. Max courted Nissan's daughter, Taube, and they married on February 6, 1946 in Kyrgyzstan.

Taube Kohn Berger, maternal grandmother of Elizabeth Pinewski, was born in Goworowo, Poland on March 15, 1924. Her father, Nissan Kohn was the representative of Goworowo at the greater county seat which was Ostrelecki. He also held the prominent position of liaison between the county tax collectors and the townspeople when their assets were being assessed. Nissan and his wife, Sara Dranica Kohn, had six children, Taube and five siblings, Chaim, Mendel, Etty, Shayna and Murray. When the war began, Taube fled with her family from Poland to Siberia where they were placed into a forced labor camp. They were released in late 1941 as a result of Operation Barbarossa. Too cold to stay in Siberia, and unable to return to Poland, the family traveled south to Kyrgyzstan and Kazakhstan. Many months later, in late 1946, Max was caught at the border and put in jail by the Communists. He was imprisoned for working in the underground and for smuggling Jews who were too weak to travel to the American Zone in West Berlin. After four months, the underground arranged his release by bribing his jailers.

Taube and Max had a baby boy, Faibol, nine months after their wedding but he was tragically killed in Berlin by a drunk driver when he was only twenty months old. The couple then moved to the American Zone in Germany where they lived in the Foehrenwald DP camp, outside of Munich. Their daughter Anita, Elizabeth's mother, was born in June 1949. Four months later, on October 11, 1949, with the help of the Hebrew Immigrant Aid Society the Bergers arrived in the United States. They lived in Coney Island, then Sheepshead Bay and had two more sons, Morris (1951) and David (1955). The Bergers finally settled in Miami Beach in 1969.

During their courtship, Max had learned that Taube had two brothers, Chaim and Mendel, working as tailors for the Russian army. He was determined to return them to their family. In late 1945, he had false papers prepared and went to their base and heroically brought them back to Kyrgyzstan under the pretense that they were prisoners of war and that he had instructions to take them.

(clockwise)
Max Berger. Berlin, c.1946-47.

Taube, Max, Max's sister Rivka
and baby Faibol. Berlin, 1947.

Taube holding baby Anita.
New York, 1950.

Taube and Max. Munich, 1949.

לשנה טובה תכתבו
A happy New-Year
תש"ח Berlin 1947-48
להתראות בארץ ישראל

Max Berger's New Year's Card
from Berlin, 1947-48.

542464

A.E.F. D.P. REGISTRATION RECORD

Original ☑   Duplicate ☐

A.	B.	C.	D.	E.	F.	G.	H.	I.	J.

For coding purposes

(1) Registration No. 5299447

BERGER, Taube

M. Single ☐   Married ☑
F. Widowed ☑   Divorced ☐

POL-Jew.

(2) Family Name   Other Given Names   (3) Sex   (4) Marital Status   (5) Claimed Nationality

15.3.1925   GOWOROWO   POLAND   Jewish   (8) Number of Accompanying Family Members:

(6) Birthdate   Birthplace   Province   Country   (7) Religion (Optional)

(9) Number of Dependents: KOHN   Nisan   DRAJNICA   SARA

(10) Full Name of Father   (11) Full Maiden Name of Mother

(12) Desired Destination   Palestine

(13) Last Permanent Residence or Residence January 1, 1938.   GOWOROWO. Wwa   POLAND

City or Village   Province   Country   City or Village   Province   Country

WORKER

(14) Usual Trade, Occupation or Profession   (15) Performed in What Kind of Establishment   (16) Other Trades or Occupations

a. POL   b. Jew   c.

(18) Do You Claim to be a Prisoner of War   [ ]

(17) Languages Spoken in Order of Fluency

(19) Amount and Kind of Currency in your Possession

(20) Signature of Registrant: T Berger

(21) Signature of Registrar   _____   Date: 31.10.46   Assembly Center No.

(22) Destination or Reception Center:

(23) Code for Issue | 1 | 2 | 3 | 4 | 5 | 6 | 7 | 8 | 9 | 10 | 11 | 12 | 13 | 14 | 15 | 16 | 17 | 18 | 19 | 20 | 21 | 22 | 23 | 24 | 25 | 26 | 27 | 28 |

Name or Number   City or Village   Province   Country

(24) Remarks

DP-2

American Expiditionary Force DP camp registration of Taube Kohn Berger. October 31, 1946.

Silver tea set brought from Germany in 1949.

184

MICHAEL PINEWSKI

Joseph (Yosef Arieh) Hecht, grandfather of Michael Pinewski, was born on April 10, 1927 in Ruscova, Romania. He was one of five children born to Mordechai and Chaya (Fishman) Hecht. Mordechai was a transporter of freight and cattle and Chaya was a homemaker. Joseph grew up in a religious home with an open door for anyone in need of a meal or a place to sleep. Joseph attended school until 2:00 o'clock every day and then cheder in the afternoon. In 1940, when the Hungarians occupied Ruscova the Jewish children were no longer allowed to attend school so young Joseph began working with his father. He remembers that year putting on tefillin for the first time at his Bar Mitzvah and going straight to work from the synagogue. He worked with his father throughout the Hungarian occupation which lasted until 1944 when the Germans came into Ruscova. Joseph and his family were then taken to the Vishava ghetto for approximately four weeks. From there the Hechts was loaded into freight cars and taken to Auschwitz. Upon entering the barracks, Joseph was stripped naked, shaved and tattooed. His mother and two youngest siblings were killed on the day of their arrival. From Auschwitz, Joseph was taken to Lagischa. a sub-camp of Auschwitz where he was beaten very often and starved. Surviving Lagischa, Joseph was then taken to Buna, which was the largest Auschwitz sub-camp. In Buna, many were executed and others fell victim and died from hard labor, starvation, mistreatment. From Buna, Joseph was forced on a death march which lasted about six days. After the march he ended up in Flossenburg for approximately two months. From Flossenburg he was forced on another march and to Veterfelt from where he was liberated on April 23, 1945. He was the sole survivor of his family. Joseph spent the next seven months in a DP camp, working in the kosher kitchen. In December 1945, he returned to Ruscova, and found there a few friends and cousins who had survived and also briefly returned. This group made the difficult trek back to Germany on foot, climbing many mountains and crossing many borders. After some time, Joseph left Germany and sailed on the SS *Marine Tiger* ship to the United States, arriving on December 25, 1947. He lived for a time with relatives and began work as a butcher.

Joseph and Blanche Slomovits, who were both from Ruscova, and had known each other growing up, met once again in New York.

Elementary school photo. Ruscova, Romania. late 1930's.

Blanche Slomovits Hecht was born on June 10, 1928 in Ruscova, Romania to Baruch and Laya (née Fried) Slomovits. Baruch was a grocer and cattle dealer and Laya was a homemaker. Blanche had five siblings, Yankel, Riza, Lazer, Pearl and Yitzchak, and the children grew up in a religious home surrounded by a large extended family. Baruch Slomovits died of a heart attack when Blanche was very young. Her oldest brother, Yankel, was then sent to Chernivtsi to work and help support the family. Blanche attended school until the Hungarian invasion in 1940, was sent to a ghetto in the spring of 1944 and then was transported to Auschwitz four weeks later. The family was immediately split up. Blanche's mother and two youngest siblings were taken in one direction; her brother Lazer was taken in another. Blanche herself, having been separated from her older sister, Riza, ran to her sister's side when the guard's back was turned. This bold act saved her life. From Auschwitz, Blanche was taken to Gelsenkirchen to work. Surviving the bombings and shootings there, she was then sent to a munitions factory where she worked twelve hours a day one week, and twelve hours a night the next. Blanche was liberated on the street in Gelsenkirchen. Blanche spent some time in Germany after the war, and arrived in the United States on March 14, 1948 on board the SS *Marine Flasher*. She traveled under her mother's maiden name, Fried. She was only nineteen and listed as "stateless."

Blanche and Joseph Hecht were married November 10, 1951. They settled in Brooklyn and raised their children Mark, Carol and Barry there. When their youngest was eleven they also took in another child, Robert Reiss, whom they raised lovingly with the rest. Joseph earned a living as a butcher and then opened up a retail store named LBJ. For the next seven decades and counting they continued the Hecht family tradition of keeping an open door to anyone in need.

Blanche and her brother Yankel were reunited in the late 60's when a random encounter in the Soviet Union between Yankel and a Hecht acquaintance revealed that the siblings were both alive and living on different continents. Neither Blanche nor Yankel knew that the other had survived the war.

Ship manifest of the SS Marine Flasher. Blanche Fried and her sister are listed as "stateless."

Joseph Hecht's arm with Auschwitz number and the bracelets with same number worn by his daughter, Carole Pinewski and his granddaughter, Robin Gelberg.

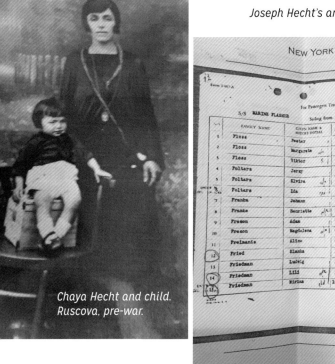

Chaya Hecht and child. Ruscova, pre-war.

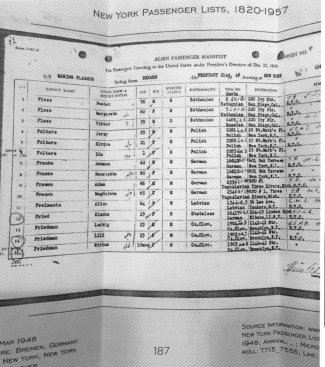

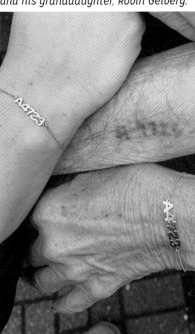

SHAUL RABINOWITZ

Michael Rabinowitz, father of Shaul Rabinowitz, was born in 1909 in the shtetl of Delyatichi, Poland on the banks of the River Niemen. He was one of eight children born to Esther Hannah and Berl Rabinowitz, who were in the lumber business. The shtetl's remoteness afforded its Jewish inhabitants a relatively peaceful existence during WWI, until 1916, when it became the front between the warring armies. Overnight, the residents became homeless. The Rabinowitz family underwent years of wandering and privation, during which Michael's teenage brother and sister died of hunger and typhoid fever. Returning to Delyatichi at the end of the war, the Jews found a devastated shtetl and barren fields. Consequently, Michael and his family relocated to Vishay. Michael attended a traditional cheder in Delyatichi, followed by more modern and strongly Zionist education in Vishay. The values of Judaism and love for Israel guided his psyche and actions throughout his life. Most of the extended Rabinowitz family emigrated from Lithuania over the years before and after WWI. Michael immigrated to South Africa in 1925, where he engaged in business and Zionist activism.

On a visit to Palestine in 1937, he met Yehudit Danieli, the youngest daughter of Rehovot founders. He returned in 1940 to marry her. After living in South Africa for twenty-eight productive years, the couple made *aliyah* in 1968, and settled in Rehovot. As in South Africa, Michael was involved in charitable and Zionistic projects in Rehovot, and forged close and deep ties with the Chief Rabbi of the town, Rabbi Simcha HaCohen Kook. In their friendship, mutual trust and respect prevailed, despite the fact that Michael and Yehudit joined the Conservative (Mesorati) Shul in Rehovot, where Michael served as president for a few terms.

The few extended Rabinowitz family members who remained in Lithuania were murdered in the Holocaust. Among them were Michael's aunt and uncle, Fraidl (née Rabinowitz) and Yuda Gajewski, and his first cousins Rivka, Nathan, Velvel, Esther, Rachel and Issher Koziol – all residents of the shtetl of Radishashok, whose Jews were massacred in a nearby forest on September 30, 1941.

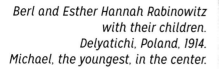

*Berl and Esther Hannah Rabinowitz
with their children.
Delyatichi, Poland, 1914.
Michael, the youngest, in the center.*

Songbook and address book of Michael Rabinowitz.
Lithuania, 1925. This first entry in the songbook contains
the nine stanzas of the original poem Tikvatenu by
Naftali Herz Imber written in 1877 in Zloczow, Poland and
then, in a shorter version, adopted as the anthem of the
Zionist movement in 1897.

Many years after Michael's death in 1987, his son Shaul found this letter, addressed to Chief Rabbi Kook, filed carefully among his father's many papers.

This poignant letter is entitled "An Everlasting Testimony and Memorial," and dated 5 Elul 5736 or August 31, 1976. Written in flowery and sometimes archaic Hebrew and sprinkled with Biblical and liturgical references, an aging survivor writes to Rav Simcha Ha-Kohen Kook[1] praising his wisdom and learning, and his position as the crown of Rehovot's inhabitants in his new role as the city's chief rabbi. The writer notes that he, in particular, is most fortunate to benefit from this Rav's wisdom and learning "having traversed the valley of weeping,[2] blood, fire and billowing smoke[3] and gases, rivers and rivers of blood and tears. It is a small consolation to see the glorious crown of the nation of Israel beginning to rebuild once again....".

The letter ends with a heartfelt request, never articulated, but clearly implied, that Rav Kook officiate at his funeral.

"As I have described above, I endured during the years of the terrible Shoah all the stages of the Inquisition, and I was left without children and most cruelly stripped of all that was holy and dear to me "God gives and God takes May God's name be blessed forever."[4] He then asks that "when I return to my Maker and to all who 'in their death were not parted'[5] and though I am reluctant to impose upon the Rav yet you must recognize this request that comes from the heart, I ask ...." The sentence ends with a pregnant ellipsis. Your student who honors and loves you,

Chanoch ben Pinchas Traiman

- Translated by Shaul Rabinowitz

1 Grand-nephew of Rav Avraham Yitzhak Kook. Rav Simcha assumed this position in 1974 after his brother, Rav Shlomo Kook, the former chief Rabbi of Rehovot, was killed in a car accident with his wife and two of his children.

2 Psalm 84:6
3 Joel 3:3
4   Job 1:21
5   II Samuel 1:23

MARK RAMER

Leon (Lonik) Ramer, father of Mark Ramer, was born on April 8, 1919 in the town of Kety, Poland. His parents were Yetti Rendl Bokshorn and Solomon Ramer, who was a merchant. The youngest of seven children, he was orphaned at a young age and was living with his eldest married sibling when Hitler invaded Poland in 1939. He was taken to five different camps that were part of the Gross-Rosen concentration camp complex. He met his wife Sophie (Zosia) Kling in the camps when she accidentally fell into a hole and he rescued her. Sophie, born on November 14, 1921 in Czarhnov, Poland, was the daughter of Moshe and Feygele Kling. Leon liked to joke that Hitler was his matchmaker. Leon's older siblings Samek, Rugia, Frieda and Sala and their children and one spouse all perished in the Holocaust. Another brother, Poldek, survived the war in Siberia where he contracted tuberculosis and he later died in Israel in the 1960's.

Leon and his brother Arnold survived the camps along with Sophie and were liberated in 1945. The couple was married after the war and settled in Walbrzych, Poland. There their son Mark was born in 1947 and their daughter Yola in 1954. In 1958 they were able to leave Poland and they lived in the Jewish ghetto of Venice for nine months waiting to procure the papers to immigrate to Israel. Once there, however, the Ramers found life was very difficult and so, soon after Mark's Bar Mitzvah, they immigrated once again, arriving in New York in 1961 and settling in Jamaica, Queens. Leon worked at first in a bakery, then in a pajama factory, and then, by patiently traveling from one sporting goods store to the next, often with his son in tow, he established Ramer Sports. This grew into a successful business importing a great variety of sports equipment including ankle weights and the ever popular ball – the famed Pensy Pinky. Tragically, Yola died of a brain tumor in 1969 at the age of fifteen. Mark lived his parents' dream by graduating from Queens College and then NYU Dental School and marrying another dentist, Naomi Fuchs, in 1986. Leon retired in the early 90's and passed away at 100 in December 2019 shortly after the untimely death of his beloved and loving son, Mark Ramer. He left grandchildren and great-grandchildren eager to carry on the family tradition of love for community and the state of Israel.

Mark Ramer dedicated his life to making a better world,
guided by Theodor Herzl's motto "If you will it, it is no dream."

Moshe Kling, Sophie's father.

Solomon (Shlomo) Ramer, Leon's father.

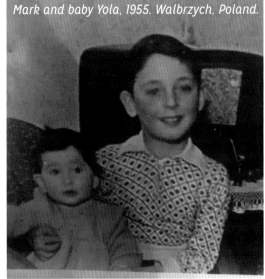
Mark and baby Yola, 1955. Walbrzych, Poland.

Sophie (left), her twin brothers, and their mother, Feygele.

Sophie's twin brothers, Shudek and Yudek Kling.

Marriage of three couples in 1945. Sophie in white with Leon behind her. Arnold Ramer, Leon's brother, is standing beside him in center of photo.

ever-popular Pensy Pinky rubber ball.

ALLEN ROSENBERG

Jack Rosenberg, father of Allen Rosenberg, was born on March 15, 1920 in Wolszczowa, Poland. Jack was one of eight children born to Pessel Apelevich and Abraham Rosenberg, who was a tailor. He was nineteen when the Nazis invaded his town and was immediately transported to work in an ammunitions factory in a camp close by and soon after to Auschwitz, where he performed similar work. Jack remained in Auschwitz until a final death march. Luckily, he managed to fall off the line and escape to a nearby farm and hide there. He hid for only a short time as the Allied victory soon followed. He then spent one year in Hamburg, hospitalized with tuberculosis and related illnesses. Released from the hospital he remained for a time in Germany and, with a surviving first cousin and several other young men, made a living trading on the black market. Jack immigrated to the United States in 1952. At first in the dry-cleaning business, he later went into the truck and auto parts trade in New York and became quite successful. In May 1960 he married Simone Sabbah in New York. The couple had one child, Allen.

Jack Rosenberg

THE UNITED STATES OF AMERICA

ORIGINAL
TO BE GIVEN TO
THE PERSON NATURALIZED

No. 7617787

CERTIFICATE OF NATURALIZATION

Petition No. 676407

Personal description of holder as of date of naturalization: Date of birth March 15, 1920 ; sex male ; complexion medium , color of eyes hazel , color of hair black , height 5 feet 4 inches; weight 130 pounds; visible distinctive marks scar on left side of neck & cheek Marital status married former nationality Polish

I certify that the description above given is true, and that the photograph affixed hereto is a likeness of me.

Jack Rosenberg
(Complete and true signature of holder)

UNITED STATES OF AMERICA }
SOUTHERN DISTRICT OF NEW YORK } ss:

Seal

Be it known that at a term of the District Court of The United States held pursuant to law at New York City on September 5, 1956 the Court having found that

Jack Rosenberg

then residing at 808 West End Avenue, New York, N. Y. intends to reside permanently in the United States (when so required by the Naturalization Laws of the United States), had in all other respects complied with the applicable provisions of such naturalization laws, and was entitled to be admitted to citizenship, thereupon ordered that such person be and (s)he was admitted as a citizen of the United States of America.

In testimony whereof the seal of the court is hereunto affixed this 5th. day of September in the year of our Lord nineteen hundred and 56 , and of our Independence the one hundred and 81st

HERBERT A. CHARLSON
Clerk of the U. S. District Court.

By _____ Deputy Clerk.

It is a violation of the U.S. Code (and punishable as such) to copy, print, photograph, or otherwise illegally use this certificate.

DEPARTMENT OF JUSTICE

GABRIELLA SAFDIEH

Gabriella Safdieh's grandfather, Joseph Tykocinski, was born on February 18, 1917 in Falenica, Poland to Breindel and Moshe Leizer Tykocinski, who owned a hardware store and lumber-yard. He had four siblings – Sarah (who was killed in Treblinka with her husband and child), Irena and Psachiah (who went to Israel after the war) and Paula (who immigrated to America). Joseph's son Mark wrote of his father's travails in *God, Faith and Identity from the Ashes: Reflections of Children and Grandchildren of Holocaust Survivors*, edited by Menachem Z. Rosensaft (2015).

The seminal story was my father jumping from a moving train heading to the Belzec death mill from liquidated Tarnow, delivering himself, his younger sister, and three other family members through a barbed window opening, machine gun fire as staccato background….
My father was not consumed with bitterness against the Jewish shoe store owner in Budapest to whom he was delivering false Christian papers but who turned him in to the Gestapo. And soon after the liberation of Buchenwald, when an American soldier handed him a gun and motioned to an SS guard bound up on the ground, my father turned it away. Even after Auschwitz, even after Buchenwald, he couldn't take a life, even that life….
Almost two decades ago, I videotaped my father's war experiences. In the course of the extended seven-hour interview, he broke down crying, but only once, and not where one might have expected. He was stoic as he described the horrific liquidation of Tarnow; the hiding and running; his escape, across Czechoslovakia, from Poland to Hungary; the brutality of Auschwitz; the liberation from Buchenwald. It was early in the war and he had decided to head east to find safety. His father followed the horse-drawn cart for miles, repeating the priestly blessing, **"Yevorechecha Hashem v'yishmerecha…"- "May the Lord bless you and watch over you,"***– over and over. A clearing in my father's emotional space suddenly flooded with a rush of raw emotion, the memory of his father's love channeled through an unshakeable, intuitive belief in God. For my father this was what was unbearable, making room for the dialectic of his father's resilience versus vulnerability, within the swirl of his love and faith…. This was the narrative thread that I will treasure most.*

After liberation Joseph went to a DP camp in Germany where he met Guta (Gitel) Rosencweig. Guta was born on September 9, 1920 in Lencznerow, Poland to Chany Lea and Jonathan Rosencweig. The eldest of eight children, she grew up in Zawiercie, Poland (Marszalkowska St.), where her father owned a candy store on Blanowska St. She was active in Zionist youth groups and, after her mother died, was busy caring for her younger siblings. She was imprisoned in Auschwitz-Birkenau for thirteen months, and then transferred to Bergen-Belsen, where she was liberated by British troops. Only one brother, Jacob, survived, and he too died shortly after the war's end.

Guta married Joseph Tykocinski in 1947 and the couple lived in Munich, where their daughter Annette (originally Hannah) was born in 1948. They immigrated to the U.S., docking in New Orleans, in 1950. They initially went to Los Angeles, but then moved to New York City where Joseph's sister Paula Ziemba lived. Their son Mark was born in 1952. Joseph ran a chicken farm in Lakewood, N.J. in the early years, until he became a real estate developer of single-family homes, apartments, and shopping strips.

Guta Rosencweig (top row, first on left)
with her Zionist youth group.
Gdud Massada. Lencznerow. mid- 1930's.

Guta Rosencweig (front row, first on left)
Zionist youth group. Ramat Hashofet.
Doar Afula. Lencznerow. mid-1930's.

Guta and Joseph Tykocinski
wedding photo., 1947.

Guta and Joseph. Munich. post-war.

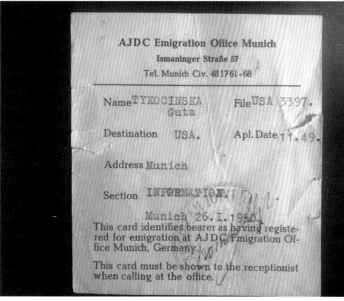

AJDC Emigration Office Munich

Ismaninger Straße 57

Tel. Munich Civ. 48 17 61-68

Name TYKOCINSKA   File USA 3397.
     Guta

Destination   USA.   Apl. Date 11.49.

Address Munich

Section   INFORMATION.

Munich 26. I. 1950
This card identifies bearer as having registered for emigration at AJDC Emigration Office Munich, Germany.

This card must be shown to the receptionist
when calling at the office.

Guta Rosenscweig DP camp registration card.

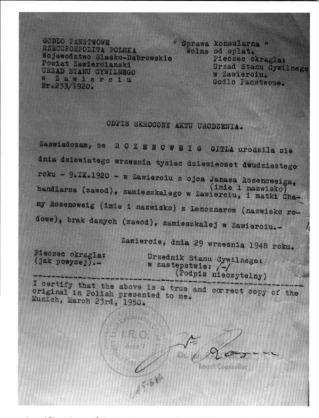

GODŁO PANSTWOWE   " Sprawa konsularna "
RZECZPOSPOLITA POLSKA   Wolne od opłat.
Wojewodztwo Slasko-Dabrowskie Pieczec okragła:
Powiat Zawiercianski   Urzad Stanu Cywilnego
URZAD STANU CYWILNEGO   w Zawierciu.
  w Zawierciu   Godło Panstwowe.
Nr.233/1920.

        ODPIS SKROCONY AKTU URODZENIA.

Zaswiadczam, ze R O Z E N C W E I G G I T L A urodziła się
dnia dziewiatego wrzesnia tysiac dziewiecset dwudziestego
roku - 9.IX.1920 - w Zawierciu z ojca Janasa Rozencweiga,
                                      (imie i nazwisko)
handlarza (zawod), zamieszkalego w Zawierciu, i matki Chany Rozencweig (imie i nazwisko) z Lencznerow (nazwisko ro-
dowe), brak danych (zawod), zamieszkalej w Zawierciu.-

              Zawiercie, dnia 29 wrzesnia 1948 roku.

Pieczec okragła: Urzednik Stanu Cywilnego:
(jak powyzej).-   w zastepstwie: /-/
                              (Podpis nieczytelny)

I certify that the above is a true and correct copy of the
original in Polish presented to me.
Munich, March 23rd, 1950.

Certification of Guta Rosencweig's birth and background.
March 23, 1950.

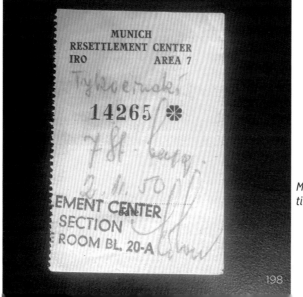

MUNICH
RESETTLEMENT CENTER
IRO   AREA 7

Tykocinski

14265 ✳

7 St - bg

2. 11. 50

EMENT CENTER
SECTION
ROOM BL. 20-A

Munich resettlement center
ticket. November 2, 1950.

American Joint Distribution Committee
ID card for Guta Tykocinski. Munich.
January 26, 1950.

A.E.F. D.P. REGISTRATION RECORD

Guta and Joseph with baby Annette.
Sailing to New Orleans. 1950.

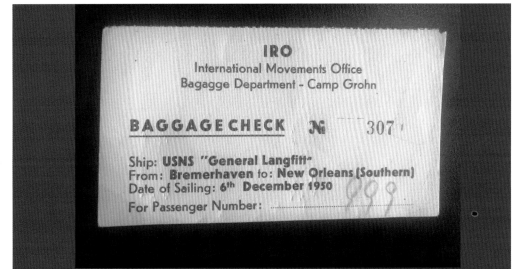

Bagggage claim check on the
USNS General Langfitt

IRO
International Movements Office
Bagagge Department - Camp Grohn

BAGGAGE CHECK № 307

Ship: USNS "General Langfitt"
From: Bremerhaven to: New Orleans (Southern)
Date of Sailing: 6th December 1950

For Passenger Number: 999

SAUL SAFDIEH

Saul Safdieh's grandfather, Aaron Shampan, was born in Sierpes, Poland on September 13, 1916 to Devorah and Yakov Shampan, who earned his livelihood as a wheat farmer. The family was prosperous and the three Shampan children, Aaron, his sister Reuchel, and his brother Reuven, grew up secure and comfortable. The Nazi invasion brought an end to this existence. Aaron, twenty-three at the start of the war, spent time in the Warsaw ghetto and in the Majdanek concentration camp. He jumped off a moving transport train, hid on a gas tank, and joined a passing work detail, which by pure chance, created for him a band of lifelong friends. In one camp he was luckily assigned to kitchen duties and, risking his own life, was able to sneak some sugar to a close friend named Sam Feldman, sick with appendicitis. By dissolving tiny measures of sugar into his water ration each day, Sam managed to survive. Aaron's act of selflessness had saved Sam's life.

After the war ended, Aaron found himself the sole survivor of his entire family. He worked for a short but profitable time in Germany where he met and married another survivor, Bella Jakubowicz, in December 1945. Shortly thereafter, the couple sailed on the third post-war army ship to America, the SS *Marine Perch*.

Bella Jakubowicz was born in the small shtetl of Chmielnik, Poland on December 10, 1924 to Feigel and Isaac Jakubowicz who supported his seven children working on a goose farm. When the Nazis invaded and demanded one young person from each family for a work detail, seventeen-year-old Bella magnanimously volunteered to go instead of an older sister who already had a suitor. This act of chesed saved Bella's life. By the end of the war, her parents and all her siblings were dead. Bella worked in the kitchen of the Skarzysko work camp from October 1942 to January 1944 and was kind enough to share her meager rations with a woman named Franya whom she had befriended in the camp. From January 1944 to January 1945 she worked in the Czestochowa labor camp. She was then transported to Bergen-Belsen and ran away from there two weeks before liberation, first hiding in the forest and then fleeing to Manheim until the war's end. Her travails included jumping off a moving transport as well as enduring for many months the hazardous fumes and chemicals of an ammunition factory. Bella's work ethic was exemplary as was her kindness. Free at last, she joined her one remaining living relative, her uncle Harshel Jakubowicz, who had married Franya. In a burnt-out shell of a destroyed German shul on Rosh Hashanah 1945, Bella met Aaron Shampan. She always said that she liked this particular young man because he was wearing clean shoes. By the first night of Chanukah they were married. By 1946, they were in New York.

The young couple settled in Boro Park and later raised their three children, Phyllis, Jack and Susan, in Queens. Aaron worked at first as a custom peddler, selling goods from his car and allowing his customers to pay in installments, a precursor to credit card transactions. He later went into real estate.

At Aaron Shampan's funeral in 1992, his friend Sam Feldman paid tribute to the man who had saved his life. "Not like father to a son, not like a mother to a daughter, was Aaron to me. We were more than brothers."

When asked what brought her to a prayer service after so much tragedy and suffering, Bella told her children, "If you don't believe in something, you are no better than a "chaya" - a beast."

Band of brothers, Aaron Shampan, third from left, and friends. At liberation.

...vorah Shampan. Sierpes, ...e-war.

Shampan siblings. Left to right: Reuchel, Reuven and Aaron. Sierpes, pre-war.

Wedding photo. Aaron Shampan and Bella Jakubowicz. Germany, first night of Chanukah, 1945.

Aaron and Bella, en route to America. 1946.

BLIMA SAFRIN

Avram Chaim (Henry) Gamss, the father of Blima Safrin, was born in Pzeworsk, Poland in July 1920, one of the twelve children of Paya Nesha and Aron Gamss, who was a merchant.

When it became clear that the only chance of escaping deportation was to go into hiding, the patriarch of the family, grandfather Aron, decided that like the patriarch Jacob before his dreaded encounter with his brother Esau, the Gamss family was best off separating into smaller groups. Thus it was that Avram Chaim joined three single brothers (Mordechai, Norman and Benny), a married brother and sister-in-law (Itcha and Leah Gamss) and a married sister and brother-in-law (Tsivia and Leibish Engelberg) along with seven small children (Sally, Lola, Miriam and Feigla Engelberg and Sara, Rita and Nachum Gamss) in the attic of Stanislaw (Stashik) and Maria Grajolski, a Polish farmer from nearby Urzejowice. The Gamss family entered the attic in the summer of 1942. In September they learned that the rest of their family had been killed. Grandpa Aron's advice had saved the group in the attic. For two years these fifteen souls existed in this tiny space and endured extreme heat and cold, near starvation and constant fear of discovery. Leah and her baby son both perished in the attic and a desperate attempt to save Tsivia's baby, Feigla, was also unsuccessful. When then war ended, the survivors from the attic emerged, alive but altered forever. Initially they could not even straighten their bodies and walk normally due to the fact that for twenty-four months they had remained stooped under the four-and-a-half foot ceiling of their hiding place.

The family's return to Pzeworsk was short-lived as the townspeople threatened to kill any and all surviving Jewish neighbors. Avram Chaim and his extended family traveled from Poland to Czechoslovakia to Romania to Hungary to Austria and finally across the Alps to Italy where they waited in the Cremona DP camp until papers came through allowing them to immigrate to the United States. Avram Chaim arrived in New York in 1948 and was soon married to the sister of a woman Tsivia had befriended in the DP camp, Chana Kessler.

Chana Kessler, the mother of Blima Safrin, was born on January 1, 1923 in Ungvar, Czechoslovakia. Chana was one of the four children born to Chaya Ruchel and Moshe Yehuda Kessler, who was a craftsman. When the Nazis invaded, Chana's sisters, Hilda and Fayga, were sent from Ungvar to stay with an aunt, but Chana's decision to stay home was a fateful one. She and her parents and little brother were deported to Auschwitz. Only Chana survived the death camp. After liberation, Chana and her sisters were reunited and, after a brief time in a DP camp, they each immigrated to the United States. Chana arrived in 1948.

Chana Kessler and Avram Chaim Gamss married in 1951 and settled in Brooklyn where they raised three daughters, Paya, Ruchie and Blima. Avram Chaim remained a pious and hard-working Jew all his life. Despite living through the horrors of the Holocaust, Chana and Avram Chaim built a life and a home filled with warmth and deep love for their children, community and each other, with tremendous gratitude to Hashem.

In 1988 the story of the Gamss family in hiding was made into an award-winning documentary "Voices from the Attic," produced by Debbie Goodstein, daughter of Lola. In 2009 Rita Lurie, another survivor from the attic, co-wrote the memoir Bending Towards the Sun with her daughter, Leslie Gilbert-Lurie. These two ventures into the territory of loss and trauma are poignant and heartbreaking evidence of the emotional scars of the Shoah and their infiltration into the psyches of second and third generation survivors.

The Gamss family, Tsivia, Isaac, Chaya Shaindl, Paya Neshe, Shia Moshe, Aron, Max, Yossel, (second row) Blima holding Norman, Rachel (Paya Neshe's mother), Leibish, Benny and Henry.

Hilda and Hannah Kessler

(from left to right) Norman Gamss, Sonia Gamss, Max Gamss, Sara Gamss, Isaac Gamss, Clara Gamss, and Avram Chaim Gamss, Italy, c.1946.

MARTY SCHAFFER

Lilly Goldstein Schaffer, mother of Marty Schaffer, was born in Chust, Czechoslovakia on April 16, 1923, one of five children of Sheindel and Mordechai Goldstein, who was a jeweler. When the war began, the Goldsteins were transported from their home and the parents and two brothers were killed. Details as to how and where are unknown. Lilly herself was sent to work in a bomb factory and then to Auschwitz with a younger sister, who perished there. While in Auschwitz, Lilly experienced many horrors including a beating over the eye by the infamous Dr. Josef Mengele, a beating which left her with impaired vision for the rest of her life. She later testified against Mengele with the United Restitution Organization, created to aid survivors. She reunited with her older brother Nathan in the Föhrenwald DP camp and it was there that she met Gerson Schaffer, another survivor.

When she was liberated, a soldier handed her a chocolate bar and it was at that moment that she realized she'd survived.

Gerson Schaffer, father of Marty Schaffer, was born August 1, 1919 in Szczebrzeszyn, Poland one of the eight children of Roiza and Joseph Szafir, who was a tailor. When the Germans entered their town, Gerson's parents urged him to run into the nearby woods and there he remained for the remainder of the war, fighting with the partisans and living in the forest, foraging for food and shelter. He was wounded twice, once in the forehead and once on his forearm, the scars remaining visible on him all his life. The emotional scars stayed with him as well and he refrained as much as possible from ever talking about his experiences or what he endured. When the war ended, his parents and six siblings were dead and only one brother survived. In Föhrenwald DP camp Gerson worked as a tailor. He and Lilly Goldstein were married on December 16, 1945 and their eldest son, Joseph, was born in the camp. When they immigrated to the U.S., the Schaffers settled in East New York and another son, Marty, was born in 1952. Experienced with tailoring, Gerson initially worked for a distant cousin in a clothing factory.

Striking out on their own, he and Lilly repaired damaged handbags and sold them from a pushcart, an endeavor which led to the opening of a dry goods store which Lilly's head for business transformed into a success. The Schaffers raised their two boys in Brooklyn and left a legacy of endurance and perseverance in the face adversity.

(opposite page, clockwise)
Gerson Schaffer, (left), with friends. Undated.

Marriage photo of Lilly Goldstein and Gerson Schaffer.
Marriage certificate in English.
German marriage certificate,
Föhrenwald DP camp in Wolfrathausen, Germany. December 16, 1945. 12 Tevet 5706.

Heiratsurkunde

Standesamt Wolfratshausen _____ Nr. 86/1948

Der Schneider Gerszon Szafir _____

_____, wohnhaft in Wolfratshausen, Föhrenwald

geboren am 1.August 1919 _____

in Szczebrzeszym, Polen _____

(Standesamt _____ Nr. _____), und

die Schneiderin L₁la Goldstein _____

_____, wohnhaft in Wolfratshausen, Föhrenwald

geboren am 16.April 1923 _____

in Chust, CSR _____

(Standesamt _____ Nr. _____),

haben am 25.März 1948 _____

vor dem Standesamt Wolfratshausen _____

_____ die Ehe geschlossen.

Vermerke: _____

Wolfratshausen _____, den 25.März 1948

(Siegel)   Der Standesbeamte:

Wimbald

Gebühr RM -.60

Reg. Nr. 387/48

Druck 1255 a. (112646)
_____nalschriften-Druckerei, München 4, Barer Straße 22

Marriage certificate issued to bride
S H A F I R Ella nee Goldstein
and bridgeroom
S H A F I R Gerson
Ceremony performed by:
Rabbi Friedman Cwy Nusen

F Ö H R E N W A L D
on
16 day of December 1945
certified by:
N.Herzke Hönig
chief rabbi of Föhrenwald.

WILLY SENDERS

Herman (Herschel) Senderovic, father of Willy Senders, was born on December 25, 1916 in Trebušany, Czechoslovakia to Yita and Avrum Dovid Senderovic, who was a teacher. Yita died in childbirth when Herman was very young and his maternal grandparents, the Lerners, helped to raise him. There were five siblings and a second marriage produced another half-sister. With an elementary school education, Herman spent the years prior to the war doing a number of odd jobs and at age fifteen struck out on his own to seek a better life in Košice, where he worked in a grocery store. By 1938 he was back home and when the Hungarians took over in 1939 Herman was sent to a series of labor camps where he dug ditches in Hungary and cleared forests in Russia. In 1943 he volunteered to serve in the Czech army and was given the responsibility of supervising the distribution of supplies, in particular gasoline. In 1945, still in uniform, he returned to his birthplace to find his home ransacked and his father and grandparents gone.

After the war, in Ostrowa, Herman reunited with a girl he knew from home, Hana Zola, and they married on June 28, 1947 and had a son, Abie. A few years later, fearing the communists, the young family escaped on foot to Austria where they lived for four years in Vienna and produced another son, Willy. When their papers finally came through, the Senderovics immigrated to the U.S. on the USS *Constitution*, and landed in Philadelphia on Memorial Day 1954. Now with the shortened name Senders, Herman learned the language, and earned a livelihood as a grocery store owner. He and Hana had two more children, Elaine and Bobby, and they raised them all in a sheltered, loving and observant household in Philadelphia.

Hana Zola Senders was born on March 4, 1921 in Negrava, Czechoslovakia which was situated near Munkacs. Her father, Yitzhak Zola, owned a small farm which produced most of the family's needs. Her mother, Ruya Katz Zola, died giving birth to her fifth child in 1934 and Yitzhak's second marriage produced four more sons. The large family lived in a small house consisting of three bedrooms and a kitchen and in 1940 when Yitzhak was sent away to a labor camp, Hana left home and found a job as a seamstress in nearby Munkacs. Shortly after Passover in 1944 Negrava's Jews were forced into the ghetto of Munkacs and a few weeks later they were all transported by cattle car to Auschwitz. Upon arrival, Hana held tight to her youngest brother Mordechai's hand until it was pulled away and he was sent to his death. Her grandmother, father, step-mother and four half-brothers perished there too. Hana was assigned the number A11682 and the job of cooking and cleaning for Nazi officers, first in Auschwitz and then in Freudental. After liberation she traveled to Ostrowa where her modest manner impressed her *landsman* Herman Senderovic and, together they forged a future.

Herman and Hana Senders raised their children and grandchildren
to "Remember who you are and where you come from."
The Senders family celebrates their arrival in the United States on Memorial Day each year.

Avrum Dovid Senderovic. Trebušany, pre-war.

Yita Senderovic. Trebušany. Early 1930's.

Herman (in necktie) with friends. Trebušany, 1930's.

Herman on a motorbike. Košice (?), 1938.

Herman in the Czech army with Russian medals, 1944.

Hana and Herman, wedding photo. Ostrowa, June 28, 1947.

Chanukah celebration in Vienna. Herman and Willy, top left. c.1952

Austrian passport of Wilhelm Senderowicz. September 28, 1951.

Kiddush cup brought to U.S. from Vienna.

MIRA WECHTER SENNETT

Shosha Lev, Mira Sennett's mother, was born in the spring of 1917 in the small village of Siemiatycze, outside Bialystock. Her mother, Elka (née Melamed), was a teacher and her father, Mishka was a shoemaker. One of four children, Shosha left her family in 1936 to join the *Hachshara* (preparation) Kibbutz Borochov in Lodz, hoping that her elder brother Michel, serving then in the Polish army, would someday join her. The members of this Kibbutz, all young, fervent Zionists, came from every corner of Europe, hoping to gain fluency in Hebrew, learn necessary skills and then realize the dream of immigration to Palestine. Shosha, a graduate of a Polish gymnasium, was assigned to the kibbutz's lending library. She soon met her soulmate, a young poet from Bialystock named Joshua.

Kalman Yerchamiel Wechter, Mira's father, was born in the spring of 1914 in the town of Kelz. He was the eldest of the seven children of Malka and Avram Wechter who were orchard keepers for the local Polish landlord. At sixteen Kalman struck out on his own to apprentice as a tailor in the textile center of Lodz. In Lodz the young Kalman became acquainted with Zionist leaders and followers all dreaming of charting a new life of Jewish dignity in their own homeland. He joined the Kibbutz Borochov and, now a master tailor, mentored the sewing workshop which produced uniforms for the Polish army.

In the summer of 1938 Kalman was issued two permits to emigrate by The Jewish Agency. He stood up in the dining hall of the kibbutz which was filled with 450 members and shouted to Shosha across the room, "Shosha, du vielst Liebe oder Palestine?" Do you want love or Palestine? Shosha, looking in Joshua's direction, responded softly but firmly, "Palestine." Kalman and Shosha were married in Siemiatycze in January 1939 and, laden with farewell photographs and touching messages from their fellow Kibbutzniks, they sailed for Palestine.

Most of these beloved friends from the Kibbutz Borochov perished in the Shoah. The last of the survivors of the Lodz ghetto were transported to Treblinka on the tenth of Teveth 1942. Of the extended Lev family, only Shosha survived. Witnesses say that 34 members of the family, three generations, were in one line heading to the gas chambers. Kalman too lost almost his entire family. Only his youngest brother Moshe survived by jumping off a cattle car headed to Treblinka. He miraculously found his beloved, Genya, who was hidden in a hayloft. Moshe, Genya and their baby Sarah fell into the joyful, waiting arms of Kalman as they disembarked from the *Exodus* in 1947.

Shosha and Kalman joined Kibbutz Givat Brenner and established the collective's sewing workshop. Their only child, Mira, was born in 1943. In 1949 the Wechters moved to Tel Aviv where they established one of Israel's most successful textile manufacturing centers and were also instrumental in hiring Jewish refugees from Arab countries. In 1958 the Wechters immigrated to the United States and settled in the Bronx where Mira continued her education at the prestigious Bronx High School of Science, Barnard, The Jewish Theological Seminary and Columbia University. Mira Rosenfeld Sennett became a master teacher of special education and Judaic studies and had a profound impact on American Jewish youth, both on and off campus.

Kalman Wechter, an expert in fabrics, was fond of saying "Torah is Der Beste Skhora," Torah is the best merchandise.

סקירה סטטיסטית
על מצב הקבוץ שע"ש "בורוכוב", בלודז

בנוגע למספר, הגיל, המין, ההשכלה הכללית והמקצועית, מצב ההתעסקות
של החלוצים-ות ומשלח יד הוריהם.

(המצב בחודש אקטובר 1934)

המספר הכללי

מין	מספר	% אחוז
בחורים	146	54
בחורות	124	46
ס"ה	270	100

הגיל

בן (בת)	מספר	% אחוז
18—22 שנים	154	57
23—26 "	95	35.2
27—30 "	21	7.8
ס"ה	270	100

השכלה

איזה	מספר	% אחוז
טכניקום וסמנריום	6	2.2
מקצועי	22	8.1
גבה	8	3
תיכוני	45	16.7
עממי	157	58.1
למוד ביתי	32	11.9
ס"ה	270	100

הכשרה מקצעית

איפה	מספר	% אחוז
בבתי-ספר	28	10.4
אצל בעלי מקצוע	115	42.5
ס"ה	143	52.9
בלי כל הכשרה	127	47.1
ס"ה	270	100

		מספר	אחוז
	18—..	122	45.2
	19—24	55	20.4
	ס"ה	270	100

	מספר	אחוז
סוחרים	17	4.1
בעלי-מקצוע	65	24
מקצועות-חפשיות	24	8.9
בלי התעסקות	45	16.6

Kalman and Shosha. 1939. "Uber im yam, un a man" (Going overseas unmarried) was ill-advised according to this popular saying.

The Lev siblings. Left to right: Michel, Leah, Liba and Shosha. Siemiatycze, 1933.
On the back "Bederech le-hachshara" – on the road to Hachshara.

(opposite page)
Kibbutz Borochov in Lodz.
Shosha Lev, second row, second from left,
Kalman Wechter, second row, extreme right. 1936.

Statistics published by the Kibbutz
analyzing the makeup of its membership.

New Year's Greeting
from Michel Lev
to his sister Shosha.
September 25, 1936.
Serdeczne Zyczenia
Noworoczne –
Cordial wishes for the New Year.

Lev Family. Left to right: Leah, Elka, Shosha, Michel, Mishka, Liba.
All but Shosha perished. Siemiatycze, 1929.

The Wechters. Right to left: Sarah, Malka, Hadassah, a dentist,
and her husband. Warsaw, 1936. All perished in Treblinka in 1942.

BARBARA SILBER

Shlomo (Solomon) Scheiner, father of Barbara Silber, was born on May 2, 1918 in Koshitza, Poland, one of three sons of Alter Yechiel and Devorah Scheiner. Alter Yechiel died in 1920. Shlomo and his brother Alter Yechiel lived with their maternal grandparents (Yitzhak Yeshaya and Chava Itzkowitz) in Krakow. Shlomo attended the Yisodei HaTorah cheder associated with the Aguda and Gerer chassidim in Krakow until 1939. After the Nazi invasion, he cut his *peyes* (sidelocks) and removed his armband so as to walk about the city freely. He was twenty-one years old. In 1941 he left Krakow and survived by traveling through smaller towns, first to his grandparents and then to his mother in Plashuv. On March 18, 1943 he was deported with 5500 others to Auschwitz-Birkenau. Time and time again Shlomo survived Dr. Mengele's selection process and he was ultimately sent to one of the *lager* or work camps which consisted of groups of 200 men each. Sadly, the most notoriously cruel of the kapos in his *lager* was the Jewish one. For four months he worked at various jobs including sorting the contents of suitcases and then he was transferred to work in a nearby coal mine. On January 17, 1945 he fled a death march and returned to Krakow on foot to search for his mother. Miraculously, through a Red Cross list, Shlomo was reunited with her and his younger brother after the war. His older brother Yaakov was killed with his wife and children shortly before liberation.

And so, Shlomo Scheiner, age twenty-seven, began again. Having never lost his integrity or his humanity, he somehow found a suit to wear and a pair of *tefillin* to *daven* with and for the next five years (1945-50) worked for the U.S. government at DP camps across Germany and testified at war crime tribunals in London.

Rachela Gruenglas, was born on July 10, 1928 in Tarnubczek, Poland, the youngest of the three children of Malka and Moshe Gruenglas, who owned a sugar mill outside of town. In 1940 Malka and the three children were forced to run for their lives and ended up in Siberia where they lived under very harsh conditions for the remainder of the war. Moshe was at the mill when his family was driven out and they were later told that he was killed in Auschwitz. After the war, the Gruenglases spent some time in the Landsberg DP camp where Rachela met Shlomo Scheiner.

They married in Landsberg on September 11, 1949. Together with the Gruenglas family, the young couple immigrated to the United States. They settled in Brooklyn, and Shlomo became a manufacturer of ladies raincoats. The Scheiners raised three daughters, Sherry, Bella and Barbara, in a loving, observant home teaching them that "above all else, one should always remain a *mensch*."

Shlomo Scheiner told his children that one night in deepest agony he dreamed that Eliyahu came to him and recited the prayers of Motzei Shabbos which somehow pulled him from the brink of despair and death. For the rest of his life these prayers were especially meaningful to him.

Wedding invitation of Rachela and Shlomo Schiener.

Wedding of Rachela and Shlomo Scheiner. Landsberg DP camp. September 11, 1949.

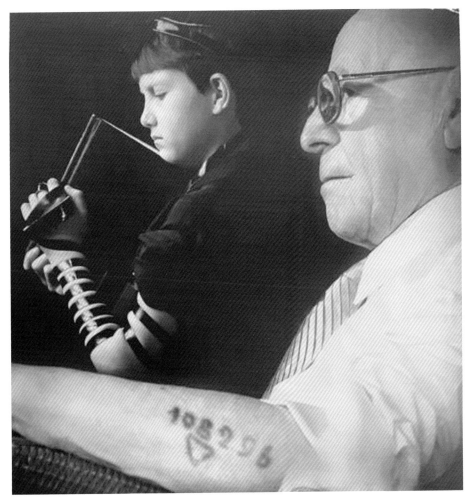

Shlomo Scheiner at his grandson Alexander Silber's Bar Mitzvah. New York. December, 2004.

Rachela and Shlomo Scheiner, undated.

> **"You turn my mourning into dancing. You undid my sackcloth and, with joy, gave me strength."**
> — Psalm 30

MENDY SILBER

Abraham Silber, the father of Mendy Silber, was born on January 28, 1912 in Rozwadow, Poland. He was one of three children (Abraham, Kalmen and Nettie) born to Chaya Ita (née Greenbaum) and Yehuda Silber, who was in the textile business. The family was living in Dusseldorf before the war. Kalmen was in Denmark at the start of the war and was able to reach the U.S. safely. The rest of the family was sent back to Poland, made their way to the Russian side and were sent to a labor camp in Siberia. Despite the awful hardships, the Silbers survived, along with a young niece and nephew. Shortly after liberation, in 1946, Chaya Ita died and Nettie moved to Israel. Abraham and his father, after three years in the Bergen-Belsen DP camp, were brought to the U.S. by Kalmen and settled in Williamsburg, Brooklyn. In June 1953 Abraham married another survivor, Sara Feinstat, and they had two children, Mendy and Chaya. Abraham worked for his brother Kalmen in the sweater business and then went on to establish his own knitting mill.

Sara Feinstat Silber, the mother of Mendy Silber, was born in Solec, Poland on July 10, 1922 to Devora (née Segal) and Menachem Mendel Feinstat who was a *schochet*, a butcher. One of ten children, Sara attended Polish gymnasium and then the original *Bais Yaakov* in Krakow, founded by Sara Schenirer. When the war began, the Feinstats were living in Bielsko. They fled from town to town – Mielec, Sandomierz, Dombrowa, Tarnow and Krakow. They were barred from entering the Krakow ghetto, an act that probably saved their lives. The family then fled to Stopnica. In September 1942 Sara was sent to a forced labor camp in Skarszysko-Kamienna, the Hasag ammunition factory. Two years later she was sent to Leipzig to another branch of the factory and in April 1945 she was forced on a death march. Miraculously, she survived. Of the twelve members of the family, six children remained. Their parents and four married siblings, and a dozen nieces and nephews were murdered. After liberation Sara was in the Bamberg DP camp and then spent some time in Israel. She arrived in New York in approximately 1950, and married Abraham Silber in 1953.

In the labor camp, the prisoners were fed a crust of bread and a bowl of watery soup daily. When Pesach came, Sara decided to refrain from eating the bread for the eight days of Yom Tov, even though she was practically starving. She kindly gave her portion each day to a Polish prisoner who worked at a nearby machine. He was so touched by her generosity that he made for her a simple ring fashioned from the grey, dingy metal they used to make bullets. Sara treasured this ring all her life and never took it off. It served to remind her of the great sacrifice she was able to make and the mitzvah she was still able to perform even in the midst of horror and inhumanity.

Abraham Silber (far left), watching a group of 500 children, including his own niece and nephew, leaving Bergen-Belsen DP camp, without their parents, for Palestine. Fall, 1947.

Wedding of Abraham Silber and Sara Feinstat. New York. June, 1953.

Sara and Abraham Silber. New York, undated.

ESTHER KAHAN SMITH

Esther Kahan Smith was born on Sukkot in 1927 in the small town of Vişeu de Sus, Romania. Her mother, Yenta Tessler Kahan, died soon after childbirth and her father Yosef Hakohen Kahan, the prosperous owner of a general store, gave the newborn Esther to his childless sister and brother-in-law, Mirrel and Moshe Yaacov Fischer to raise. Esther grew up in the loving home of this shoemaker and his wife. She attended a cheder and then a public school supplemented by Jewish studies in the evenings. Moshe Yaakov died in 1944 and before a stone could be put on his grave, the entire Jewish population of the town was transported to Auschwitz. There the notorious Mengele pointed Mirrel to the left and seventeen-year-old Esther to the right and in that moment Esther lost the only mother she had ever known. From May to November 1944 Esther and her half-sister Betty (Batya) were in Auschwitz and then they and about 250 other young women were transported by train to Torgau (a subcamp of Buchenwald) where they labored twelve hours a day in a munitions factory nourished only with scraps of bread and soured soup.

Soon after being liberated by the Russian army in 1945, Esther and Betty were smuggled by a Jewish clergyman to what he believed to be the safer, American side. The women first returned to their hometown where they found their brother. They sold their home, traveled to Vienna and then with the help of HIAS were transferred to the Leipheim DP camp. There Esther met Baruch (Ben) Smith, another survivor, who was born in Ulanow, Poland and who had survived the war in Siberia. Through HIAS Esther and Betty obtained visas to the United States and arrived in Boston harbor aboard a U.S. naval ship in 1949. They moved to Brooklyn and worked as seamstresses in the garment center. Baruch Smith arrived soon after and the couple married in January 1951. Working as a tailor for the designer Pauline Trigère, Baruch supported his wife and two children, Jane, born in 1954 and Morris, born in 1957. Esther, in her nineties, is a beautiful, effervescent woman insanely proud of her many grandchildren and great-grandchildren and never far from her book of Tehilim and her *Artscroll* chumash and siddur.

When Esther was deported to Auschwitz she hid a picture of her late mother in her shoe,
but when the new arrivals were disinfected, the precious photo,
her only image of her mother, was destroyed.

Gravestone
of Yenta Tessler Kahan,
Vişeu de Sus, 1928.

Yosef Ypsip Kahan, Esther's father. C.1930.
Mirrel Fischer, Esther's aunt. C.1930.
Moshe Yaacov Fischer, Esther's uncle. C. 1930

Betty's sister, Goldy Kahan, her cousin Raisy and an unidentified friend (r to l). Vişeu de Sus, Hungary, 1930's.

Rachel Kahan, Esther's stepmother. c.1930.

(Below) Leipheim DP camp friends. Esther third row, second from left. Her sister Betty in front of her and her brother, Sam, next to Betty at the end. 1947-48.

Leipheim tailor shop. Esther, front row center. 1947-48.

The dining hall at Leipheim DP camp. Esther third from right.

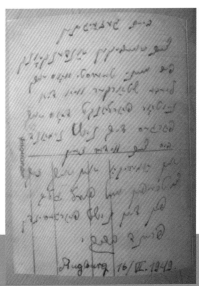

Farewell postcard from Baruch Smith to Esther Kahan as she leaves for America in 1949. In Yiddish he pleads "Do not forget me." Augsburg DP camp, June 16, 1949.

Vor- und Zuname: **Eszter Kahan**   Haft-Nr. 46105

Beruf: **Beamtin** geboren am: 10.10.26 in: Felsöviso

Anschrifts-Ort:

Eingel. am: **19.11.44** Uhr von **Auschw.** Entl. am: ___ / ___ Uhr nach ___

Bei Einlieferung abgegeben:

			Koffer	Aktentasche	Paket
Paar Schuhe, halb	Schlüpfer, Makko	Mantel: Tuch	Paar Handschuhe: Stoff	Effektensack	
Paar Schuhe, hohe	Leibchen	„ Leder	Handtasche	Invalidenkarte Nr.	
Paar Schuhe, Haus	Korsett	„ Pelz	Geldbörse	Invalidenquittung	
Paar Schuhe, Überzieh	Strumpfhaltergürtel	Jacke: Tuch	Spiegel	Arbeitsbuch	
Paar Strümpfe, Wolle	Unterrock	„ Leder	Messer	Photos	
Paar Strümpfe, Seide	Bluse	„ Pelz	Kamm	Schreibpapier	
Paar Söckchen	Kleid, Rock	„ gestrickt	Ring		
Hemd	Schürze: Kittel	Hut	Uhr m. Kette		
Hemdhose	Schürze: Träger	Mütze	Uhr m. Armband		
Büstenhalter	Taschentuch	Schal	Halskette		
Schlüpfer, Seide	Pullover	Paar Handschuhe:Wolle	Armband		
Schlüpfer, Wolle	Trainingsanzug	Paar „ Leder	Koffer		

Bemerkungen: ___

Abgabe bestätigt: Effektenverwalter:

KL. 88/9.44 15a.r.oo

Personal effects card for Esther Kahan, Buchenwald.

Ung. Jüdin

Konzentrationslager   Art der Haft: ___ Gef. Nr.: 46105

Name und Vorname: Kahan, Ester

geb.: 10.10.26 zu: Felsöviso

Wohnort: Felsöviso, Arbaten. 10.

Beruf: Beamtin   Rel.: jüd.

Staatsangehörigkeit: Ungarn   Stand: led.

Name der Eltern: Josef Kahan, Jnse Kahan   Rasse: jüd.

Wohnort: Felsöviso

Name der Ehefrau: ___   Rasse: ___

Wohnort: ___

Kinder: ___ Alleiniger Ernährer der Familie oder der Eltern: ___

Vorbildung: 6 j. Volksch.

Militärdienstzeit: ___ von — bis ___

Kriegsdienstzeit: ___ von — bis ___

Grösse: 160   Nase: normal   Haare: braun   Gestalt: ___

Mund: normal   Bart: ___   Gesicht: rund   Ohren: normal

Sprache: deutsch, ungarisch, rumänisch   Augen: grün   Zähne: ___

Ansteckende Krankheit oder Gebrechen: ___

Besondere Kennzeichen: ___

Rentenempfänger: ___

Verhaftet am: 1.5.44   wo: Felsöviso

1. Mal eingeliefert: 28.5.44 KL ___ 2. Mal eingeliefert: 2.11.44 BUCHENWALD

Einweisende Dienststelle: 19.11.44 von Auschwitz

Grund: ___

Parteizugehörigkeit: ___ von — bis ___

Welche Funktionen: ___

Mitglied v. Unterorganisationen: ___

Kriminelle Vorstrafen: ___

Politische Vorstrafen: ___

Ich bin darauf hingewiesen worden, dass meine Bestrafung wegen intellektueller Urkundenfälschung erfolgt, wenn sich die obigen Angaben als falsch erweisen sollten.

v. g. u.   Der Lagerkommandant

Kahán Eszti.

KL/42/8.44 200.000

Buchenwald intake form for Esther Kahan

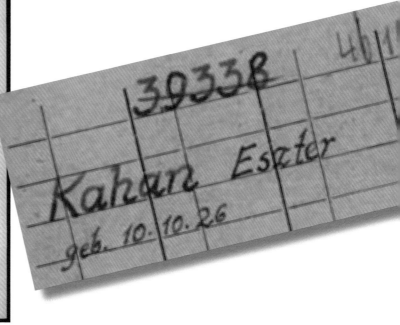

30338   46...

Kahan Ester

geb. 10.10.26

Prisoner registration card for Esther Kahan

Number card for female prisoners, Buchenwald.

Displaced persons registration card.

JOHN STEINDECKER
Michelle Spielfogel

John Steindecker was born in Paris on October 10, 1936, one of the three children of Charles and Erna Salomon Steindecker. Charles was in the banking business and worked for the family firm of Steindecker Frères. With the outbreak of war in Europe, Charles was called up to join the army of France. When the Nazis took over Paris, Erna and the three children, Lillian (b. 1933), John and Olivier (b.1939) left for Marseille. Soon thereafter Charles was demobilized and immediately joined his family. The Steindeckers traveled to Spain and then to Portugal. From Lisbon they boarded the *Dixie Clipper* and flew to New York with twenty-one other transatlantic passengers, landing at La Guardia air field on July 2, 1941. The voyage was recorded in the New York *Times* the following day. "Six of the passengers aboard the *Dixie Clipper*… were ordered to Ellis Island when two of the three children of Mr. and Mrs. Charles Steindecker, French refugees, were found to have chicken pox." Erna's father, Ivan Salomon, who had been a very successful tobacco leaf merchant in Holland and who managed to get to Montreal and then New York by 1940, helped establish the young family in Manhattan where they settled on Central Park West. Charles partnered with Raymond Bauman, formerly of Strasburg, to form the company of Charles Raymond and Co. which manufactured vitamin chocolates for the U.S. army. John was educated at Manhattan Day School, then TA (the Yeshiva University High School) and then New York University.

John married Rebecca Falk on September 29, 1964 and they raised their three children, Jimmy, Jeremy and Michelle, in Manhattan.

Ivan Salomon, Erna's father

Therese and David Steindecker, Charles' parents.

YANKEE CLIPPER OFF WITH 9 FOR LISBON

Sir Gerald Campbell Leaves for First Visit to England Since the War Began

36 HERE ON DIXIE CLIPPER

Six of 21 From Europe Held at Ellis Island—Lawyer Back, Unable to Reach London

The Yankee Clipper, carrying nine passengers to Lisbon and twenty-seven to Bermuda, left the Pan American Airways marine terminal at La Guardia Field a few minutes after 1 P. M. yesterday, and within two hours the Dixie Clipper, returning from Lisbon with twenty-one transatlantic travelers and fifteen Bermuda passengers, took its place at the dock.

Sir Gerald Campbell, director general of the British Information Service in the United States, was one of the outgoing transatlantic passengers. Sir Gerald, who was accompanied by John Wheeler-Bennett, an assistant in the information service, said he had not been in England since the outbreak of war and that he was going to report to his superiors. He will return within a month.

Drafted in French Indo-China

Major Louis Castex, manager of Air France Transatlantique, was returning to Europe, concluding a year's trip around the world on commercial airlines. Major Castex's trip was interrupted eleven months ago while he was in French Indo-China by a mobilization order that made him chief of a school for training fliers. He described the French Indo-China Air Force as "very weak."

Other transatlantic passengers included Joseph Y. Curtis, State Department courier; J. Frater Taylor, a British industrialist on special business for his government, and Harden G. Cooke, assistant general manager of Press Wireless, Inc., bound for an indefinite stay in England. The clipper, commanded by Captain Audrey Durst, also carried 300 two-day old chicks for a Bermuda farmer and 2,327 pounds of mail.

Six Sent to Ellis Island

Six of the passengers from Lisbon aboard the Dixie Clipper, which docked at 3:06 o'clock, were ordered to Ellis Island when two of the three children of Mr. and Mrs. Charles Steindecker, French refugees, were found to have chicken pox, and Miss Maria del Pino, Spanish citizen en route to Manila, could produce no transit visa.

Frederick Bunn, a lawyer, of 93-49 222d Street, Queens Village, Queens, returned to New York after waiting ten weeks in Lisbon attempting unsuccessfully to get air passage to London on legal business for a private client. Dr. Howard Florey, Professor of Pathology at Oxford University, and Dr. Norman Heatley, both British subjects, said they came here on "medical business," but would not say whether it was official. Miss Catherine Dreyfus, 21-year-old French actress, who said her great-uncle, Albert Moissan, was Napoleon's last companion in St. Helena, also was on board. The plane carried 2,288 pounds of mail.

The New York Times
Published: July 3, 1941
Copyright © The New York Times

Marriage of Charles and Erna. Paris, 1932.

Charles in his New York office. 1942.

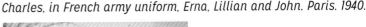

Charles, in French army uniform, Erna, Lillian and John. Paris. 1940.

John and Lillian. Paris, 1939.

Newspaper article describing the arrival of the Steindeckers to New York. July, 2, 1941.

221

ARTHUR TALANSKY

Kalman Talansky was born on October 19, 1924 in Pittsburgh, one of the five children (Ida, Abe, Kal, Moishe and Shoshana) of Rabbi David and Rebecca Skodnick Talansky. Kal was raised in Williamsburg, Brooklyn where his father was the rabbi of a small shul on Floyd Street and he and his brothers attended Yeshiva Torah Vodaath . Rabbi Talansky, born and educated in Russia, arrived here as a young man in 1919 and was forever grateful to his new homeland for the opportunities that it afforded him. When the U.S. entered the Second World War, he encouraged his older son Abe to enlist and supported Kal when he was drafted. Rabbi Talansky himself went to the draft board and volunteered to be a chaplain in the Navy but was rejected because of his communal and family responsibilities.

Rabbi Talansky worked hard to help refugee children from Europe when they arrived in America. He brought many of them home and his younger children often gave up their own beds for months on end to accommodate the orphans who crowded in. In October 1943, 400 rabbis marched on Washington to bring President Roosevelt's attention to the atrocities being committed by the Nazis in Europe. Rabbi David Talansky was amongst them.

Kal, in the meantime, went to camp Upton in New York, then to New Orleans for basic training. The Jewish chaplain in New Orleans was Rabbi Herschel Schacter, who wrote home to the Talanskys, reassuring them that their son was keeping true to his Jewish traditions as best he could. The young trainee also got packages of food and loving letters from the pretty girl he had met at a Young Israel dance on the night before the attack on Pearl Harbor. Her name was Irene Weisinger. In the spring of 1944, Kal landed with his unit on Utah beach. He spent most of the war in France and briefly reunited with his brother Abe in Verneuil. He returned home after marching through Belgium, Germany and Austria. He arrived at Fort Dix in 1946 and to his father's delight, his tefillin were still with him. He married Irene in 1947, established a successful aluminum window business, and raised their three children, Debbie, Arthur and Beth, in Queens, N.Y.

Megillah scroll given to David Talansky by his future father-in-law Leib Skodnick as part of his daughter Rebecca's dowry. Uman, 1919.

Private first class Kalman Talansky.

Kalman Talansky in the army in France. 1944.

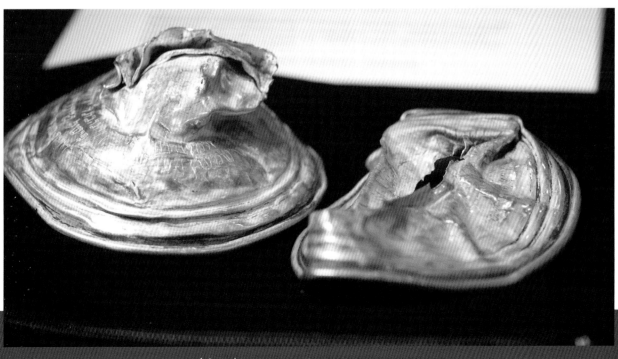

(above) Remnants of silver torah rimonim found in a destroyed synagogue by Kalman Talansky while stationed near Lyon, France, 1944

(opposite page)
March of the Rabbis in Washington D.C., October 1943.
Getty Images - The LIFE Picture Collection
Photographer: Thomas D. McAvoy

Rabbi David Talansky, extreme left, with children brought to America from Morocco and Tunis in order to attend the Mir Yeshiva. Standing in the center, bearded, is Rabbi Kalmanowitz, dean of the Mir Yeshiva and a strong advocate of Sephardic youths who were being persecuted in their native lands. Shaking his hand is Avrohom Portal, a native of Marrakech, who studied at the Mir and established its first high school.

ISRAEL WAHRMAN

Sarah Herskovitz Wahrman, mother of Israel Wahrman, was born on August 15, 1922 to Freida and Yaakov Elimelech Herskovitz in Ilnica, Czechoslovakia. When she was a baby, they moved to Orechova where her father became close to Rabbi Yoel Teitelbaum, the future Satmar Rebbe. The Herskovitz family, with its eight brothers and sisters, finally settled in Coltova, in the vicinity of Tornalya.

In Coltova, Yaakov Elimelech worked as the region's *shochet* (ritual slaughterer) traveling by bicycle to eighteen neighboring villages in all sorts of weather. In addition, since Coltova was lacking a rabbi, he served as the spiritual leader of the community and he even functioned as the town's master clock repairman. Both Sarah's parents were models of chesed in their community. An excellent student, Sarah aspired to enter gymnasium for higher education but these plans were thwarted by the Hungarian invaders. In addition, with the new order prohibiting *shechita* (ritual slaughter), the family was forced to earn a meager living from shearing rabbit fur and weaving it into yarn.

Attempts to immigrate to Palestine, to African countries, to the United States all failed. On May 18, 1944, the entire family was moved to a small shared room in the Tornalya ghetto. Food was scarce and the eldest son was taken to forced labor. After three weeks, the Herskovitz family endured the horrific journey in cattle cars to Auschwitz. Brother, father, two sisters and Sarah were sent to the right by the infamous Dr. Mengele and Freida and the three youngest children to the left, to the gas chambers. Then Sarah was sent to a slave labor camp in Plasov, Poland. Six weeks later she and her sisters were transported back to Auschwitz, where they saw their devout father. Even in the midst of the horror of Auschwitz, Yaakov Elimelech was known to arrange *minyanim* (prayer quorums) and to wisely advise others to eat the *trayf* (non-Kosher) rations in order to stay alive. At Guben, the next labor camp, working with fine wires, Sarah managed to fashion beautiful jewelry from discarded materials. Bartering these creations, she procured extra food for herself and her sisters, which enabled them to survive. The three girls then endured a horrific death march to Bergen-Belsen. Liberated on April 15, 1945 by the British, Sarah was too sick to return to her home and she and her sisters sailed to Sweden to recuperate.

Of the eight Herskovitz children, five had miraculously survived. Helped by an aunt and uncle in Gary, Indiana, Sarah and her sisters sailed to the U.S. on the SS *Stockholm* and arrived in August 1948. Living with her older sister in Detroit, Sarah met and married another survivor, Shlomo Wahrman, on June 7, 1949. They raised their three boys in Brooklyn and Queens. Sarah Wahrman's inspiring memoir *Hope Never Dies* was published by Artscroll in 1999.

Sarah learned from her father the efficacy of prayer even in the face of death.
" Even if a sharp sword rests on a man's neck, he should not desist from prayer." (Brachot 10A)

The Herskovitz family.
Coltova, c. 1940.
(Sarah is standing behind her father)

Jewish patients at the clinic in Arkiva, Sweden.
Sarah and her sister Golde (bottom row, left). c. 1946

(right to left)
Sarah, her sister and a friend (later sister-in-law). Sweden,
c. 1946

Rabbi Shlomo Wahrman, father of Israel Wahrman, was born on August 1, 1926 in Leipzig, Germany. He was the eldest of the three children (Shlomo, Pepi and Siggy) of Rivka and Yosef Wahrman who had emigrated from Galicia in 1925. Yosef Wahrman was a devout Jew descended from Torah luminaries including Rabbi Shlomo Kluger, the *magid* of Brody. He operated a silver shop on the Nordstrasse but also served as a chazan and a *schochet* (ritual slaughterer) in Leipzig, secretly continuing to perform *schechita* (ritual slaughter) even after it was outlawed by the Nazis. The children attended the famous Carlebach school and donned the traditional brown caps of Jewish youth in Leipzig. Shlomo's childhood was a happy and secure one, though by the mid 1930's, he and his schoolmates became accustomed to the taunts and physical assaults of the *Hitler-Jugend* (Hitler youth). Like many of Leipzig's Jews, the Wahrmans made attempts to emigrate, first to Palestine, and then, when Yosef's sister in America sent affidavits, they eagerly awaited their visas to the U.S. On Kristallnacht kind neighbors hid the children as mobs outside chanted "Death to the Jews." On the day after Pesach, April 11, 1939, they sailed from Hamburg on the SS *Roosevelt*. After a brief time in Brooklyn the family moved to Cincinnati, Ohio. Shlomo Wahrman studied for many years with Rabbi Eliezer Silver, one of the leading rabbis of the time, who was president of the Union of Orthodox Rabbis of the U.S. and Canada. He also studied in the Beth Medrash Govoha in Lakewood, New Jersey, and became a rabbi and educator. He married Sarah Malka Herskovitz, and they raised three sons, living in Brooklyn and later in Queens.

Rabbi Wahrman authored thirteen scholarly books and numerous scholarly articles. He served as the Rosh Yeshiva of the Hebrew Academy of Nassau County for decades until his retirement. His memoir *Lest We Forget: Growing Up in Nazi Leipzig 1933-1939* was published in 1991 by Artscroll.

Shlomo Wahrman's parents,
Rivka and Yosef Wahrman. Leipzig, 1930's.

Candelabrum brought from Germany by Yosef Wahrman and
made by him from melted silver German coins.

RABBI ELIE WEINSTOCK

Arthur Goldschmidt, the grandfather of Rabbi Elie Weinstock, was born on June 14, 1915 in Sprenglingen, Germany to Johanna and Jonas Goldschmidt, who was the *shochet* (ritual slaughterer) for the town's predominantly Orthodox Jewish families. Arthur had three siblings: a sister, Inga, and two brothers, Leo and Fred. He was sent at age twenty, in 1935, to Denmark for *hachshara* (preparation for Aliyah). By 1937, however, a friend advised him not to wait any longer for a visa to Palestine, but rather to get to the U.S. He arrived on the SS *Deutschland* on April 24, 1937. Arthur immediately set about trying to bring his family to the States. The situation meanwhile in Germany was worsening by the day. Ritual slaughter was prohibited as was shopping in Aryan stores. The children were thrown out of their Volkschule. After the terrors of Kristallnacht, the family was desperate to leave. It took another two years, but in March 1940 Arthur and his older brother succeeded in bringing his parents, grandparents and younger siblings to the States. In 1943 Arthur Goldschmidt enlisted in the United States Army to serve the country that had provided safe haven to them all.

In 1942 Arthur married Florence Gerber, a distant cousin, who was born in America. The family settled in Brooklyn where they raised their two daughters, Karen and Joan. Arthur earned a living in sales and retail.

Arthur Goldschmidt was a dedicated "shul Jew," attending daily minyan and serving as a Gabbai. When he moved to Dallas in 1973 for business, he helped establish the Orthodox shul in the city years before it became the community it is today.

Corporal Arthur Goldschmidt, in the U.S. Army. 1943.

The Goldschmidt home. Sprenglingen, Germany.

Johanna and Jonas Goldschmidt.

AVRUM WEISS

Jack Weiss, father of Avrum Weiss, was born on March 15, 1922 in Lancut, Poland. He was the eldest of the three children born to Chaya Reich and Mordechai Yehuda Weiss, who was a baker. His brother Yisroel was born in 1927 and his sister Reizel in 1930. Educated in a *cheder* and in the local public schools, Jack worked alongside his father in the bakery until the Nazis invaded when he was seventeen. By October 1939, Jack, his father and his brother made the decision to head east towards Russia. Reizel was hidden in nearby Nemerov with a Christian family and Chaya, who remained in Lancut, was most probably shot with the remainder of her townsmen in January 1943. The three Weiss men continued east to Siberia and then south to Uzbekistan and then ever further east, always one step ahead of the fleeing masses.

Olga Weiss, Avrum's mother, was born on December 5, 1922 in Doronezh, Russia. She was one of three children, Olga, Pola and Misha, born to Zalman Gershinsky and his wife Zippora. In 1940 Olga was preparing to enter the University of Kiev with a scholarship earned through her work as a communist leader of her region. Learning of the imminent arrival of the Germans, she too fled east with her father and sister. Misha was conscripted into the Russian army and was killed in May 1943. Zippora had died before the war in a Moscow hospital.

Like their Biblical ancestors, Jack met his wife Olga at a watering well deep inside Russia. His brother Yisroel also met Pola. The two brothers married the two sisters and they, with their fathers, all remained in Russia until the end of the war. Afterwards the Weisses spent several years in a DP camp in Germany till the proper papers were procured. Yisroel and Pola were aboard the first legal ship to the newly formed state of Israel in 1948 and the remaining Weisses immigrated to the United States in 1950. Jack and Olga settled in Brooklyn, opened a take-out food business and raised two sons. Zalman Gershinsky, after spending five years in the Gulag, immigrated to Israel in 1953.

(left to right) Yisroel and Jack Weiss in the DP camp. Note: Jack's uniform of the military police of the camp. c.1949.

Pages from a calendar given to Jack Weiss in Siberia. The creator of the precious calendar hoped that perhaps Jack would survive while he would not. The calendar notes the special prayers and blowing of the shofar in the month preceding the Jewish New Year in 1946. The calendar page ends on the eve of Rosh Hashanah.

Courtesy, Yad Vashem, The World Holocaust Remembrance Center

ROSALIE WEISS

Jack (Yaakov) Mikulincer, the father of Rosalie Weiss, was born in Uzhorod, Czechoslovakia on January 20, 1923. He was one of the eight children of Leah and Eliezer Mikulincer, a veteran of the Austro-Hungarian army. The Mikulincers owned and operated two bakeries in the town. Jack attended cheder and public school and, as a young man, worked alongside his father in the family bakery. The Mikulincers were known for their hospitality. Eliezer Mikulincer was always the last man to leave shul on Shabbos, making sure he could take home any people who did not have a place to eat. Challah and soup was always plentiful for their many shabbos guests.

In 1941, the Nazis took away all work permits for Jews, so at the tender age of eighteen, Jack left for Budapest where he found work as a baker. Returning to Uzhorod in 1944, Jack was placed into a forced labor squad, or Munka Tabor, and sent with a unit of 120 men to dig foxholes for the Germans in the Ukraine. Horrified to hear of Nazi atrocities, he escaped to the east and joined the Russian army. His superb language skills were soon recognized and Jack began to work for the NKVD, the Russian secret police, interrogating captured German soldiers.

When the war ended, Jack returned to Uzhorod and found his home ransacked. Of the family of ten, only Jack and three siblings had survived.

Jack left for Prague and once again found work in a bakery. In a Mizrachi-run Hachshara center in Cheb, Jack met Feigy Mittleman, another survivor. Feigy was born on July 1, 1926 in the very small town of Shtareschtuzitzu, Czechoslovakia and was one of the five children of Shloime and Reizel Mittleman. Her family ran a liquor store and a grocery. In 1944, Hungarians confiscated their property and, after a brief stay in Uzhorod, the Mittelmans were transported to Auschwitz where Feigy's parents and youngest brother perished.

Feigy and Jack were married in the kitchen of Feigy's sister on June 26, 1947 and left for Israel via Italy shortly thereafter. Jack served in the Israeli army for twenty-six months and was wounded in the War of Independence. Their daughter Rosalie was born soon afterwards. The family found Israel inhospitable to religious Jews and in 1955, unable to get a license to open a bakery in Acco, they immigrated to Sidney, Australia, where another daughter, Aviva, was born. In 1961 the Mikulincers finally arrived in the United States. Jack then opened a kosher bakery in Brighton Beach, Brooklyn.

A sadistic sergeant overseeing Jack's forced labor unit gave each laborer a small, grayish bar of soap and told the men that these soaps were made from the bodies of their dead relatives. For Jack Mikulincer this was a watershed moment. The horrific words of this German officer strengthened his resolve. He would survive to avenge the death of the kedoshim..

Shloime Mittleman in Austro-Hungarian army uniform.
The Hungarian flag was not sewn onto the caps of Jewish soldiers.

Jack Mikulincer, left, with his commanding
officer, in the Israeli army.

Jack and Feigy Mikulincer wedding photo.
Uzhorod, Czechoslovakia. June 26, 1947.

The wedding certificate from New South Wales
which explains "The parties to this marriage
were previously married to one another at
Kraslice, Czechoslovakia on Twenty seventh June 1948
according to the Laws of the Jewish Faith.
It was not possible for them at that time to have
a civil ceremony. This marriage has been performed in
order to place the legality of their union beyond doubt."

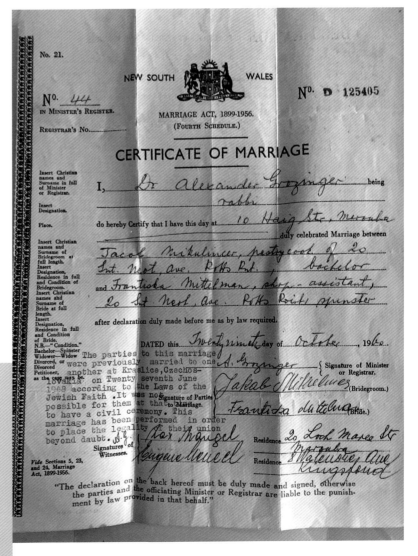

AVI WILENSKY

Yera Weksberg Hammer, maternal grandmother of Avi Wilensky, was born in Sosnowiec, Poland on January 1, 1926. She was one of five children (Bella, Manya, Yera, Yonah and Chaim) born to Rochel and Isser Weksberg, who owned and operated a textile store. Yera was just thirteen when the Nazis invaded Poland in 1939. Shortly thereafter, she and six hundred other girls were taken to Neustadt in Czechoslovakia to work in a textile factory. A year later, she was transferred to Blechhammer and assigned to kitchen duties. The access to food was literally a lifesaver since she could barter bread for anything from soap to leather shoes. One day, forty girls were transported to Auschwitz by truck. Within an hour they were brought back to Blechhammer when the *Judenalteste* (camp elder) prevailed upon the German commander of the camp to return them to their jobs. As a result, Yera has two numbers on her arm, one she received on first arriving, and a second upon her return.

On January 21, 1945 the camp was evacuated as Russian soldiers drew near. Yera was forced on a death march for thirteen days in deep snow and frigid weather. She arrived in Gross-Rosen where she found a brother and a cousin. Later still, she was sent to Bergen-Belsen block 199 where a Jewish block commander cruelly beat the young girls. Once again Yera was lucky to be assigned to the kitchen. Though deathly ill with typhus, she was able to survive by securing extra rations. Yera was liberated by the British on April 23, 1945. She returned to Poland briefly, sold her home, went to Lodz and then ended up in Cham, Germany. In Cham she was introduced to Nathan Hammer, through her one surviving brother, Yonah. The couple married in Cham in 1945. Yonah, Yera's only surviving relative, was tragically murdered with a hammer blow to the head by a German smuggler.

*In June 1981 at the first World Gathering of Holocaust Survivors in Israel, Yera Hammer was approached by the actor Robert Clary (of **Hogan's Heroes** fame) who came to thank her for sharing her rations and thus saving his life at the Blechhammer camp.*

Nathan Hammer was born in Krakow, Poland on February 5, 1911, one of the five children of Reizel and Beirish Hammer, who owned a shoe polish factory. Nathan was a brilliant young man who attended the Yeshiva Chochmei Lublin and then the prestigious Jagiellonian University in Krakow. At the outbreak of war he was a businessman with a wife and two children. He was sent to Plaszow and then to the labor camp of Flossenberg where he worked making parts for fighter planes. He survived a death march and at the end of the war found that he was the sole survivor of his family.

Yera and Nathan left Germany for the U.S. in 1949. HIAS sent them to Richmond, Virginia but they eventually settled in Passaic, New Jersey where Nathan established a successful ladies sportswear business and the couple raised two children, Bernard and Rosalie.

*One night, Nathan Hammer was ordered by a sadistic guard to assemble an airplane engine by sunrise or else face death. Nathan attempted but failed. Exhausted and hopeless, he fell asleep. By his account, he dreamed that night of an engineering expert who demonstrated what needed to be done. Nathan awoke and with the instructions still in his brain, succeeded in assembling the engine. His life was saved. This miraculous story was included in Nachman Seltzer's **Incredible Series**.*

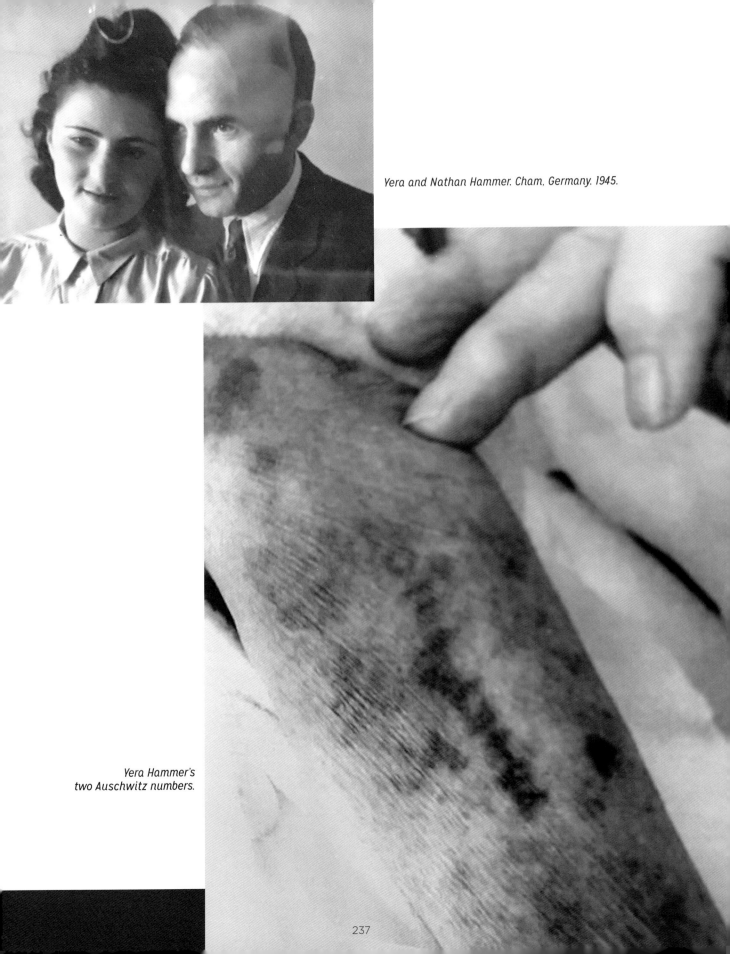

Yera and Nathan Hammer. Cham, Germany. 1945.

Yera Hammer's
two Auschwitz numbers.

RABBI SIMCHA WILLIG

Ella Weiss Willig, grandmother of Rabbi Simcha Willig, was born on October 2, 1923 in Oswiecim, Poland, the youngest of the ten children of Duvid and Sarah Weiss. Rabbi Duvid Weiss spent his days in the Bet Medrash and functioned as a shamesh for the Shiniver Rebbe. Sarah Weiss was the family's breadwinner and an exceptionally successful entrepreneur who succeeded in many businesses including the production of chocolates. Preceding Ella were Chatcha (Chaya Yehudis - born December 17, 1889), Hymie, Chatzkel, Aidel, Esther, Yocheved, Lili, Lipa, and Moshe. In 1920 the family home was ransacked by Polish soldiers and the family's life savings stolen. The next years were financially challenging. As the family continued to struggle to get by, Duvid left to Antwerp with two daughters, Esther and Yocheved, and then continued to the United States, joining his son Hymie who had arrived in 1920 with the Strettener Rebbe. In 1934 Duvid was able to send for Sarah and the four youngest children. The family settled in Brownsville, Brooklyn and Ella, only eleven, went on to school with her cousin Hymie's daughter, Shani. Duvid and Sarah began life anew and Duvid earned a living as a chazan. On June 12, 1946 Ella married Jerry (Yaakov) Willig and they had four children, Mordechai, Temi, Chava and Dovid.

Chatcha, Chatzkel and Aidel along with their young families remained in Poland and fell victim to the Nazi killing machines. Chatzkel, musical and athletic, is remembered as the family's champion who would defend his father and siblings when taunted and threatened by antisemitic bullies. Almost no details remain regarding his fate. Similarly, about Aidel we know only that she married a man named Wolf Yaakov Datner. Of Chatcha a bit more is known. A brilliant linguist and musician, Chatcha had married Moshe Mayer Ziegeltuch, a *sofer* (scribe), in 1930 and had given birth to her only child, a girl named Bracha Temma, in 1939. In nearly flawless English Chatcha wrote to her youngest sister Ella in New York, describing her delight in her new baby and her yearning to be reunited with her family. The letter intimates that communication between the Weisses in America and the Weisses in Europe was ongoing. This letter, written in 1940, was the last and it is highly likely that Chatcha and her baby Bracha with "the sweet eyes" were murdered not long after.

The first line of Psalm 30 is traditionally translated as "I will extoll you, Lord, for you have lifted me up." For the Weiss family the line reads more appropriately "I will extoll you, Lord, for you have impoverished me." The reason for this alternate translation is the family's fervent belief that had they not been left penniless by their hooligan attackers, they would never have emigrated and most likely they would never have survived.

Weiss family - Sarah, Dovid and eight children. Oswiecim, Poland, c. 1920.
Eldest brother Hymie is already in America so Sarah placed a small photo of him on her chest. Ella is not yet born.

Opposite page: letter written by Chatcha in Poland to sister Ella in New York. 1940.

Inset: Chatcha Weiss Ziegeltuch with baby Bracha Temma. Poland, 1940.

grow larger than you'll be the
"Kale majdet", the beautifullest in
N. York and — when God will help
me to be there — I'll look for you
to make you happy. Oh, how happy
I'll be than! To be togather with you
all, not alone as I'm now. Why you
don't send me a picture of you all?
I'm very curious to see you all. Is
mother all right?   What
will be with Li   is
When they dont
don't go married
wise enough
No wonder that   strang
to her "she'd neve   as
I heard (!) she is
good girl — isn't? My sweetheart Ella
forget all pains and take care on mother
because children are so long happy and
lucky — how long they have parents, God
save them. It will come better times for
you also. I wish you a happy new year —

EVA WOLF
Eda Frenkel

Eva Wolf's mother, Ethel Dondushansky, was born on November 8, 1911 in Ednitz Bessarabia, Romania to Yocheved and Dov Dondushansky. She grew up in an affluent home along with her siblings, Azriel, Malkah, Yosef, Ari and Rosa. On April 14, 1934, Ethel married Elias Davidman, who was born in Yareshev, Russia on June 5, 1914 to Rose (née Pinkovetsky) and Samuel Lazer Davidman. The young couple left for Palestine soon after their wedding and settled in Jerusalem, where their son Samuel, was born in the old Hadassah Hospital on March 30, 1936. The Davidmans were able to save Ethel's siblings, Azriel, Yosef and Malka, from Hitler's grasp, by bringing them to Palestine. The others, her parents and Ari (age 15) and Rosa (age 12), all remained in Romania and perished in 1942. Elias' too lost his mother in the Shoah; his father had died prior to the war. His siblings escaped in a variety of ways. His sister, Sheva, left Russia with her daughter on a children's Aliyah. His brother, Levi, fled to Brazil via Portugal under an assumed name. A half-brother, Abraham, went to Palestine to join Kibbutz Heftziba. Other older half-siblings had immigrated to America even before Elias was born.

Elias had spent the war years in South America. After the war ended in Europe, he flew to New York via Panama on a Pan American plane landing on May 10, 1946. He then arranged for Ethel and their son to follow. They sailed via Alexandria, Egypt and arrived in Miami, Florida on the SS *Saturnia* on March 11, 1947. The family settled in Queens and their daughter Eva Rose was born in New York City on January 7, 1948. Elias worked in the import-export of textiles from the U.S. to South America and was aided greatly by his facility with languages. On the long road that brought him from Yareshev, Russsia to Jamaica, Queens he managed to pick up Russian, Yiddish, Hebrew, Arabic, Spanish and Portuguese.

Eva recalls, " When I was growing up we went to the same synagogue in Jamaica, Queens that the Ramers went to. Mark and I shared memories of this 'survivor's shul,' as he called it. I remembered once 'needing' to tell something to my mother during yizkor. I went back in to her section of the shul and I was devastated by the sound of crying I heard from the women. I will never forget it. I was very young. It may have been 1951."

(left), Yocheved and Dov Dondushansky. Ednitz Bessarabia, Romania. pre-war.

(above), The Davidman family. Elias is the baby in front of his mother. Yareshev, Russia. 1915.

AFFIDAVIT IN LIEU OF
MARRIAGE CERTIFICATE

STATE OF NEW YORK }
COUNTY OF NEW YORK } SS.:

ROSE GOODMAN, being duly sworn, deposes and says:

I am a housewife and reside at 200 West 95th Street, Borough of Manhattan, City of New York.

I am a citizen of the United States, having been naturalized on August 10th, 1944 in the United States District Court for the Southern District of New York, at New York City, New York, as evidenced by Naturalization Certificate No. 6218590.

I am sixty-five years of age. I arrived in the United States on December 25, 1934.

I am making this affidavit as proof of the date and circumstances of the marriage of ELIAS DAVIDMAN. I do hereby certify that ELIAS DAVIDMAN was married on April 14th, 1934 in Edinti, Bessarabia, Roumania, to ETEL DONDUSHANSKY. I was living in the town of Edinti at the time of the said marriage and remember the Davidman's marriage.

Sworn to before me this
1st day of March, 1946.

Rose Goodman

Harry Rosengin
NOTARY PUBLIC

Ethel and Elias Davidman. Ednitz, c. 1933-34.

Ketuba of Ethel and Elias Davidman. 12 Cheshvan, 5694.

An affidavit (dated March 1, 1946) used in lieu of a marruage ceritficate signed by a woman now living in New York who witnessed the wedding in Romania in 1934.

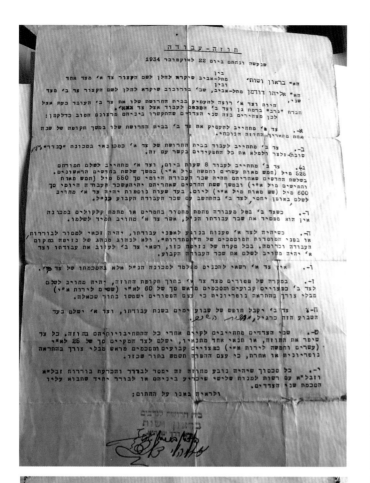

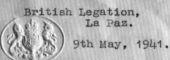

Employment contract for Elias Davidman in a sock factory in Tel Aviv. October 22, 1934.

Letter dated May 9, 1941 from the British consulate in La Paz, Bolivia to Elias Davidman advising him that those residents of Palestine who might be seeking Palestinian citizenship had to apply before July 24, 1941.

Elias Davidman application for a Nonimmigrant Visa to the United States for the purpose of conducting business October 30, 1945. Elias gives his permanent address as Cochabamba, Bolivia.

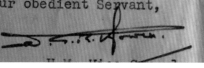

British Legation,
La Paz.

9th May, 1941.

Sir,

I should be obliged if you would take such steps as are possible to warn natives of Palestine who wish to apply for Palestinian citizenship under the Order in Council which came into force on July 25th 1939 and have not yet made their application, that they must do so before July 24th 1941.

The Order in Council applies to "persons of over 18 years of age at the 6th August, 1924, who were born within Palestine and acquired on birth or subsequently and still possess Turkish nationality, and on the 1st August, 192[ ] were habitually resident abroad and have since maintained an unbroken personal connexion with Palestine and intend to resume permanent residence in Palestine" and who do not possess any other nationality except Turkish nationality.

Forms of application may be obtained from this Legation on request.

I am, Sir,
Your obedient Servant,

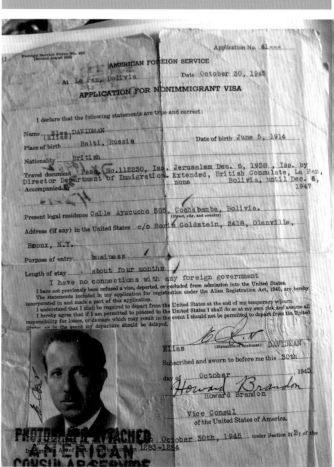

AMERICAN FOREIGN SERVICE

At La Paz, Bolivia   Date October 30, 1945

APPLICATION FOR NONIMMIGRANT VISA

I declare that the following statements are true and correct:

Name (Elias) DAVIDMAN

Place of birth Balti, Russia   Date of birth June 5, 1914

Nationality British

Travel document Pass. No.112230, Iss. Jerusalem Dec. 6, 1938. Iss. by Director Department of Immigration. Extended, British Consulate, La Paz, Bolivia, until Dec. 6, 1947
Accompanied by none

Present legal residence Calle Ayacucho 505, Cochabamba, Bolivia.

Address (if any) in the United States c/o Boris Goldstein, 2418, Olanville, Bronx, N.Y.

Purpose of entry business

Length of stay about four months

I have no connections with any foreign government

I have not previously been refused a visa, deported, or excluded from admission into the United States.
The statements included in my application for registration under the Alien Registration Act, 1940, are hereby incorporated in and made a part of this application.
I understand that I shall be required to depart from the United States at the end of my temporary sojourn.
I hereby agree that if I am permitted to proceed to the United States I shall do so at my own risk and assume all responsibility for losses, or damage which may result in the event I should not be permitted to depart from the United States or in the event my departure should be delayed.

Elias DAVIDMAN

Subscribed and sworn to before me this 30th day of October 1945

Howard Brandon
Vice Consul
of the United States of America.

GEET WOLF

Isaac Engel, (Moshe Eliezer Engel), father of Geet Wolf, was born on March 16, 1921 in Zwolen, Poland, one of three sons of Yita Leah (née Bonhardt) and HaRav Avraham Yehoshua Aryeh Engel, who was an ordained but nonpracticing rabbi, and worked in the hardware business. Yita Leah was a direct decendant of HaRav Simcha Bunim Bonhardt of Peshischa and HaRav Yitzhak Kalish of Warka, of the Amshinov Hasidic sect. Isaac grew up amongst a very large, loving, extended family of devout Jews and attended *cheder* as well as public school. He was eighteen when the Nazis invaded Poland, and soon after the ghetto in Zwolen, was created. By October 1942 it became clear that the Zwolen ghetto was to be liquidated. Isaac locked his parents and younger brother, Simcha Bunim, into a hidden attic chamber, provided water and bread for them and hoped they would thus escape deportation. His older brother, Gabriel Zeev, had already gone into the underground. Because he had working papers, Isaac was confident that he would not be seized when the townsfolk were ordered into the marketplace. He was sorely mistaken. Isaac was one of the first five hundred Jews to be marched to the Garbatka railroad station, but he and another boy managed to escape in the dust storm created by the massive march. A farmer who owed a debt of kindness to Isaac's father sheltered him for a few days. Returning to Zwolen to look in vain for his parents and brother, Isaac eventually concluded that they had been taken to Treblinka. Later still he learned that his older brother had been shot. For the next few years Isaac worked in the manufacture of ammunition in a series of labor camps in Policzna, Skarzysko, and Czestochowa. In December 1944, he was transferred to the horrific Gross-Rosen concentration camp, then to Nordhausen. In March 1945 he was chosen to help in the manufacture of V1 and V2 rockets at Dora. Conditions and rations for that short period were better than at any other time. Soon after, on April 15, 1945 he was liberated form Bergen-Belsen by the British army. It was in the Bergen-Belsen DP camp that he recuperated and met his wife, Adela, whom he married in 1946. Their daughter Toby was born in the Bergen-Belsen DP camp later that year. Until they immigrated to the U.S. in 1949, Isaac made a living supplying yeast to local bakeries. In the U.S. the young family settled in Detroit, Michigan where two more daughters, Chaya and Geet were born. Isaac trained as a *shochet* (ritual slaughterer) and went into the kosher poultry business.

Adela Engel, mother of Geet Wolf, was born in Olkusz, Poland. She was the sixth of seven children born to Rabbi Menechem Mendal and Toiba Ehrenfried. Adela was an excellent seamstress who had plans to go to work for her uncle, a tailor on the Champs-Élysées in Paris but the Germans invaded Poland and her dream was not to be. During the war, Adela worked in Sosnowitz in the Held Workshop, sewing uniforms for the Wehrmacht. Later she was interned in the Shatzlar Labor Camp in Czechoslovakia making textiles. Her parents and three brothers were murdered in Auschwitz. One of her surviving brothers introduced her to Isaac in the Bergen-Belsen DP camp after liberation. In Detroit, Adela helped her husband in the poultry business while they raised their three girls.

Jews of Zwolen being marched to the Garbatka train station. September 29, 1942.
The awaiting trains took them to Treblinka. This incredible photograph was given
to Geet Wolf by a local historian when she visited Zwolen in 2013.

HERSH WOLF | MYRON WOLF

Henry Wolf, father of Hersh and Myron Wolf, was born on September 19, 1919 in Munich, Germany, the only child of Regina and Wilhelm Wolf who was a kosher butcher. He attended the Frankfurt yeshiva of Rabbi Samson Raphael Hirsch. After Kristallnacht, Wilhelm was arrested and taken to Dachau, but Regina successfully appealed for his release on the grounds of his loyalty to Germany as a former Luftwaffe pilot who was awarded the Iron Cross after World War I. Leaving everything behind, the family immediately fled to England, obtaining visas because England needed butchers. While staying in London, near Gateshead, they were arrested and sent to the Isle of Man, suspected of being enemy aliens, German spies. Henry, still a teenager, was separated from his parents and shipped to Canada along with a large group of fellow German yeshiva boys. Imprisoned upon arrival, these young men were eventually released after the Toronto Jewish community reacted with outrage and protest. A kindly local Rosh Yeshiva named Rabbi Abraham Aharon Price took the homeless boys under his wing and enrolled them all in his Yeshiva Torah Chaim school and boarded them in the yeshiva dormitory. On weekends the local Torontonians hosted the refugees. On the first Shabbos of this arrangement, Henry and his good friend, Sam Nussbaum, were assigned to the home of Frimet and Morris Spiegel. It was a fateful weekend, for Sam eventually married Gilda Spiegel and Henry wed Rae Spiegel. Rae was an ardent Zionist, founder of the Shomer Hatzair of Toronto and the first woman to ever teach Hebraic studies in the Etz Chaim Yeshiva of Toronto.

Henry and Rae married on June 6, 1944 and Henry graduated from the University of Toronto at that time. Their first child, Myron, was born in Canada in 1945. The young family then moved to Providence, Rhode Island where Henry earned a Ph.D in applied mathematics at Brown University. They then settled in Forest Hills, N.Y. when Henry became a professor of math at Hofstra University. Soon after, the elder Wolfs, who had remained in England, immigrated to the United States and moved to Washington Heights, to live amongst their German compatriots. Three more boys were born to Rae and Henry in the States - Hershel in 1951, Barry in 1956 and Danny in 1958. After working for the Republic Aviation Corporation on Long Island, Henry started his own engineering company and worked for the remainder of his life in research and development for the American space program. He was subcontracted by NASA for the Apollo space mission as well as the space shuttle. He died in 1991 at the age of 72.

While very ill and in the hospital, Henry, a fighter and survivor till the end, told his Rabbi, "I didn't let those damn Nazis beat me and I'm not going to let this cancer beat me either."

Henry & Rae Wolf, Toronto, 1944.

Henry Wolf, graduating from Brown University with a Ph.D.

Henry Wolf in front of one of his projects, the space shuttle Enterprise, Cape Kenedy, 1976.

ALEX YUSUPOV
Inna Abramov │ Julie Yusupov

Zoya Shamilev Yusupov, Alex Yusupov's mother, was born in Zhuravskaya in the Stavropol region on September 16, 1923, one of two daughters of Avshalom and Adoso (Hadassah) Shamilev. The family lived in the ethnically diverse Kabarda region of the western Caucasus and were part of an ancient community of Jews in the area who were known as Mountain Jews (Gorskie Evrei). The Shamilevs worked in an efficient and productive *Kolkhoz* (kibbutz) known as Bogdanovka. On their way through to the oil fields of the Caspian, Nazis stopped to liquidate the region of its Jews. On Erev Yom Kippur, 1942, while all able-bodied men were away fighting in the Russian army, Nazis gathered the 472 remaining men, women and children of Bogdanovka and murdered them at the mouth of a pit that the victims had dug themselves. Zoya's mother, father and sister Zina were thus exterminated. Zoya herself, recently married at seventeen, was at the time in the nearby town of Nalchik which was temporarily spared a similar fate because the Nazis were unsure of the ethnic composition of this Jewish community. To their credit, their Nalchik neighbors tried to ward off the Nazis by claiming that these Jews were a people of Persian descent and followers of Islam. The ruse worked for a while. In the meantime, before the city was bombarded, its Jews dug trenches to hide in and by hiding in such a pit by day, Zoya saved her own life. Her husband, Mikhail Khanukayev, a principal of a school and therefore exempt from army duties, was a patriot who volunteered to serve. Tragically, he was killed in action on the Russian front. Left a widow with one son, Slavik, Zoya first lived with her mother-in-law and then with an uncle. She supported herself as a conductor on a bus line in Nalchik.

In 1954 Zoya married Simcha Yusupov, an attorney, and together they raised four more children, Alex (b.1955), Anna (b.1957), Sophia (b.1959), and Albert (b.1964). Simcha passed away in 1982 and Zoya moved to Pyatigorsk with her two younger children. Two of her sons served in the Soviet army, Alex in 1972 and Albert in 1987. Anna immigrated to America in 1980 and settled in Long Beach. On July 4, 1991, forty days before the fall of the Soviet Union, the rest of the Yusupov family followed. Zoya Yusupov, survivor of the Bogdanovka massacre, widowed twice, mother of five, transplanted in her late sixties, lived a life marked by courage, selflessness and generosity. When she died at the age of 96, her many children and grandchildren and great-grandchildren were astonished at the number of lives she had touched and the lasting impact she had made.

In 2005 at the Sheepshead Bay Holocaust Memorial a stone was dedicated to commemorate the atrocity in Bogdanovka. Alex Yusupov, Zoya's son, worked for five years to create this monument "in memory of the victims of this unspeakable crime."

Mindavid Yonatan Shamilev, Zoya's great grandfather in traditional Cossack uniform, the cherkesska, with cartridge pockets holding ornamental bullets.

Zoya's grandfather, Israel Shamilev, left, and his father, Mindavid Yonatan Shamilev.

Avshalom Shamilev, Zoya's father, left, with unidentified man and woman.

Zina Shamilev, Zoya's sister.

Zoya Shamilev, seated, with her mother, Adosa Shamilev, standing.

Zoya Yusupov. Nalchik, U.S.S.R.. c.1950.

Memorial to the martyrs of Bogdanovka which included Adosa, Avshalom and Zina Shamilev.
This monument, erected in 1990, stands on the exact spot where all Jewish residents of the village Bogdanovka were killed.

Zoya Yusupov, 81, whose parents and other relatives were victims of the Holocaust, cries at an unveiling ceremony at the Sheepshead Bay Holocaust Memorial Park yesterday. (AP)

Zoya Shamilev at a memorial dedication in Brooklyn, New York. New York Post. Monday, May 9, 2005.

TJ ZUCKERMAN

Philip Zuckerman, TJ Zuckerman's grandfather, was born in 1903 in Kolbuszowa, Poland to Rivka and Isaac Zuckerman. In 1920 he came to the United States by himself and built a successful business supplying felt to hat makers.

On July 16, 1933, Philip, his wife and two relatives were attacked by Nazi storm troopers in Leipzig, Germany, when they stopped to watch a passing parade. The Zuckermans were attacked because they were identifiably Jewish. The story was picked up by the *Times* since Zuckerman was an American, identified himself as such, and while recovering from serious injuries, asked the American Consul to come to the hospital to take an affidavit about the assault.

George S. Messersmith, American Consul General, wrote to the Secretary of State on July 26, 1933 about the attack on Philip Zuckerman, his wife, father-in-law and sister-in-law. The Consul General notes that although the German government and Party leaders have tried to reduce the physical attacks on Jews, *"it has been a favorite pastime of the S.A. men to attack the Jews and one cannot avoid the plain language of stating that they do not like to be deprived of their prey."*

In 1935 Zuckerman returned to Europe, this time to Poland, with a professional film crew to film Jewish life in four villages. He intended to show the film at the annual fundraising dinner of the Kolbuszowa Society that year. https://youtu.be/aw1BlnKSbLs

Philip Zuckerman

NO. 1454

AMERICAN CONSULATE GENERAL,

Berlin, Germany, July 26, 1933.

SUBJECT: Report on the attack on Philip Zuckerman,
a naturalized American citizen.

STRICTLY CONFIDENTIAL.

THE HONORABLE

THE SECRETARY OF STATE,

WASHINGTON.

SIR:

I have the honor to inform the Department that
on Sunday, July 16, 1933, Mr. Philip Zuckerman, a
naturalized American citizen residing in Berlin, was
attacked in Leipzig by S.A. men and severely beaten.
Mr. Zuckerman was accompanied at the time by his wife
who is not an American citizen, and by her father and
sister. According to the affidavit executed before
Consul Geist of this Consulate General on July 20, who
saw Mr. Zuckerman in the hospital in Berlin, not only
Mr. Zuckerman but his wife, father-in-law, and sister-
in-law were knocked down and beaten by the S.A. men.

The attack on Mr. Zuckerman was first brought to
the attention of this Consulate General by Mr. Busser,
the Consul at Leipzig, and immediately after our receipt
of the information concerning the attack Consul Geist
called on the State Secret Political Police to bring

the

Letter from the American Consul General to the Secretary of State regarding the attack on Philip Zuckerman. July 26, 1933.

The New York [Times]

Copyright, 1933, by The New York Times Co.

NEW YORK, SATURDAY, JULY 22, 1933.

[H]ITLER TROOPERS BEAT NEW YORKER

Our Consul General Protests Attack on Philip Zuckerman and Wife in Leipzig.

PUNISHMENT IS PROMISED

But Authorities Declare Walter Orloff of Brooklyn Must Stand Trial for High Treason.

BERLIN, July 21.—George S. Messersmith, United States Consul General, lodged a strong protest with the German authorities today against the maltreatment of Philip Zuckerman, an American citizen of the Jewish faith, by Nazi storm troopers in Leipzig.

Mr. Zuckerman, whose American home is at 69 East Third Street, New York City, owns a business establishment in Leipzig that imports American furs. He requested Consul Raymond H. Geist to come to his bedside in a West End hospital to take his affidavit concerning the assault on him.

Mr. Zuckerman, who was bandaged and spoke with difficulty, related that last Sunday he was walking down the Brushlstrasse in Leipzig with his wife and two other relatives and that they stopped to watch a passing parade of storm troopers.

"One of my relatives wears a long beard, making it easy to pick him out as a Jew," he continued. "When the tail of the column had passed us, several storm troopers dropped out of the ranks, rushed back and assaulted us all. They hit me with their fists.

Cried "I Am an American!"

"I cried out, 'I am an American!' But more storm troopers swarmed up—it seemed to me that there were a couple of hundred of them—I was trampled on and that was all I knew. When I came to I found myself in a drug store.

"An eye-witness who gave me his name later told me that the troopers had kicked me in the head. My wife was also beaten unconscious. I remained in Leipzig for some days because the doctor said that I had concussion of the brain and

Chaco Mediators' Lives Insured at $54,000 Each

By The Associated Press.

GENEVA, Switzerland, July 21.—The lives of the members of the League of Nations Gran Chaco commission were insured against death and disease today for 200,000 Swiss francs (about $54,000) each.

The commission is charged with negotiating to bring about an end to the war between Bolivia and Paraguay over the Gran Chaco territory.

6 NAZI AIRPLANES IN AUSTRIAN 'RAIDS'

Leaflets Attacking Dollfuss Government Are Scattered Over Five Border Towns.

NEWSPAPER SUPPRESSED

But Authorities Declare Treason Charge Against Walter Orloff of Brooklyn Must Be Pushed.

VIENNA, July 21.—Five "raids" by German airplanes on Austria took place this evening.

Planes coming from Munich appeared almost simultaneously over five Austrian towns along the German border—Reutte, Innsbruck and Kufstein in Tyrol, Reid in Middle Austria and Bischofshofen in Salzburg—and dropped masses of leaflets attacking the Austrian Government.

At Reutte and Innsbruck Austrian defense airplanes went up in pursuit, but proved quite ineffective. The Austrian Government will protest to Berlin, as it has on previous occasions, doubtless with the same negative result.

The first newspaper of the Christian Social party to be brought under the censorship, the Kaerntner Tagblatt, leading provincial organ of Chancellor Dollfuss's party, was seized today. The confiscation is an indication of the difference in outlook between the authorities in Carinthia, where the Nazis are strong, and the central gov-

HULL WILL PLEAD FOR PRICE RAISING

Will Make Appeal on Final Day of Economic Parley for World Action.

GROUPS MAY TAKE UP IDEA

Committees of the Conference Are Expected to Study Problem During the Recess.

WASHINGTON, July 21.—An appeal by Secretary Hull for international action to raise prices was scheduled today as the final action on behalf of the United States before the recess of the World Economic Conference in London on July 27.

The proposed statement by Secretary Hull is tentatively set for delivery on the last meeting day of the conference. It is planned that in this way the United States will put forcefully before the major nations of the world its renewed hope for some concrete eventual accomplishment.

At the same time, the projected statement is intended to serve as a reiteration of the contention of this Government that much can be done without discussion of stabilization of exchange or currency.

Form Is Left to Hull.

In the preparation of his final appeal Secretary Hull is reported in well-informed quarters to have asked whether President Roosevelt wished him to make any special appeal to the delegates. President Roosevelt is reported on equally good authority to have left the form of the statement to Secretary Hull.

Incidentally, it is remarked in official circles that President Roosevelt is satisfied that Secretary Hull has accomplished all that could be expected under the circumstances.

The proposed statement by Secretary Hull will not take the form of a resolution or other formal document, this being impossible under the rule preventing the introduction of new resolutions between now and the adjournment date of the conference. Instead, it is described as a projected appeal "to the reason of the governments."

On the basis of this tentative decision it is regarded as improbable that anything will be said by Secretary Hull or the other American delegates to the conference on the

NY Times front page article about the incident involving Philip Zuckerman. July 22, 1933.

The Kolbuszower Relief Association in conjunction with the Kolbuszower Young Men's Benevolent Society presents a pictorial review of Kolbuszowa and surrounding towns.

Although we have made this glorious country as our second home living under far better conditions and enjoying more freedom with the American flag, we still feel and consider in the depths of our hearts our native towns with all its shadows and faults as the sunny spot of the first happy years. Looking upon the schools, synagogues and all the other unique features prevalent in our idealistic towns we feel as a shock of pride would touch us and many a tear relieves our very sensitive hearts while looking at these pictures and recalling the first episodes of our life.

-- Introduction to the Philip Zuckerman film

Please note:
follow this link to see
this historic film,

https://youtu.be/aw1BlnKSbLs

(QR code below)

OPEN CAMERA OR QR READER
& SCAN CODE

דע מאין באת

Know from whence you came...

Pirkei Avot 3:1   פרקי אבות ג:א

Country	City	Family				
AUSTRIA	Klagenfurt	M. Gertner				
	Vienna	S. Boyarsky,	M. Bernstein	F. Klausner		
BELGIUM	Antwerp	D. Fridman, M. Junger	G. Gross,	E. Hollander,	H. Kleinhaus,	A. Lindenbaum
	Brussels	J. Nessim				
CZECHOSLOVAKIA	Bustina	S. Burian				
	Chust	M. Schaffer				
	Cinidavo	J. Boyarsky	W. Senders			
	Cop	J. Boyarsky				
	Dubová	S. Fox	B. Kest			
	Ilnica	I. Wahrman				
	Irshava	B. Hollander				
	Kivijazd	J. Boyarsky	B. Hollander			
	Košice	R. Kestenbaum				
	Negrava	W. Senders				
	Porúbka	H. Klein				
	Rad	A. Klein				
	Slatina	S. Fox				
	Shtaraschtuzitzu	R. Weiss				
	Stuzice	J. Boyarsky				
	Trnava	R. Kestenbaum				
	Trebusany	W. Senders				
	Ungvar	B. Safrin				
	Usť-Čhorna	S. Luger				
	Uzhorod	R. Weiss				
	Vilchovitz	B. Kest				
	Vonihove	R. Cooper				
FRANCE	Paris	J. Steindecker				
GERMANY	Berlin	H. Goldschmidt	G. Gross			
	Frankfurt	D. Friedman	E. Rennert			
	Hamburg	H. Goldschmidt	E. Kremer			
	Karlsruhe	D. Ottensosser				
	Kiel	B. Peyser				
	Leipzig	J. Kestenbaum	I. Wahrman			
	Markelsheim	D. Ottensosser				
	Munich	H. Wolf	M. Wolf			
	Sprenglingen	E. Weinstock				
HOLLAND	Scheveningen	H. Kleinhaus				
HUNGARY	Bekescaba	F. Frenkel				
	Kállósemjén	A. Gaspar				
	Negresti	J. Gruenfeld				
	Nyiregyhaza	A. Gaspar				
	Sasvar	S. Cohen				
	Sirma	S. Cohen				
LATVIA	Mogilev	J. Packin				
	Riga	J. Packin				
LITHUANIA	Marcinkonys	A. Pilevsky				
	Rudniya	A. Pilevsky				
	Swinzian	A. Lindenbaum				
POLAND	Będzin	F. Gleitman	M. Gleitman	B. Samuels		
	Belchatów	D. Hershman				
	Belitza	S. Golden				
	Brok nad Bugiem	A. Pines				
	Chrzanow	F. Gleitman	B. Samuels			
	Chelm	J. Meer				

Country	City	Family			
POLAND	Chmielnick	S. Safdieh			
	Chorzele	E. Pinewski			
	Chrzanów	F. Gleitman	B. Samuels		
	Delyatichi	S. Rabinowitz			
	Dubowa	S. Luger			
	Falenica	G. Safdieh			
	Felsztyn	A. Billet	M. Kremer		
	Goworowo	E. Pinewski			
	Kamoyonka-Strumilowa	N. Gaspar	S. Talansky		
	Kelz	M. Sennett			
	Kęty	M. Ramer			
	Kielce	R. Kestenbaum			
	Kolbuszowa	TJ Zuckerman			
	Koshitza	B. Silber			
	Krakow	E. Pines	A. Wilensky		
	Krasnik	T. Pines			
	Lancut	R. Kohn	A. Weiss	A. Lindenbaum	
	Lencznerow	G. Safdieh			
	Lodz	D. Hershman			
	Lvov	F. Distenfeld	N. Gaspar	S. Talansky	
	Olkusz	G. Wolf			
	Ostróg	L. Marshak			
	Oswiecim	S. Willig			
	Ozorków	D. Gelbtuch			
	Połtusk	A. Pines			
	Piotrików	S. Boyarsky			
	Pzeworsk	B. Safrin			
	Rozwadów	S. Pilevsky	E. Pines	M. Silber	
	Rzeszów	E. Hollander	H. Kleinhaus		
	Shumsk	J. Goldberg			
	Siemiatycze	M. Sennett			
	Sierpes	S. Safdieh			
	Skálat	B. Gelbtuch			
	Skawina	S. Gross			
	Solec	M. Silber			
	Sosnowiec	J. Kaplan	A. Landy	A. Wilensky	
	Stanislawów	D. Fridman			
	Starachowice	R. Kestenbaum			
	Suwałki	R. Kleinhaus			
	Swinzian	A. Lindenbaum			
	Szczebrzeszyn	M. Shaffer			
	Tarnogród	T. Pines			
	Tarnoruda	B. Gelbtuch			
	Tarnów	H. Heller	J. Kestenbaum		
	Tarnubczek	B. Silber			
	Trzebinia	S. Gross	R. Kleinhaus		
	Tuliglow	D. Billet			
	Vilna	S. Begelman			
	Voronezh	A. Weiss			
	Warsaw	D. Fridman	H. Heller	E. Kremer	A. Feinman
	Węgrów	R. Born	R. Distenfeld		
	Wieliczka	M. Bernstein			
	Wohyn	J. Bendavid			
	Włoszczowa	A. Rosenberg			
	Werynia	S. Goldman			
	Zawiercie	G. Fridman			
	Zolkiew	R. Born	R. Distenfeld		
	Zwoleń	G. Wolf			
ROMANIA	Ednitz	E. Wolf			
	Ruscova	L. Capobianco	M. Pinewski		
	Rozavlea	D. Ohayon	B. Erber		
	Vişeu de Sus	E. Kahan			
RUSSIA	Tambov	D. Kalter	J. Wilensky		
	Voronezh	A. Weiss			
	Yareshev	E. Wolf			
	Zhuravskaya	A. Yusopov			
SWITZERLAND	Basil	A. Feinman			

A society without memory is like a journey without a map. It's all too easy to get lost.

Judaism is a religion of memory. The verb zachor appears no fewer than 169 times in the Hebrew Bible. "Remember that you were strangers in Egypt." "Remember the days of old." "Remember the seventh day to keep it holy." Memory, for Jews, is a religious obligation....

Often I am asked – usually in connection with the Holocaust – is it really right to remember? Should there not be a limit on grief? Are not most of the ethnic conflicts in the world fuelled by memories of perceived injustices long ago? Would not the world be more peaceable if once in a while we forgot?

My answer is both yes and no, for it depends on how we remember.

Though the two are often confused, memory is different from history. History is someone else's story. It's about events that occurred long ago to someone else. Memory is my story. It's about where I come from and of what narrative I am a part. History answers the question, "What happened?" Memory answers the question, "Who, then, am I?" It is about identity and the connection between the generations.

In the case of collective memory, it all depends on how we tell the story. We don't remember for the sake of revenge. "Do not hate the Egyptians," said Moses, "for you were strangers in their land." To be free, you have to let go of hate. Remember the past, says Moses, but do not be held captive by it. Turn it into a blessing, not a curse; a source of hope, not humiliation. To this day, the Holocaust survivors I know spend their time sharing their memories with young people, not for the sake of revenge, but its opposite: to teach tolerance and the value of life. Mindful of the lessons of Genesis, we too try to remember for the future and for life....

One of the greatest gifts we can give to our children is the knowledge of where we have come from, the things for which we fought, and why. None of the things we value – freedom, human dignity, justice – were achieved without a struggle. None can be sustained without conscious vigilance. A society without memory is like a journey without a map. It's all too easy to get lost.

I, for one, cherish the richness of knowing that my life is a chapter in a book begun by my ancestors long ago, to which I will add my contribution before handing it on to my children. Life has meaning when it is part of a story, and the larger the story, the more our imaginative horizons grow. Besides, things remembered do not die. That's as close as we get to immortality on earth.

-- Rabbi Lord Jonathan Sacks, The Times (UK). July 2004

Ordinary Objects | Enduring Legacies

The Atlantic Beach Collection

As we move further and further from the Holocaust, it is harder and harder to make the experience seem "real" to the next generation. There are fewer survivors to tell their stories. Learning the history and commemorating *Yom HaShoah* are sacred responsibilities. At the same time, these experiences may sometimes lack a feeling of personal connection. I had the privilege of taking one hundred 8th graders to *Yad Vashem*. The most impactful moments were when students came into close proximity with the actual objects that had been through the Shoah and when they encountered a familiar name or place. There is nothing more powerful than personal items and personal stories.

Sue Talansky has done an incredible service by collecting the objects and stories of the Atlantic Beach community, giving so many a more personal and powerful sense of connection to our past. She demonstrates how ordinary objects are key to enduring legacies.

-- Rabbi Elie Weinstock
The Jewish Center of Atlantic Beach

———————————————————

Each person, photograph, letter, and object incorporated in this masterful collection tells a story, a story that the world needs to know. Each story must be shared, as the Torah teaches us never to forget what has happened to us and our ancestors -- to pass it along.

The images and texts in this work, meticulously organized by Sue Talansky, bring us back to the horrors of the Holocaust and simultaneously highlight the humanity of the men, women, and children who lived during those terrible times. When we open this book, when we read about or gaze upon the well-curated photos of these personal objects, we keep alive the individual narratives of those herein, and others too.

Each individual victim and survivor of the Holocaust is represented here, in this important volume, because this personal and precious book reminds us about the value of each person, each family, each item, and each story.

-- Rabbi Simcha Willig
The Jewish Center of Atlantic Beach